GLIMPSES OF HOPE

DISLOCATIONS

General Editors: August Carbonella, *Memorial University of Newfoundland*; Don Kalb, *University of Utrecht & Central European University*; Linda Green, *University of Arizona*

The immense dislocations and suffering caused by neoliberal globalization, the retreat of the welfare state in the last decades of the twentieth century, and the heightened military imperialism at the turn of the twenty-first century have raised urgent questions about the temporal and spatial dimensions of power. Through stimulating critical perspectives and new and cross-disciplinary frameworks that reflect recent innovations in the social and human sciences, this series provides a forum for politically engaged and theoretically imaginative responses to these important issues of late modernity.

Recent volumes:

For a full volume listing, please see the series page on our website:
https://www.berghahnbooks.com/series/dislocations

GLIMPSES OF HOPE

The Rise of Industrial Labor at the Urban Margins of Nepal

Michael Hoffmann

berghahn
NEW YORK · OXFORD
www.berghahnbooks.com

Published in 2023 by
Berghahn Books
www.berghahnbooks.com

© 2023 Michael Hoffmann

Library of Congress Cataloging-in-Publication Data

A C.I.P. cataloging record is available from the Library of Congress
Library of Congress Cataloging in Publication Control Number: 2022036411

British Library Cataloguing in Publication Data

A catalogue record for this book is available from the British Library

ISBN 978-1-80073-810-2 hardback
ISBN 978-1-80073-811-9 ebook

https://doi.org/10.3167/9781800738102

CONTENTS

ACKNOWLEDGMENTS

This book emerged from several postdoctoral projects, which I undertook at various institutions in Germany after the completion of my PhD at the London School of Economics in 2012. These included the Max Planck Institute for Social Anthropology, the Department of Social Anthropology at the University of Cologne, the re:work Colloquium at Humboldt University in Berlin, and the Center for Interdisciplinary Research (ZIRS) at the University of Halle in Germany. I am grateful to the people that I encountered throughout my fieldwork in Nepal, and to those at the above institutions who helped me develop the ethnographic material into a book. Most of all, I am thankful to the various employers, unionists, workers, and respected state officials who helped me in my research in both Nepalgunj and Pokhara in Nepal. The modern food-processing company near Nepalgunj allowed me to spend ten months of fieldwork in their factory, and I owe a great deal to management for giving me permission to conduct my research there. In Pokhara, I also want to thank the contractors, food factory owners, and sand-mine contractors for their help in my research inquiries. I have refrained from citing their names to protect their identities. For getting me in touch with locals in Nepalgunj, I thank Irantzu and Safik, and also the family of an influential landlord for hosting me throughout the period in Nepalgunj. I am deeply grateful to Kucchat Chaudhary who worked for me as a research assistant throughout the period in Nepalgunj. His comments in the field were insightful and proved highly valuable while I was writing the ethnographic material back at the various academic institutions in Germany. I also would like to thank professor Jonathan Parry, my former PhD supervisor and colleague, for visiting me for a few days of joint fieldwork in Nepalgunj. His guidance as a mentor both at the London School of Economics and at the Max Planck Institute for Social Anthropology in Halle, and afterward, really helped put the fieldwork data into perspective. His provocative questions were always sharp, insightful, and thought provoking.

I am also deeply indebted to the various institutions that funded me during different stages of the research and writing of this book. I would like to thank Chris Hann, Susanne Brandstädter, Andreas

Eckert, and Burkhard Schnepel for inviting me to their respective academic institutions and for the many productive discussions we shared. At the Max Planck Institute, I benefited from very insightful discussions with my colleagues in the Industry and Inequality Group. I would like to particularly thank Dina Makram-Ebeid, Eeva Keskülä, Dimitra Kofti, Andrew Sanchez, Christian Strümpell, and Tommaso Trevisani for their many comments on the various papers from this work that I presented and the stimulating discussions I had with them. I am especially grateful for sage advice from Christian Strümpell at various critical junctures throughout the writing of this book.

At the University of Cologne, I would like to thank Susanne Brandstätter, Jean Baptiste Pettier, Tijo Salverda, and Oliver Tappe for their comments on my work. I also would like to thank Clemens Greiner for inviting me to join the research group at the Global South Studies Center at the University of Cologne. I would like to thank my colleagues within this group, including Sabine Damir Geilsdorf, Ulrike Lindner, Gesine Müller, Oliver Tappe, Felix Wemheuser, and Michael Zeuske. My thoughts on industrial labor were particularly shaped by a research stay at re:work; I thank Andreas Eckert and Jürgen Kocka for inviting me to the institution and for creating an extremely supportive research and working environment. My research group there was very nurturing and I received very helpful comments from my colleagues, particularly from Hannah Ahlheim, Görkem Akgöz, Beate Althammer, Om Barak, Alina-Sandra Cucu, Ulrike Freitag, Oisin Gilmore, Preben Kaarsholm, Bridget Kenny, Tim Kerig, David Mayer, Benedetta Rossi, Caroline Rotauge, Juliane Schiel, Daniel Tödt, and Michael Zeuske. Thanks also to Felicitas Henschke and Farah Barakat for creating a stimulating working environment by organizing fun group activities throughout my stay at re:work. My ideas on industrial labor were also influenced by short trips to a textile factory and a mine in Kenya with the re:work team to assist at a summer school in August and September 2018. This experience gave me a better understanding of industrial labor in another sociocultural and political context and helped put the situation of labor in Nepal into perspective.

I would like to thank my research assistant, Mohan Bujrel, for his enthusiasm and insightful comments throughout my research in Pokhara. His comments while doing fieldwork have significantly impacted the research agenda of this book project. In addition, I am grateful for all those managers, workers, and contractors working in and around the Industrial Area of the city for supporting my research and listening, often very patiently, to my questions. Similarly, I would like to thank the workers in the sand mines close to the city for allowing me to gain insight into their lives and for supporting my research.

Parts of this book have been published in different forms in a book chapter and a journal article. Chapter 1 is a revised version of "From Casual to Permanent Work: Maoist Unionists and the Regularization of Contract Labor in the Industries of Western Nepal," in *Industrial Labor on the Margins of Capitalism: Precarity, Class, and the Neoliberal Subject*, edited by Chris Hann and Jonathan Parry (2018). Similarly, parts of chapter 7 have been used in "Digging for Sand after the Revolution: Mafia, Labor, and Shamanism in a Nepali Sand Mine," *Dialectical Anthropology* 45(2): 117–133. I gratefully acknowledge permission to reprint revised versions of both, and I appreciate the comments and critical suggestions made by the anonymous reviewers of both the edited volume as well as the journal article.

I also would like to mention how grateful and lucky I am that some old friends helped in supporting my research: I am grateful for Tommaso Dolcetta for a visit throughout fieldwork and shooting some stellar photos of the factories examined, one of which is featured on the cover of this book. While working on the last ethnographic chapter of this manuscript, I have learned much from exchanges with Rocco Santangelo, and I thank him for his insights on this chapter. I also would like to thank Kiran Hacker for all the editorial work on the book. His comments on drafts were always insightful and his fine-tuned editorial work was excellent. Finally, I wish to thank my family for their enthusiasm and encouragement throughout the entire period in which this book project emerged.

NOTES ON THE TEXT

I have used pseudonyms throughout for most informants except for those who are known as public figures in Nepal. I have also anonymized company names and location names to grant confidentiality for my informants. In some cases, I have invented new names for people I have written about in previous publications to avoid the duplication of individual names throughout the text.

To protect my informants, I also refrained from using images taken throughout the various fieldwork trips. I strongly believe that most of my informants would embrace this important privacy-enhancing decision and that the employers of the factories would prefer there to be no images in this book. This is not because they feared my writings on the conditions of labor in their factories, but rather because employers were keen on protecting their technology from competitors, for understandable reasons.

The first instance of all Nepali, Hindi, and Tharu words are italicized, and thereafter italics are dropped. For the sake of simplicity, the plural form of Nepali, Hindi, and Tharu words is denoted by the addition of an *s*. English translations have been used where they are adequate to convey the meaning of the original terms.

Financial costs are given in the original currency, either Nepali rupees (NR) or Indian rupees (IR), followed by an estimated conversion to euros. Throughout fieldwork, exchange rates between the Nepali rupee and other currencies fluctuated considerably. At the beginning of my first longer period of fieldwork for this study, in October 2013, 1 euro was roughly equivalent to 134 NR, 1 US dollar to 99 NR. At the start of my second fieldwork period in October 2018, I could buy 1 euro for 133 NR and 1 US dollar for 115 NR. By the end of my fieldwork in early March 2020, 1 euro was roughly equivalent to 125 NR, 1 US dollar to 113 NR.

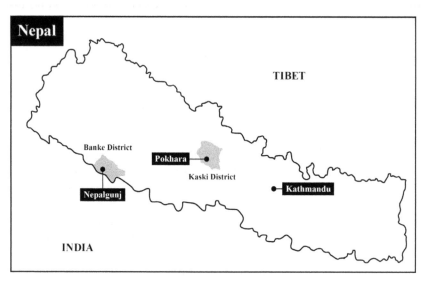

Map 0.1. Map of Nepal © Michael Hoffmann.

INTRODUCTION
The Noodle King

In his book *Making It Big* (2016), Binod Chaudhary, Nepal's most successful businessman and "Noodle King," tells his story of entrepreneurial success and reflects on the hurdles he had to overcome to build a business empire and eventually become Nepal's first billionaire. According to the book, Chaudhary comes from a family of the Marwari caste who originally immigrated to Nepal from Rajasthan at the end of the nineteenth century. Chaudhary's grandfather, Bhuramal Das, laid the foundation for his later success; after a devastating earthquake struck Nepal in 1934, he began a formally registered textile company. The grandfather spent a lot of time training his son, Lunkaran Das—Chaudhary's father—in the art of business, and Lunkaran Das later expanded his grandfather's business beyond the Kathmandu clothing store into a profitable enterprise. The strategy of Lunkaran Das was to diversify the family business, and so he entered the construction business in Kathmandu. He won important contracts in 1968 and established a high-quality retail store called Aron Emporium in Kathmandu. The companies founded by Chaudhary's grandfather and father formed the basis for what has today become the Chaudhary Group of companies.

Binod Chaudhary grew up in this environment and learned the art of craftsmanship not in school but in his family's retail store. In the 1970s, when tourists were flocking into Kathmandu, Chaudhary seized the opportunity and started his own business: a discotheque called Copper Floor. This found quick success and provided Chaudhary with connections to the rich and powerful of Kathmandu. With his new access, he learned an important lesson: dealing with the elite can be extremely profitable. It is a theme that runs through Chaudhary's autobiography. Thus, Chaudhary describes how a few years later, in 1979, through good relations with the political class, he managed to obtain a license to import and assemble parts for Panasonic radios. In return, Chaudhary had to support the Thapa government in its campaign to maintain the Panchayat regime.

Political patronage—as Chaudhary emphasizes at various points in his book—proved to be important in the development of his business empire. Through many clever "deals" over his forty-year career, Chaudhary developed a business empire whose greatest assets were majority stakes in the Nepalese Nabil Bank and in Chaudhary Group Foods, the producer of Wai Wai noodles. By 2020, Chaudhary's food company, Wai Wai, had factories in India, Bangladesh, and Serbia, with another under construction in Egypt. Chaudhary's net worth is now about 1.5 billion US dollars, making him the 1,513th richest person in the world in November 2020, according to Forbes (2020).

Chaudhary's autobiography—which he refers to in the book's acknowledgments as the Chaudhary Group's company biography—represents a classic rags-to-riches story of a self-celebrating and highly successful businessman. In this sense it is not surprising that the book's publication was followed by stern critique from left-wing scholars. In an insightful review of the book, Shubhanga Pandey (2015) pointed to the irony of claiming to "make it big" despite Chaudhary having been born into a family with an already thriving business.[1] Furthermore, Pandey critiqued Chaudhary's open admiration for neoliberal, authoritarian personalities, reminding the reader that Chaudhary was loose with his historic facts and gave little attention to other leading figures within the Chaudhary Group. Building upon such criticism, I chose *Making It Big* as an entry point for another reason: at the heart of Binod Chaudhary's rags-to-riches narrative is the omission of the experiences of workers in his food-processing factories and urban construction sites, in addition to the hoarding of the value that has been extracted through their labor.

This book deals with the experiences of those working in food factories and on construction sites—new sites of employment in Nepal that are similar to those that make up Chaudhary's empire. It is based on eighteen months of anthropological fieldwork undertaken between 2012 and 2020 on the margins of two cities in Nepal: Nepalgunj, a border town located in the western lowlands region (Tarai), and Pokhara, a picturesque city at the foothills of the Annapurna mountains in the central hill region (Pahad). Taking inspiration from E. P. Thompson's classic *The Making of the English Working Class* (1963) and Jonathan Parry's work *Classes of Labour* (2020), this book ethnographically and ethno-historically explores various aspects of Nepal's industrial and urban modernity. More specifically, this book examines how Nepal's recent urbanization has contributed to the rapid growth of certain basic consumer industries such as food manufacturing and water bottling, as well as urban construction and related sand mining. The expansion of these new industries has been accompanied by a rising middle class that has increasing purchasing power and is changing its patterns of consumption. Instead of searching for universal explanations for the contemporary predicament of labor in the Global South (Mollona et al. 2010), this book explores these new work environments in the Nepali context. By doing so, the book aims to develop a more general understanding of the entanglements between urbanization and (industrial) working-class formations and how these are embedded in broader political contexts. More precisely, this book aims to provide answers to the following five questions.

1. As the rapid urbanization of Nepal has given rise to a growing urban middle class with increased purchasing power, what industries have emerged on the fringes of Nepal's cities? What are the working realities in such industries? More specifically, how does the composition of these emerging working classes relate to the consumption patterns of the new middle class?
2. If we look closely at the new work environments in modern food-processing factories, water-bottling plants, the construction industry, and sand mining, how do their respective working classes relate to each other and to the urban middle class?
3. What types of politics of labor have emerged in the new industries that are driven by the urban boom and the growing middle class? How have labor unions begun to challenge inequalities at work and make an impact on the everyday life of workers, as well as on the politics of labor?
4. How do people working in different positions within the industrial hierarchy deal with the fact that Nepal has become increasingly embedded in a broader global context? How does uneven development play out at the local level?
5. How do workers deal with uncertainty and insecurity triggered by the broader context of the Maoist revolution and the earthquakes of April 2015?

Throughout the book, I aim to explore answers to these fundamental questions regarding the development of Nepal's working class on the margins of urban spaces. Such questions emerged largely after a reflection upon five larger surprises that I encountered throughout my fieldwork. The first surprise was the rapid process of urbanization that I observed during my travels in Nepal between 2012 and 2020. Land prices in many places skyrocketed, with urbanization occurring in large municipalities like Kathmandu and Pokhara, in small villages along the east–west Mahindra highway, and even in some border towns. This urbanization fostered a growing middle class that often lived in residential villas in the towns. What struck me, however, was the growth in several associated businesses alongside the urban boom: the food and beverage industry produces the most revenue in the country, water-bottling factories have sprung up, construction is booming, and sand is being extracted from the rivers of the country. This surprisingly rapid urbanization gave rise to a core concern in this book: who is enabling the consumption patterns of the new middle class? In a country that lacks large-scale industries such as steel and coal mining, and where the rate of labor emigration is high, such a question should be relevant to academics and the broader public alike.

The second surprise during my fieldwork was the composition of the working classes in the industrial and urban work environments that I visited. As I learned over the years, in many of the new working environments the laborers saw themselves primarily as wage workers, instead of identifying predominantly along the lines of caste, ethnicity, or gender. Of course, there are differences among sites, as the various ethnographic chapters of this book will show. But what is striking is that the division between permanent and contract labor is highly important—at least in the food and water-bottling industries. The book will go into more depth on how this division between permanent and contract labor plays out in different settings.

My third surprise was the role of labor politics within the work environments. I was surprised to learn that in the food-processing companies, labor politics was very militant in the immediate aftermath of the Maoist revolution but declined in the years after. As I will show in detail throughout the first four chapters of this book, radical labor unions entered the factories and pressured management to give permanent status to a workforce that was mainly contract laborers. This signifies, as I will later elaborate, that the appearance of Maoists on the political stage has profoundly shaped the politics on the shop floor of various industries across the country. In comparison with other industrializing countries, I argue that Nepal is an outlier in terms of its industrial development trajectory. In certain industries a reverse of the current global neoliberal trends can be seen—a shift from casual to permanent labor, and a broad politics of labor among the workers.

The fourth surprise was related to the importance of uneven development between Nepal and other countries in the Middle East and Southeast Asia. This global context had a direct impact upon everyday experiences in the examined workplaces. This theme will crop up in all the chapters of the book and raise some important questions in the conclusion regarding the sustainability of militant labor politics in an environment that is embedded in a broader political economy of the Global South.

The fifth and final surprise was the creative and imaginative ways that people at various levels of the labor hierarchy engaged with uncertain futures. For example, I discovered that some industrialists in the lowland have used the geomancy practice of Vastu Shastra to "bring their factories in line with earthly energies" and heighten industrial output (see chapter 3). At the same time, many young workers try to escape the toil of industrial or urban working environments by migrating to distant places. To cope with the uncertainties involved in these difficult work trips, they consult with shamanic priests to figure out the most auspicious day for departure (see chapter 7). This secondary level of analysis will be discussed further throughout the book. Before turning to a more in-depth explanation of these surprises, I will begin the discussion by laying out two histories that are fundamental to the understanding of industrial and urban working classes in Nepal: the history of Nepal's "slow" industrial revolution and of Nepal's urbanization process.

Stocktaking of Nepal's Industrial Revolution

The history of Nepal's industrial development is relatively short. It goes back to the year 1936 when—after the formulation of the Nepal Companies Act—the Biratnagar Jute Mills were established (Jha 2016). This first industry was followed by other early industrial ventures in the 1930s and 1940s that largely fared badly or had to shut down quickly. By the early 1950s, "modern industry consisted of a few dozen small and medium sized firms, employing no more than 20.000 persons—less than 1 per cent of the total workforce" (Shah 1981:1063). This inaugural phase of industrialization was followed by the establishment of a few more government-owned industries in the 1950s and 1960s, particularly after the government of Nepal launched its first five-year plans in 1956 (Shah 1981:1064). Often such industries were established with the support of either China or the USSR (Jha 2016).

From 1960 to 1990 the country witnessed the rule of the Panchayat regime. During this period, few industries were established in the country. This may seem surprising, as throughout this time other "developing countries" embarked on courses of import-substituted industrialization. Such a course, for example, led to mass industrialization in neighboring India (Khilnani 1997). In Nepal, however, as outlined by Mallika Shakya, "the three national economic plans covering the period from 1956 to 1970 failed to trigger industrialization" (2018:19). This failure of the ruling royal family to trigger industrialization was rooted in at least two different reasons. First, it is certainly related to the royal family's preference to siphon off hefty profits from the few industries established throughout that period. This is from anecdotal observations by the aforementioned industrialist Binod Chaudhary, who described the climate of industrialization before the restoration of multi-party democracy in 1990 as follows: for every industry being set up, two taxes apparently had to be paid: first the official one, and then the one for the royal family, who often wanted to have a 50 percent partnership in any new industry (2016:107–108). This in turn gave little incentive to the landowning elites to transition into small-scale industrialists or for large-scale capitalists from abroad to invest in Nepal.[2]

Second, the lack of industrial development in Nepal at that time should be considered in light of the Cold War as well. Neither the United States nor the USSR had an interest in developing Nepal, as both saw Nepal as a comfortable cushion between the emerging powers of India and China. For instance, Narayan Khadka (2000) writes about USAID during the Cold War period, the agency through which America not only supported Nepal's development efforts but also helped Nepal maintain its independence and neutrality.

It was only at the end of the Panchayat regime, after Nepal's first Jana Andolan (People's Movement) in 1990, that industrial development in Nepal really took off. While this process is still little understood due to a lack of research, two ethnographies provide some insights. First, Mallika Shakya's (2018) illuminating work on the rise and fall of Kathmandu-based industrial garment production shows how a treaty between the United States and Nepal that granted quotas to Nepal for exports of garments stimulated the emergence of a large garment industry that employed tens of thousands of workers in Kathmandu in the 1990s. Second, my own previous work on the Kailali district area shows that while few brick factories were already established in the early 1980s, large numbers of brick kilns in the area were only being established from the 1990s onward (Hoffmann 2018a:171).

Most industries established across the country in the early 1990s were either located in the lowland area of Nepal or in urban centers in the hills. The reason for this restriction was that large swaths of the country remained unsuitable for industrial development due to the difficult hilly or mountainous terrain. Despite this disadvantage for industrial development, the idea of an "industrial future," also described as the "transition from an agricultural-based economy into an industrial society," has been a central promise of a number of politicians from a broad spectrum in Nepal. Its core idea—that Nepal can industrialize despite its geographical location—goes back to a 1930s study by a team of Swiss geographers led by the geologist Tony Hagen. Hagen argued that Nepal was "rich" in natural resources, particularly energy reserves, that could be exploited to start the industrialization process (Hagen 1969).

This uneven distribution of industrial development faced another challenge between 1996 and 2006, when Maoist insurgents fought a guerrilla war against the state. Throughout the insurgency, several industries were firebombed, industrialists were kidnapped for ransom, and often a voluntary donation (*chanda*) was asked of industrialists to keep the party's coffers filled. Some industrial laborers were involved in the conflict between Maoists and the state, while others used the opportunity to press their demands at sites of small-scale production, such as brick kilns (Hoffmann 2014a). In the wake of the insurgency, industrialization remained stalled; many of the industrial elite in the country were suspicious about the fragile peace until the dissolution of the people's army and its integration into the Nepal royal army in 2011.

Hence it is not surprising that so little industrial development has taken place across the country. According to a 2011 survey undertaken by the Bureau of Statistics of the Government of Nepal, approximately 250,000 people worked in the manufacturing economy in Nepal. The food and beverage, tobacco, and textile industries made up a large bulk of the workplaces within Nepal's manufacturing landscape (Gautam 2018:40). The construction sector was found to be the largest part of the informal economy. Obviously, such industrial and urban sites of employment were not distributed evenly around the country but occurred at certain nodal points: in or around large and midsize cities, along stretches of the highway, or close to border towns in the lowland area. This is because in such places there are larger markets and a growing urban middle class that consumes the few locally produced or processed goods. Let us now look more closely at the urban development process in Nepal.

Boomtown Nepal: From Shangri-La to Concrete Jungle?

Many of the Nepalis I have met over the years prefer to live in, or close to, an urban area. The stance that I heard from many was that life in or close to a city offered more modern facilities such as schools and hospitals, and made life easier. Given such frequent statements of desire for city life, it is hardly surprising that in recent years urban growth has been extremely rapid, and Nepal has become one of the top-ten fastest urbanizing countries in the world. Admittedly, compared to other countries, up till recently Nepal was still ranked among the top-ten least urbanized countries in the world. According to a recent study by the United Nations (2014:53), the level of urbanization raised from 8.9 percent to 18.2 percent within the period between 1990 and 2014. Despite this increase of urbanization, Nepal still ranked as the 6th least urbanized country in the world by 2014. However, as the same report highlights, Nepal is the only non-African country among the top ten fastest urbanizing countries in the world in the estimated period in between 2014 and 2050. It is projected to urbanize at an average annual rate of 1.9 percent over that time period (ibid 2014: 68). It is thus little surprising that a Nepali English-language newspaper headline recently proclaimed that "Nepal is going urban" (Koirala and Koirala 2019).

Importantly, Nepal's urbanization follows an uneven pattern. Urbanization occurs above all in the Kathmandu Valley, the Pokhara Valley, the Inner Tarai Valleys, and in market and border towns located on highway junctures between the east–west highway and the five main north–south corridors.

The economic consequence of this urban development is not limited to growth in local construction industries. Instead, urbanization is arguably the driver of other industries, such as the modern food-manufacturing industries, bottled-water industries, and sand-mining industries. The former is evidenced by studies in neighboring India showing that urbanization leads to an increased intake of modern industrially processed foods (see Bren d'Amour et al. 2020). The latter is evidenced by chapters 5 and 7 of this book, which show that the history of producing industrially processed bottled water and extracting sand is of relatively recent origin and corresponds to Nepal's recent urban growth. Of course, there are other consumer goods that are in much higher demand in an environment of rapid urbanization. But this study limits its focus to the histories of modern food manufacturing, bottled-water processing, housing construction, and sand mining.

By engaging in the linkages between urbanization and the growth of small-scale domestic industries, this analysis aims to move beyond conventional studies that highlight the effects of urbanization on consumption (e.g., Donner 2011) and to focus instead on the production of commodities that are consumed. A central concern of this book is to get to a better understanding of the work behind such middle-class consumption patterns. My aim is not to provide another account of how the new middle class of Nepal emerged, but rather to explore the consequences of rapid urbanization and middle-class formation on local labor forces. After all, the consumer goods purchased by the new middle class must be produced somewhere, and my aim is to shed light on the specific labor regimes required to realize such consumption patterns. Hence, I argue that urbanization combined with the formation of a middle class has profound effects for labor; urbanization creates both "opportunities" as well as new exploitative relations between capital and labor.

The Study of Nepal's Middle and Working Classes

The study of class has never been a central feature in anthropological studies of Nepal. In what has been written on the topic, little concerns the country's working classes; much of the limited scholarship on class in Nepal has been oriented around the idea of a "middle class" (Adhikari 2013; Crawford et al. 2008). Probably the first comprehensive attempt at providing a systematic analysis of the complexities of middle-class formation in Nepal can be found in the scholarly works of Marc Liechty (2003, 2017). Liechty's work indicates that Nepal's middle class was born in the 1950s, when—after the fall of the Rhana regime—expatriates and foreign organizations came to Kathmandu. In the wake of their arrival, new schools were established and global ideas were transmitted by the NGOs and foreign diplomats operating in the country. The result of this "invasion" was that Nepal's emerging middle classes strongly emphasized education and the formation of friendships with foreign professionals as a means of access to upward mobility. Since then, as Liechty (2003) shows, Kathmandu has seen the rise of a strong middle class over the last six decades, comprised of people who share a certain set of consumer practices and cultural codes that include the consumption of new forms of media, food, and sometimes even commodified sex.

Undoubtedly, Liechty's work has been fundamental not only in shedding light on the historical emergence of Nepal's middle class but also in outlining the more general relationship between (being middle) class and consumption. This book builds upon Liechty's work and contributes to an aspect of the overall conceptualization of class in Nepal that has so far been mostly overlooked: the relationship between class and production. More precisely, this monograph attempts to unearth the hidden connections between Nepal's working and middle classes. As James Carrier and Don Kalb (2015) remind us, class is a relational category, and following that, I view the two as interrelated phenomena. Indeed, one of the arguments of this book is that to understand the Nepali middle class, it is beneficial to explore the most common forms of middle-class consumption from the perspective of production. Only when one understands what happens behind the closed doors of food-related factory work and in the everyday construction sites across the booming housing industry can one understand how the rise of the middle class relates to new forms of inequality at the sites of production. While such a view may not broaden our understanding of the differentiations within the middle class, it does help conceptualize the relations between different classes.

One way to begin to consider the relationship between production and class in the Nepali context is to explore the marginal literature of a handful of scholars who have commented on the conditions of Nepal's working class (Kondos 1991; Kondos, Kondos, and Ban 1991, 1992; Seddon, Blaikie, and Cameron 2002; Shakya 2018; Hoffmann 2018a,b). Perhaps the first important work in this tradition was the 1979 book by Seddon, Blaikie, and Cameron, which commented on the general conditions of Nepal's working class and emphasized their strong links to the rural countryside. These authors' more recent works (Blaikie, Cameron, and Seddon 2005 [1980], 2002) may also warrant mentioning in a class-from-production context (even if their rather linear Marxian critique now looks quite outmoded), because they make the important point that not only is government employment a common road to middle-class status, but that the distribution of these jobs (still) disproportionately falls to high castes from the hill regions (this is also a theme discussed in chapter 2 in this book) (see also Lawoti 2005).

Finally, a spate of recent literature has emerged discussing the meaning of "working class" in the Nepalese context. For example, Mallika Shakya's (2018) discussion of the garment industry differentiated between those who worked as craftsmen and those who worked in mass manufacturing, echoing Massimiliano Mollona's (2009a) distinction between artisans and proletarians in a Sheffield-based steel plant. Shakya's work on the garment industry in Kathmandu (2018) situated garment labor within what she calls an "industrial ecosystem" that goes beyond discussions of the workplace. While such an approach includes actors like the World Trade Organization and the impacts of international trade agreements on local working realities, its downside is that its boundaries are blurred, and every shop floor becomes integrated into a wider international system of trade. The other important work on industry is a more regional view that considers how the country's rapid political change influences workplaces, while also acknowledging the various layers and hierarchies within the working class. My previous works on brick kilns (Hoffmann 2014a, 2018a) followed this approach, considering changes in the regional political economy, and concluded that the proletariat was not united but was rather split along ethnic differences. Finally, Dan Hirslund, in a discussion of construction work in Kathmandu (2021), considers labor markets to be structured by the broader political economies of the urban housing markets. My book builds upon these observations but also takes inspiration from debates about industrial labor in other countries. Above all, it is inspired by the tradition of industrial sociology that emerged from Marx's classic studies of the transformations of labor under capitalism (1977 [1848])—both those who followed him and those who critiqued him—as I will outline in the next section.

Anthropological Perspectives on Class and Industrial Labor

Some of the most influential conceptions of class can be found in the writings of Karl Marx (1977 [1848]) and Max Weber. Marx identified class in terms of property ownership and access to the means of production. In his view, under a capitalist economic system of production there were—at least in the long run—only two classes: those who owned capital and those who owned only their labor power (1977 [1848]:222). Importantly, for Marx these two classes were ultimately antagonistic, and he saw the dominant class not only controlling the access over the means of production but also exploiting the other. Hence, in order to rise, a working class needed to ultimately organize itself politically and transform from a "class in itself" into a "class for itself" through sustained class struggle. In contrast, Weber's concept of class focused less on "exploitation" and more on "life chances" (see Wright 2002). In Weber's worldview, members of a certain class shared the same life chances, which were determined by both their respective market situations as well as by the resources that individuals brought into market exchange (e.g., property as well as professional qualifications). Furthermore, in Weber's world, class was only one determinant in the political development of modern societies, and thus he pointed also to the relevance of religion and nationalism in the development of capitalist societies. Yet ultimately these different conceptions of class led both authors to make different predictions on the future of capitalist development. For Marx, the exploited working classes—deprived of the means of production— would ultimately rise up to overthrow the capitalist class. Weber, however, saw working classes only in the early days of capitalism being exploited, whereas later the relationship between capital and labor would be smoothed out.

One important strand in the critique of both Marx and Weber highlights that, in both cases, the notion of class is too structural. Accordingly, in this book I aim to also capture the lived experience of class, and in doing so I take my inspiration from the concept of class that was later popularized by the historian E. P. Thompson in his book *The Making of the English Working Class*. Thompson used class in its singular form to emphasize the growth of a working-class consciousness in Britain between 1780 and 1832. By doing so, he foregrounded the agency of ordinary people in the process of the making of a working class, going beyond a more common assertion that working classes were forged by historical forces. His impetus should not be understated. It was only after Thompson's discussion of the British working class that a substantial discourse among anthropologists surrounding the nature of class emerged, with the result that from the 1970s onward anthropologists and sociologists began challenging fundamental concepts of class and its manifestations in different societies (see, for example, Breman 1994, 2004; Burawoy 1979, 1985; Nash 1979; Kalb 1997; Parry 1999, 2020; Sanchez and Strümpell 2014).

Certainly, it is now a challenge to review this large corpus of anthropological and sociological literature on class. It is not my intention to do that here, as others have done so already, at least partly (see, for example, Carrier 2012, 2015; Carrier and Kalb 2015; Parry 2020). But instead of reviewing the literature in depth, I want to emphasize particular aspects of the debate on class and highlight the inspirations that this book draws from and builds upon. This is because, from among the aforementioned literature, this book was particularly inspired by the writings on industrial working classes by Michael Burawoy (1979, 1985), June Nash (1979), and Don Kalb (1997), as well as the work of Jonathan Parry (2020) (which I discuss in more detail toward the end of this section). Importantly, all four scholars argue in their writings against the general teleological assertions that Marx and Weber made: relations between capital and labor took different forms over different time-space complexes, and it was the task of ethnographic scrutiny to unearth such relations. Their contributions to discussions on the nature of class, however, consisted of placing a different emphasis on unearthing such a history.

First, Michael Burawoy, in his seminal book *Manufacturing Consent* (1979), highlights the centrality of the workplace in "manufacturing" consent to a specific regime of labor, and capitalist ideology more generally. For Burawoy, class was socially constructed at one's own workplace, and this construction did not only have to be mere exploitation. Rather, he examines how the exploitative relationship between capital and labor could be blurred through practices of managerial gamification of the workplace. Second, in her discussion of Bolivian tin miners—among others—June Nash revisits the older Marxian concept of class consciousness. Her work points to the importance of the interplay of culture in class formation processes, particularly highlighting how Bolivian indigenous Cholo culture informed expressions of class solidarity in Bolivia. In her view, class solidarity is not only framed at the workplace; one must take much wider processes of cultural identification into the analytical frame. Above all, as she points out (1979:332), it was the Bolivian tin miners' geopolitical situation at the periphery of global commodity chains that informed their ideas of class, exploitation, and uneven development.

Third, Don Kalb's magnum opus *Expanding Class* (1997) emphasizes the importance of analyzing class relationships from an ethno-historical perspective. Comparing Brabant's quaint central shoemaking district to its electrical boomtown, Eindhoven (home of the enormous Philips Corporation), Kalb shows the significance of working historically to analyze the development of industrial working classes in broad contexts. Moreover, by introducing the concept of "flexible familism," Kalb's work not only examines the importance of gender in class analysis but also widens the scope of what constitutes a class. In this way, Kalb's work breaks with older Marxist assertions of an essentialized class identity and paves the way for further class analysis that includes questions regarding culture, community, family, and gender.

Parallel to the emerging anthropological discourses of what constitutes class in the industrial context in the United States, South America, and Europe, a debate took place from the 1970s onward regarding the situation of industrial working classes in South Asia (see also De Neve 2005; Parry 2020). The pioneer in this debate was the British anthropologist Mark Holmstroem, who published in 1976 a case study of regular workers employed in four Bengaluru factories, thereby highlighting the importance of the division between those working in the formal economy and those toiling in the informal sector. For him, the former lived in—as he called it—a "citadel" (Holmstroem 1976) that provided safety and—relatively speaking—wealth for all those inhabiting it, whereas the lives of those toiling in the sea of the informal economy (e.g., as street hawkers, transporters, those carrying out small repairs) were marked by insecurity and danger.

This captivating image of a citadel drew attention and was dissected in subsequent years of debate. The Dutch sociologist Jan Breman, known for his now famous long-term ethnographic field studies of various forms of labor in the Indian state of Gujarat, over the years increasingly rejected it (1994, 2004), maintaining a picture of the Indian working classes that was marked by gradations of difference rather than a clear division between a labor elite and those working outside. In fact, even Mark Holmstroem himself, in his book *Industry and Inequality* (1984), began to paddle back from his strong assertion of a divided working class, now framing the relation between citadel and its outside more akin to a mountain slope, less clear-cut and sometimes even linked through kinship.

However, Jonathan Parry's (2020) seminal monograph on Bhilai's industrial working class—which forms the fourth source of inspiration for this book—provides a different image of the Indian working class that questions the "mountain-slope model." Parry found that the gulf separating those laboring as permanent workers from those employed as contract workers was huge, leading to the proposition—at least from the canvass of his field site in Bhilai—that India's working classes seemed divided into two segments: those who had permanent jobs and those who worked as casual laborers. This division was not a pure economic division, but it was experienced by both segments as living in two different life-worlds, and therefore he maintained that—for Bhilai—the Indian working class remained divided into two different working classes, thereby not only debunking Marx but also others that followed his lead (e.g., Bernstein 2006).

This book is informed by these debates on the nature and characteristics of the industrial working classes in neighboring India. I want to highlight that class in Nepal is not an alien product but a lived reality that comes with a rich vocabulary. Hence, this book follows Parry's (2020) lead and takes a very close look at the hierarchies of labor that have merged in the Nepali context. For example, chapters 1 to 3 show the importance of the division between permanent and contract laborers in a food-processing factory on the margins of Nepalgunj. These observations prompt the hypothesis that class trumps caste, ethnicity, and gender—at least for the food-processing factories in both the lowlands (chapter 3) and the mid-hills of Nepal (chapter 4). While I am in line with Parry's suggestion that "a dichotomous model of class seems too blunt of an instrument" (ibid 2020:43) to account for the division between permanent and casual workers that also pervades these industries, I argue that in the Nepali context the division between "company" and "contract" workers is likely to be less drastic than he claims, as a substantial amount of Maoist union activism has meant that a substantial number of temporary workers were enabled to acquire the status of permanent company workers (chapters 1 and 4). This confirms my earlier work on Nepal in which I claimed that working-class formation in Nepal has been deeply influenced by both the Maoist conflict (2018) and broader forms of uneven development in the wider region (Hoffmann forthcoming).

And yet this book also suggests that in other work environments, class matters less: for example, in the bottled-water plants in the Kaski district, gender and ethnicity matter more (see chapter 5); in the informal economy of Pokhara, it is again ethnic laborers who do the most backbreaking jobs, and ethnicity and gender are important factors in constituting the local working classes. In this way, the book highlights the complexity of class formations due to the entanglements of class, ethnicity, and gender, and shows how class developments, while pointing to an overarching emergence of class as a marker of self-identity, develop differently in various parts of Nepal. Accordingly, cultural conceptions of the interplay between gender, ethnicity, and work continue to play a central role in managerial decisions about who gets to work at a specific workplace and under what conditions.

Comparing Labor at Different Sites

Comparison is at the heart of the anthropological enterprise. Since the inception of the discipline in the nineteenth century, anthropologists have always compared. Yet since the 1980s, the practice of making comparisons across field sites has increasingly become contested with the rise of the so-called crisis of representation debate. Anthropologists began asking to what extent one field site can be compared with another, and in what contexts. Two camps emerged: those who reject comparison—the "comparison exiteers"—and those who insist on its validity. Within the "exiteers" camp, a prominent segment includes the followers of the influential US anthropologist Clifford Geertz (1973). They argue that one must look at the specifics of a culture and should stay within this paradigm. On the other hand, there are those who favor comparison, highlighting the commonalities rather than the differences between groups.

These broader debates within the discipline of anthropology have also influenced the anthropology of labor. Certainly, labor provokes a comparison with other settings as well as the inclination to categorize labor practices into different segments and labels. But nevertheless, most anthropological monographs focus on a specific setting, such as a factory or an industrial town. The influence of Burawoy's writings (1979, 1985) cannot be neglected. In his influential critique of Harry Braverman (1974), Burawoy pointed to the value of anthropological investigations into the culture of work at the workplace. Much anthropological writing has either followed or critiqued Burawoy while remaining within the confines of one field site. Only recently has a new brand of the anthropology of industrial labor emerged, one that makes comparisons between different cities (Parry 2020) or even countries (Lazar 2012; Parry 2020).

This monograph stands in line with this interest in comparison, and one of the central aims of this book is to cover new terrain in an anthropological comparison of labor. For example, the book asks questions such as: What is the difference between working in a food factory in the lowlands versus the highlands of Nepal? How is food-processing factory work different from working in a mafia-controlled sand mine? By focusing on such comparisons, the book aims to make a contribution to such comparative labor studies. In contrast to the aforementioned scholarship, it contributes to the marginalized field of comparative labor studies in at least three distinct ways. First, unlike most monographs of industrial labor, the book focuses on four different industries. This focus on distinct fields—both formal and informal—allows for some interesting comparisons between various sectors of Nepal's non-agricultural economy. For example, one of the findings in this book suggests that work in "mafia-controlled" sand mines is far more lucrative than work in food-processing factories or large parts of the construction sector (see chapter 7).

Second, the industries discussed have all been built within the last three decades. Most of the industries discussed only began to develop after the end of the civil war and the period of post-conflict uncertainty, the two earthquakes of 2015, and the subsequent six-month blockade of Nepal by India. Thus, an alternative reading of this book is as a way to understand the reconstruction of Nepal after the end of the dictatorship in the Jana Andolan of 1990. From this historical perspective, the book provides insights into how both employers and workers deal with the uncertainty caused by larger events. For example, we learn that food-processing companies have turned to priests to realign their factories according to the principle of Vastu Shastra, and that workers in sand mines consult spirit mediums to learn the most auspicious date on which to leave the mine and travel abroad in search of better employment prospects.

Third, a comparative view on labor and its politics in both the lowland region and the mid-hills of Nepal allows for a deconstruction of common regional stereotypes. Since the end of the insurgency period, there has been a view of the hills and highlands as being "civilized" while the lowland region—the Tarai—is somehow "wild," "full of unrest," and maybe even considered to be "dangerous." My ethnographic material shows, however, that many of these stereotypes are exaggerations and that the lowlands and highlands have much in common in terms of labor politics and the ways these stereotypes play out within the factories.

Last, a comparative view of labor allows us to make some assertions about the role of political patronage in industries. Chapter 7 of this book, for example, shows how political patronage matters in sand-mining industries. This might be familiar ground to those who are acquainted with South Asian labor politics. Jonathan Parry, for example, shows in his ethnography of mine work outside the steel town of Bhilai that the left must sometimes engage in shady deals with mine owners to advance its cause (Parry 2020). In the last chapter, we see how the new Maoist government of Nepal engages with shady deals of "dons" in the sand mines, while they remain less invested in everyday construction work (see chapter 6). That is not to say that ideology does not matter anymore in Nepal, but such an analysis allows for a more complex understanding of political patronage in Nepal's industrial and urban labor landscapes.

This book has a twofold ambition. First, it aims to shed light on the labor regimes and forms of inequality found within the emerging industrial landscape and construction industry of Nepal. Examining class-based processes in such industries over the last three decades is important because of the continuing large-scale migration of Nepalis to other places abroad. Second, it highlights the role of unions in such industries and how unions—and their associated middle-class activism—challenge inequalities at work. As a result of this ambition, one of the main insights of this book is that while the working classes are primarily from ethnic indigenous groups, the inequalities among them have been addressed by unions, particularly in the direct after-math of the "People's War." However, the labor union activism that made these gains subsequently faded over the years, and it now takes place only in certain parts of the economy. This book also contains an account of the partiality and spatiality of labor union activism in Nepal. But before elaborating on this, the next section provides a more detailed description of the two towns in which fieldwork was conducted.

The Field Sites: Nepalgunj and Pokhara

Nepalgunj is a border town in the western lowlands of Nepal and ranks among the poorest of Nepal's cities. It is known in the wider area for its predominantly Muslim population, the Madesh uprising in the aftermath of the revolution, and its local community of gold smugglers, who operate across the nearby border with India. It is not a beauty spot, but instead is known for its main artery road strewn with rubbish and lined with shops, businesses, and other half-built concrete buildings, with roads leading off into residential areas on both sides. Undoubtedly, for any visitor, the town has a slightly Wild West atmosphere, where labor migration to faraway places in the Middle East and Malaysia, as well as smuggling and cross-border trade with nearby India, are probably far more important economic activities than industrial labor. Nepalgunj is in Banke, which is one of the five districts in western Nepal where the *kamaiya* system of debt-bonded labor existed until 2000. The town's population is a mix-ture of groups such as Madheshi and Tharu, who are referred to by others and who also view themselves as Adivasis (literally "original settlers" or autochthons), along with Hindu and Muslim communities. The town is also known for its trading community and its small industrial corridor along the highway from Nepalgunj to the neighboring city of Kohalpur. It is unique in Nepal for its predominantly Muslim population, and locals refer to the Muslim neighborhood, Eklaini, as a "little Pakistan." There are many local rumors that the town hosts a few international security specialists who carefully watch the Muslim community and its madrasa schools for any activity by Taliban fighters or other extremist groups.

Pokhara, on the other hand, is in the Kaski district in the mid-western hills of Nepal and ranks among the country's most developed and prosperous towns. The city has witnessed spectacular growth from a remote village with a few thousand inhabitants in the 1960s to Nepal's second largest city with an estimated 402,000 inhabitants. Over the same period, the city has developed a massive tourism industry; early foreign tourists were adventurous hippies arriving in town via the famed "magic bus" tours along the hippie trail. Others followed later, and by 2000 an estimated 100,000 tourists came to town every year. One of the most striking elements to a tourist visiting the city is certainly the cleanliness of the streets in Pokhara, which may be unique in Nepal.

Unlike Kathmandu, Pokhara has never been a center of Nepali politics. Its residents engage mainly in tourism, trade, or self-employed businesses, and hail from a large variety of religious, caste, and ethnic backgrounds. In terms of religion, the majority of inhabitants are Hindus, followed by Buddhists, Christians, and Muslims. In terms of caste and ethnicity, the dominant groups are those from the traditional Nepali higher castes, such as Brahmins and Chhetris, as well as those from the Gurung and Magar ethnic communities who reside in rural villages on the town's outskirts. Throughout the Maoist insurgency—also called the "People's War" or the "Maoist conflict"—the town was mostly spared from bomb attacks or other spectacular forms of violence that were seen in other Nepali towns such as Tikapur (Hoffmann 2018a) and Nepalgunj (Hoffmann 2018b, 2018c).

One resident described Pokhara as a city "where all kinds of people can live together peacefully. It is like a little Switzerland." However, the innocent image of ethnic harmony conveyed by such statements has not always been totally accurate. Although there has not been a major violent inter-ethnic conflict as in Nepalgunj, a group of activists from the Gurung ethnic group fought for the establishment and recognition of an autonomous Tamuwan region in the aftermath of the Maoist revolution. In 2012, activists from this group held a conference in Pokhara,[3] which ended with the demand for a separate Gurung state, and in the following years at least one strike was held by Tamuwan activists and a road junction was decorated with Tamuwan insignia. But the activities of Tamuwan activists have been largely forgotten after the restructuring of the Nepalese state into different zones. Few of those who would be old enough to remember the group's activities like to talk about the Tamuwan idea.

Despite the differences between the two sites of my fieldwork—the Agrawal food-processing factory on the outskirts of Nepalgunj and the instant noodle factory at the margins of Pokhara—I discovered an axis of comparison that became more interesting as my work progressed: in both cities, Maoist unions had challenged the distinction between permanent and contract labor over the years. In both cases, the food-processing factories were initially run largely on the basis of casual labor. Later, when the Maoist unions began to organize in the factories and draw members from the already operating unions, the prevailing industrial labor relations were seriously challenged.

Notes on Methodology

Prior to this study, I had already undertaken a larger research project on Maoism and debt-bonded labor in western Nepal (Hoffmann 2018a). Yet my first systematic encounter with the worlds of industrial work was on an initial trip to Nepal while doing research for the Max Planck Institute for Social Anthropology in April 2013. I visited a hydropower plant bordering the districts of Accham and Dhailekh in the far-western hills of Nepal and soon learned that the construction of the hydropower plant had been stopped due to an alleged Maoist splinter group having ransacked the construction site. The development company then withdrew its workforce from the site. I then moved into the Tarai where I knocked on factories' doors, making inquiries about the possibility of doing research. Several declined to let me conduct any research for my project, but the manager in one food-processing factory was very helpful in my inquiries about industrial development and the new forms of inequalities that emerge from it. Research was carried out in this factory as well as in some adjacent food-processing factories between October 2013 and April 2014, with a short return trip in September and October 2014. This was the first phase of my research into industries and inequalities in and around the city of Nepalgunj. After carefully reviewing my ethnographic material, I decided to return to Nepal for a second round of fieldwork in October 2018 until April 2019, followed by another short trip between January and March 2020 before I had to leave Nepal due to the onset of the COVID-19 pandemic. Throughout these two trips, I decided to focus on industries in Pokhara, a city in the mid-western hills in Nepal.

The reason for this choice was that Pokhara has an industrial area, which hosts food-manufacturing factories. While waiting to gain access to such industries, I was also beginning to investigate labor in the industrial water-bottling plants of the town as well as in the informal economy of the town. In particular, I focused on the construction industry in the city and on the unregulated sand mining that was occurring in the nearby rivers. The latter two industries are closely related, as sand is one of the most essential raw materials needed in the construction industry. While weaving together these different strands of research, I began to understand that all my different research sites were related in one or another important way. First, each of these industries was linked to a growing middle class and their aspirations for modern concrete houses (which require sand), bottled water, and industrially processed foods. Second, while spending time at construction sites I learned that some of the labor in both Pokhara and Nepalgunj hailed from ethnic Tharu villages in the western lowlands of Nepal. In the construction industry I even met two Tharu construction workers who previously worked as debt-bonded laborers in the agricultural fields of Bardiya. Similarly, as chapter 2 will discuss at length, some of the former bonded laborers also worked in the food-processing factory in Nepalgunj.

One challenge in choosing these "multiple" field sites (see Marcus 1995) was my own fears and doubts that the resulting study would be lacking in the depth of ethnographic insight that one would gain from focusing on a single site. In the early phase of this study, I sometimes felt that I should have stuck to one field site and sat out my time like a mole on his hill. Nevertheless, over the course of my fieldwork, I followed the lead of chance encounters and sometimes even my own gut instincts and allowed myself to develop multiple field sites. I increasingly saw this as less of a problem. By engaging in multiple field sites, I could steer my fieldwork back to the margins of the grand anthropological tradition of comparison. Here I want to explicitly emphasize the phrase "to the margins"—not "to the core"—because in this book the anthropological tradition of comparison does not play the role it actually deserves. But it is my hope that my resulting approach will be an important contribution in advancing the debate toward a comparative analysis of labor.

Second, I must admit that the fact that there has been so little academic attention paid to Nepal's industrial landscapes facilitated and made my own gathering of ethnographic data on the industries in the region more meaningful. Spending time with employers, unionists, and workers in various industries in both the lowlands and the mid-hills produced valuable knowledge and insights that could not otherwise be obtained. The first phase of my fieldwork in the food-processing factories in Nepalgunj gave me a better understanding of workplace dynamics that proved helpful in the second phase of my research in Pokhara. I could often point out differences between work practices and discourses in the lowlands and in the mid-hills, which employers generally found interesting and sometimes even amusing. Over time I also realized that being an outsider from a European country who had gathered some small understanding of Nepali labor relationships helped me facilitate conversations with management at new workplaces. Employers who allowed me to visit their workplaces and spend time with the workers were often keen on engaging in debates comparing the industrial development in Nepal with processes in Europe.

Nevertheless, I do not want to romanticize the challenges of accessing the workplaces that I encountered throughout my fieldwork. During my first trip to the food-processing factories in Nepalgunj, I was only occasionally allowed access to the factory floors within the factory compound. The time I spent on the factory floors helped me gain an understanding of workplace dynamics, but most of my fieldwork was spent outside the factory at tea stalls where I could conduct interviews with workers. In addition, as I visited with management frequently in the beginning and later befriended Maoist unionists on the factory floor, I had to constantly renegotiate the relationships between management, unionists, and workers in the factories near Nepalgunj.

However, my experience in the lowland food-processing factories helped me later in gaining access to the factory in Pokhara. I was now aware that management was more worried about industrial espionage than about uncovering inequalities among workers. Therefore, in my initial interviews with management, I always carefully assured them that I was not interested in sharing sensitive data about the company's technology with third parties. Access to the construction sites and sand mines in Pokhara was surprisingly much easier to obtain. But access to the bottled-water factories proved difficult for several reasons, mainly related to the small size of the factory setting (see chapter 5). Probably the most challenging point in the fieldwork was when I interviewed workers in a small water-bottling plant outside of Pokhara while the employer sat next to me and prohibited me from asking in a survey about the wages in the factory. However, frequent visits to this and other water-bottling factories allowed me to learn more about both the history and character of the water-bottling industry as well as the dynamics of the factory floor.

In my first months of fieldwork in Nepalgunj, I was fortunate to be able to frequently visit the management of a food-processing factory to discuss many different aspects of work in the factory. Throughout these visits I was also allowed to visit various work areas inside the factory. Initially, a junior manager followed me around, but I was soon allowed to roam more freely inside the factory compound. It turned out that the workers were often too busy to talk while at work, and so as not to disturb their routines, I began to conduct interviews in the tea stall outside the factory gates. To get to know workers better, I initially used a survey to interact with them. With the help of my assistant, I was able to get to know a large part of the workforce inside the factory. There were several individuals who I came to know very well, including some of the Maoist unionists, the contractors of the factory, and some of the workers. For reasons of confidentiality, their personal information has not been revealed in this book. My interest in the lives of workers seemed to be taken as a sign of solidarity, and my previous work with former bonded laborers (see Hoffmann 2018a) allowed me to draw upon my knowledge of the history of the western Tarai region to get workers from the Tharu community engaged in conversations about their current situation. I also visited the houses of former bonded laborers in Bardiya and those of Madheshi workers in the villages nearby.

In the second phase of field research conducted between 2018 and 2020, I divided my time between the food-processing factory in the town's industrial zone, the water-bottling plants outside the zone, the construction sites spread all over the town, and sand mines at a nearby riverbed. The research on construction sites and sand mines began while I was waiting for a permit to enter the water-bottling plants and the food-processing factory in the industrial zone. The personal contacts of my research assistant were very helpful in this process, and they put me in touch with the contractors in the city. I often visited the day labor market in town where casual construction workers hung out in search of employment, and I was able to make friends with some of them. Since the construction industry was unionized and everyone referred to the union building as the one "near the bus station," I also visited these offices several times to get an idea of how the construction industry was organized and what labor struggles had been fought over the years.

Because sand is a fundamental part of the construction industry, my research on construction inevitably led to the sand mines that have been dug out of the rivers around Pokhara. Starting in October 2018, I frequently visited a sand mine on the Sethi river, which flows through Pokhara. After about two months, I also visited other sand mines in two villages nearby. Despite the sand mines' reputation for being run by a mafia, it was surprisingly easy to connect with sand-mine workers, and frequent visits allowed me to form friendships with some of them. Sometimes I had tea with some of the sand miners at a cooking area at the entrance to their dormitory near the river. I also met a contractor at another mine and visited his community to better understand how the contracting system works. In addition, I sometimes visited sand mines near Pokhara in the guise of a "potential investor" to get a better understanding of the going rates for sand and labor in the mines. Such roleplaying seemed to be the only way to get an accurate understanding of the investments behind sand mining.

The role of curiosity in one's own research topic is often left out of accounts of research methods, but with new research being conducted on the role of emotion in ethnographic knowledge production (Davies and Spencer 2010), it is worth mentioning. While the general assumption seems to be that anthropologists are always curious about their topic, my own experience in the field proved to be different in retrospect. While doing my fieldwork, I realized that I tended to get most interested in the experiences and discourses surrounding different forms of work after I had made a visit to a workplace. It was at this point that I could understand the basic organization of the work, and when the more productive research questions evolved, that shaped the post-fieldwork writing of this book. For example, when I was told by Maoist unionists that they had indeed given out permanent contracts to the casual workforce, I was eager to follow up and double-check with other actors such as management, workers, and state authorities in the field. In another instance, when I realized that work in the sand mines outside of Pokhara is organized by so-called dons, my curiosity in sand miners was raised sharply.

Certainly, the underlying structure of curiosity is shaped by one's journey through the academic institutions and by the people with whom one meets and works. In this sense, I believe that academic curiosity is not an individual affair but rather is socially produced by one's own history in academia. This is not to belittle my own achievements but to honestly acknowledge the influence of other academic "curiosity seekers" in shaping the course of my research. For example, the work with the Max Planck Institute group on comparing rates of permanent versus casual labor shaped the research focus of the first part of this book. The stay at re:work in Berlin, where I worked with many historians, led me later to pay more attention to local histories of industry, for example in the local construction industry in Pokhara. I also realized throughout my second period of fieldwork that staying away from social media and email accounts was productive to stimulating my own curiosity while conducting fieldwork. These heightened and lowered forms of curiosity are a part of anthropological fieldwork, and how one's own research curiosity is shaped by wider institutional frameworks in addition to the fieldwork itself remains a topic of future anthropological exploration.

Map of the Book

This book is an account of a segment of Nepal's new industrial and urban working classes. It focuses on those working in modern industrial food-processing factories, water-bottling plants, urban construction sites, and sand mines. It depicts a situation in which a particular group of people has emerged as a working population that silently operates behind the scenes of the country's rapid urbanization process. The Nepali industrial and urban working classes, which hardly existed a few decades ago, are currently taking new shape(s); new divisions between permanent and casual laborers as well as the interplay between ethnicity, caste, and gender are key to understanding the formation of these emerging working classes. The broader political context in which the working classes form must also be considered. At the same time, while Nepal's industrial and urban working classes are emerging, the country finds itself drawn into wider labor markets in distant places like the Middle East and Southeast Asia. Uneven development between countries, as well as between different regions and cities within a country, begins to impinge on the value of work and on the ways people see their personal circumstances and futures. We can only make sense of modern Nepal and its future if we begin to understand the dialectical context in which modern working classes respond to broader forces of uneven development.

Chapter 1, besides serving as an introduction to the urban context of the study, zooms in to observe the industrial food-processing factories that have sprung up on the margins of the urban municipality of Nepalgunj. We examine how working classes are divided between permanent and casual labor, and how Maoist union activism has distinctly shaped the new working class in the food industry. Chapter 2 provides a detailed description of those who were left out of union activism, while chapter 3 shows how religion functions to legitimize the emerging division between permanent and casual labor—thus opening a window into the everyday lives of workers outside of their workplace. Drawing on these chapters' insight that the post-revolutionary political context has fundamentally shaped the course of class formation in the lowland region of Nepal, chapter 4 maps out how Maoist union activism has been equally important in the formation of class in a modern food-processing factory on the edges of Pokhara. Why, for example, have unions been so successful in organizing workers in the modern food-processing industry? Why has their initial enthusiasm and authority declined in the post-conflict context? Answers to such questions are explored in chapter 4. Chapter 5 turns away from the food-processing factories and begins to examine labor in the water-bottling plants in Pokhara and the Kaski district. Here we encounter a working class that is highly gendered and ethnicized, and that has not seen much of the union activism observed in the food industries. The chapter explores the reasons for this absence of union activism and aims to capture a more nuanced picture of the impact of Maoism on manufacturing industries more generally.

Chapter 6 begins to move beyond the factory gates into the informal urban economy of Pokhara. It focuses on the construction workers in the city, the interplay of class, ethnicity, and gender, and the failure of unions to organize workers more substantially in the construction economy. Finally, chapter 7 moves into the sand mines that have been dug out of nearby riverbanks and examines the conditions of work in this lucrative industry. It further explores the themes of class formation and class politics in relation to new forms of uneven development, as well as the uncertainties that emerge from these changes. An understanding of the situation of labor in both the industrial and urban working environments leads to a key argument of the book: that Nepal's industrial and urban working classes have been profoundly shaped by broader political economies and uneven developments in the region.

Notes

1. Pandey's critique concerned the original Nepali version, which was published as *Binod Chaudhary: Atmakatha* (Nepalaya, Kathmandu, 2013).
2. Binod Chaudhary describes the relationship between industrialists and the royal family as follows: "We would invest the capital and do all the work, and the royal palace would stake a claim for a majority of the shares. They would fix their share ratio themselves and 'grant' the remaining share to us. The prevalent ratio was 49:51—49 per cent for the real investor and 51 per cent for the Palace. Anyone who would not accept such a deal was better off packing his bags and leaving the country" (2016:108).
3. This only relates to national politics. In terms of ethnic politics, Pokhara became the center of the Tamuwan movement. For example, according to one publication: "A Three-Day Conference of Indigenous Nationalities Held from 29 April in the City of Pokhara in Western 'Tamuwan' Region Concluded Yesterday Issuing a 12-Point 'Tamuwan' Declaration," https://aippnet.org/nepal-indigenous-nationalities-compre hensive-conference-concludes-with-a-12-pointdeclaration/.

PART I

Work at the Margins of Nepalgunj

— Chapter 1 —

FROM CASUAL TO PERMANENT WORK IN A FOOD FACTORY

Introduction

It was through Tarun, a friend, political analyst, and Nepalgunj native, that I first met Arjun. I had told Tarun over a chai in Kathmandu that I was interested in the history of the industries in the Banke area, and he recommended that I talk to Arjun. Taking a deep drag on a Benson Hedges cigarette, Tarun lowered his voice and explained mysteriously: "Arjun is the owner of a sugar mill in the area. The land where the mill was set up was captured by Maoist insurgents and 'the people' during the emergency period. If you visit his land today, you'll see more than a thousand families living there, but the sugar mill, the good old sugar mill, does not exist anymore."

Tarun gave me Arjun's number. I noted it down and then we changed topics. The next day, however, I remembered the conversation and rang up Arjun in Nepalgunj. He was very welcoming when I said I was a foreign researcher and interested in hearing his story. He explained to me that he was now running a new business—a petrol station in town—and invited me to come visit his new office on my next trip to Nepalgunj. The next morning, I sat in a Yeti airplane flying from Kathmandu into the hot lowland area—the Tarai—in the plains of the country. It felt familiar being back researching the area, as I had previously spent eighteen months in the Kailali district (see Hoffmann 2018a). Upon arrival, I went straight to Arjun's office at the gasoline station to get to know more of his story.

In 1984, Arjun finished his MBA from a prestigious university in New Delhi, India, and decided to return to Nepal. It was during the

rule of the Panchayat regime, and Arjun had just received a prestigious offer to work in the management department of a soon-to-be
opened airline branch office at the Tribuhvan airport in Kathmandu.
However, he decided to turn down the offer and to return to his
parents' house in the Banke district in order to become the caretaker
and manager of a sugar mill that his father ran. At the beginning the
decision to run the sugar mill was a large success. Business went
smoothly and he and his brother gradually managed to raise their
profits. But they started to face trouble after the first People's Movement when the political climate changed and multi-party democracy
was restored. People started coming on to their 800 acres of land
and eating the sugar cane. Workers began to ask for higher wages
and Arjun had to hire expensive security guards. Up to ten security
guards were protecting his business. Still, he and his brother managed to keep the sugar mill operating.

The "real problems" started with the outbreak of the Maoist insurgency. With the Maoists' influence spreading into the Terai area in the
1990s, they eventually made a visit to the sugar mill. They asked for
food and cash donations. Arjun did his best and managed to negotiate with the rebels. They had a "good relationship" for years. Yet this
relationship also got him into trouble in 2000. That year a few army
members disguised themselves as Maoists and approached one of
his workers. They asked the worker to deliver raw materials from the
sugar mill that were needed to build explosive devices. Arjun denied
having such materials, but they kept insisting. Finally, he gave in
and agreed to meet them a week later. When the time had passed,
he was surprised to see three strange characters returning to his mill
along with a group of state army personnel. He was immediately arrested and taken to a nearby army post in the neighboring Bardiya
district. There he was blindfolded, handcuffed, and badly beaten by
the army personnel. They charged him with having provided explosive devices to the Maoists and accused him of murdering more than
twenty-five people. However, he insisted on his innocence. Only after
three weeks was his painful treatment softened, and when the army
could not provide any proof of these claims after three months, he
was released from the army camp.

By late December of 2003, however, the relationship between the
two industrialists and the Maoist insurgents changed drastically.
Arjun and his brother were in the sugar mill when four men approached. They announced that they were Maoists and had decided
to appropriate the sugar mill and the adjacent farmland. They took
Arjun and his brother hostage for about half an hour before releas-

ing them. Arjun and his brother went back to Nepalgunj, and later that evening hundreds of families began squatting and settling on the land. They looted the sugar mill stores and began gradually deconstructing the sugar mill and selling the equipment. Arjun and his brother lost everything. They have never returned to the sugar mill and the police have refrained from removing the squatters from the site. Arjun explained, "You must have heard by now about Arjun Singh. He is one of the criminals who have been extorting money from us industrialists. Not only from us but also from the common people. His group not only extort money but have also kidnapped businessmen in the area."

When referring to Singh's activities, Arjun used the term "Maoist." He insisted that Singh's group was behaving like a Maoist organization and that some of his members had been in other Maoist groups previously. Arjun and his brother suffered from chronic fear. Arjun remained suspicious and mistrustful of strangers who phoned him to meet up for business. He coped with this fear by restricting his movement. As he told me: "I don't feel safe outside of Nepalgunj. In case some stranger invites me to a rural place—let's say twenty kilometers from here—I will not go, or only go after checking up on him. In a village, anything can happen, even though the police have returned. That's why we [he and his family members] restrict our movement and remain in town. At nighttime, we don't go outside, it remains too dangerous for us. Too many people have been kidnapped, and some even killed."

Moreover, Arjun was keen on emphasizing the different security status that Pahari and Deshi/Marwari industrialists enjoy. Being a Deshi, a local industrialist of Indian origin, he complained that the state treated them as "second-class citizens." He stated that the Pahari industrialists enjoyed much better security protection than the Madeshi industrialists. When I asked him to elaborate, he provided the following example: "Imagine you are being threatened by a criminal group. If you go to a local police station and you are a Pahari industrialist, the police will keep quiet and try to provide protection for you. Yet if you are a Deshi/Madeshi industrialist, then the police will leak your case to the media and your life will be in danger."

The meeting with Arjun, his experiences during the revolutionary period and its aftermath, as well as his approach to the political situation provide a unique entry point into this chapter. I attempt to further develop such themes by exploring the character and composition of class in local modern factories, and the ways in which the broader political-economic context has shaped the dynamics of work. My focus is on a couple of industrial sites along the road toward the East Mahindra highway, comprising food factories, a cement factory, and brick kilns. One of the most important industries in this industrial corridor is a modern food-processing factory that stands out for its cleanliness. It is the site of the Agrawal food-processing company, part of the large Agrawal Group that was set up in 1996 by a Marwari industrialist.[1] A portion of the company's workforce of five hundred are now employed as contract laborers and often come from far-western Tharu communities where they were previously indentured as bonded laborers.

This fieldwork concentrates on industries in and around the urban municipality of Nepalgunj in the Banke district. While the town has a large Muslim population, almost all workers in the nearby factories are Hindus who largely comprise three different groups: Indians predominantly from the states of Bihar and Uttar Pradesh, flatland dwellers (Madheshis) from the Banke district, and indigenous workers from the Tharu ethnic group in the mid and far-western lowland regions of Nepal. In this context I encountered a story slightly different from the common narrative of the global precariatization of labor (Ferguson 1999; Joshi 2003; Breman 2004; Mollona 2009a) in an era of "accumulation by dispossession" (Harvey 2003). In this Nepalese context over the past few years, labor in the food-processing industry has become more rather than less secure for the Madheshi segment of the workforce. For this ethnic group, moreover, a minimum wage has been implemented, and in contrast with the situation common elsewhere in the region, workers are now represented by leaders from their own social stratum. I argue that these changes in the situation of labor are an outcome of the Maoist revolution and the pressure that the company's Maoist union has been able to put on management—in short, a consequence of the wider political context. But, as I further argue, these results of Maoist activism have also protected workers from the intensification of labor that neoliberal conditions have promoted elsewhere (Millar 2015).

I do not claim that the Maoists have by any means solved all the problems in the factory. In fact, their union is entrenching new ethnic cleavages in the workplace. Nor do I claim that the greater labor security that I describe extends to all the western lowlands of Nepal, nor to Nepal as a whole. At other factories near my field site, labor has been casualized rather than regularized, and minimum wages are still not paid. This was, for example, the case in some of the nearby factories where the Unified Communist Party of Nepal (UCPN) Maoist union has not yet been able to organize. Where it has been able to organize, however, the situation resembles the one I describe.

The local categories that distinguish between permanent and precarious labor are important. The Nepali word *isthai* (permanent) signifies a long-term contract with a fixed, regular income. It is mostly synonymous with the Indian concept of *naukri*, and some of the Indian workers employed in the factory use this term to refer to their permanent jobs. As in India (Parry 2014:349), a *sarkari isthai* (government job) is considered best. It is well paid, provides opportunities for additional earnings from *ghus* (bribes), and is considered to be fairly relaxed in terms of the workload. There is a common Nepalese saying, "Raja ko kam kahile jaala ghaam" (When the king's work finishes, there's still sun)—that is, you can always get off early. According to another, at such a job "Kahile haatar na hune" (Hurry never comes).

But sarkari isthai is difficult to get if one does not have *aafno manchhe* (one's own people) in the government, even though the Nepali government, in the interim constitution of 2006, introduced quotas for 'backward communities and castes' that are still in effect today. They might be implemented in modern towns like Kathmandu and Pokhara, but in western Nepal the 45 percent quota for "backward" communities and castes has little effect—the situation is more like "80 percent reservation" for the upper castes. In this light, especially considering that Nepal's political economy depends heavily on "donor countries" such as Germany, the United States, and the United Kingdom, it is unsurprising that many consider working in a large international organization, or even for one of the bodies of the United Nations, the most desirable route. Such jobs are extremely well paid and sometimes involve foreign postings.

In contrast to isthai work, "contract" work comprises a variety of categories. At the district level, the Nepalese state distinguishes between three types of contract work. *Asthai kam* and *karaarkam* are both forms of temporary work: *asthai* refers to temporary work for more than one year of employment; *karaar*, to work contracts of up to one year. *Dainik jaladari kam* is daily wage work. I open my discussion with a brief description of the broad political context and an introduction to the factory I studied most intensively, and then go on to explain the role of labor law and the way the labor unions in the factory have pressed for its implementation. To get a better understanding of the type of labor relations that emerged from the conflict period, I then look at the broader structural effects of this emerging unionism. Next, I examine everyday labor relations at the shop-floor level and the way in which the Maoist revolution affected these workers. The concluding section draws out potential implications of these broader changes for labor in the region.

The Regional Revolutionary Context:
Maoist Insurgency and Post-Conflict Politics in Banke

Nepal's Maoist insurgency began in 1996 after the Nepali Congress–led government of Nepal ignored a letter composed by the Communist Party of Nepal (Maoist) that contained forty demands for change. The insurgency's main aim was to eradicate the semi-feudal, semi-colonial character of the Nepali state and society. From their bases in the hilly districts of Rolpa and Rukkum, Maoist guerrilla fighters spread their insurgency throughout the entire country. As Mallika Shakya has commented, "the Nepali Maoists targeted ethnic exploitation during their People's War between 1996 and 2006 and were the first to demand a new constitution" (2015a:1). In the initial stages of the insurgency, this exploitation of ethnic grievances meant above all that members of the Kham Magar ethnic group in the hills entered the revolutionary movement as rank-and-file fighters (De Sales 2000). However, once the revolutionaries began to mobilize support in the Banke district, their strategy became more complex: in Nepalgunj the Maoists targeted their propaganda efforts predominantly against activists aligned with Shiv Shena, a Hindu chauvinist party, in order to win support among the town's large Muslim community; meanwhile, Maoist guerrillas resorted to anti-Indian rhetoric to exploit sentiments of distrust toward the neighboring country. This anti-Indian rhetoric, as Pramoud Kantha has stressed, "had little resonance among Madheshis" (2010:161).

In November 2006 the government of Nepal and the Communist Party of Nepal (Maoist) signed a peace treaty. Thereafter, violence erupted anew in the Tarai region of southern Nepal as militant groups targeted both the state and the Maoists. This event, popularly referred to as the Madheshi Uprising, involved groups that polarized the citizenry by stirring up ethnic issues largely unaddressed during the insurgency period. These violent encounters had serious consequences for Nepalgunj, where intercommunal clashes broke out in December 2006. In 2007 three Madheshi groups created an alliance called the United Democratic Madheshi Front with the aim of transforming the lowland region of Nepal into a single, autonomous province of Madhesh (Miklian 2009:2).

These developments led to radical changes in the political topography of the Tarai lowlands. After the Constituent Assembly elections in April 2008, the newly elected Maoist movement found itself confronted by various political actors in the Madheshi movement that tried to exploit perceived anti-Madheshi sentiments for their own gain. In this expanding political matrix, Maoist-Madheshi relationships became complex and shifted over time at the central level (Kantha 2010). Yet in the lowland region of Banke, this altered political configuration also meant that Maoist cadres had to try to win over the Madheshi electorate in anticipation of the much-awaited second round of elections. These broader dynamics, as the following sections will demonstrate, had profound effects on the process of regularization of labor in local industries.

The Agrawal Factory and Its Workforce

Located in the Banke district in the western lowlands of Nepal, the Agrawal Food Company is one of seventeen industrial food-processing industries managed by the L.K. Agrawal Group, one of Nepal's largest industrial companies. This factory was built in 1995 with the help of Indian technology and skilled labor on a field site next to the highway that leads from Nepalgunj to Kohalpur. Owned by a Marwari industrialist, the relatively modern, clean, orderly factory compound presents a contrast to the disorder outside its gates. The high-walled compound, covering around twenty acres, has five distinct factory units: a flour mill, a rice mill, a mill that produces and bottles edible oils, a new unit that extracts essential ingredients for the pharmaceutical industry from herbs, and a more general food-processing unit.[2] The combined workforce comprises around five hundred persons. Within the compound there are two large accommodation blocks—one for staff and one for workers—but some local staff and workers live in the town or in surrounding villages. In the workers' block, the men (nearly all the employees are male) live in dormitory-style accommodations, packed in tightly with up to twenty workers per room.

Next to the factory compound, various other industries, including a turpentine factory, a steel-recycling unit, a cement factory, and a pharmaceutical factory, together form a small industrial corridor stretching along the main road. Compared to Nepal's largest industrial area—located at Biratnagar in the eastern Terai—it is small, but in the context of the western Terai, these factories represent the vanguard of the industrial revolution in the area. Economically, however, cross-border smuggling and labor migration to the Gulf states remain more prevalent than industrial development.

In the early days, the company's vision was guided by paternalist values. It promised that local people would make up 50 percent of its workforce, though that promise was never fulfilled. At that time its workforce was overwhelmingly Indian. "Seventy-five percent Indian workers from Bihar, twenty-five percent workers from Nepal" is how one local villager estimated the proportions. Today these ratios have changed: Indian workers now work as supervisors and machine operators in the factory, while Nepalis have the simpler jobs of machine helpers, packers, and cleaners. There are two principal sorts of Nepali workers: local Madheshis and Tharus, the latter overwhelmingly employed as *paledars* (loaders) in the factory.

There are two crucial cleavages within the workforce. The first is between the privileged Indian supervisors and machine operators (mostly from Bihar, Uttar Pradesh, and Rajasthan) and the less affluent local "sons of the soil" often employed as simple laborers, mainly machine helpers and packers.[3] Nationality matters, but so, too, does the distinction between Madheshi and Tharu. The salience of ethnicity is hardly surprising, given the current political climate outside the factory gates and the wider politics of ethnicity in the area. The Madheshi Uprising of 2006–2007 changed the way local people think about themselves: whereas Madheshis were previously looked down upon, the term has now become an assertive political identity (Miklian 2009).

Both skilled and unskilled laborers have isthai work. However, the differences in pay, even among workers with comparable levels of skill, are enormous. While an Indian machine operator often earns a middle-class income and sends his children to private schools in Uttar Pradesh or Bihar, a Madheshi machine operator doing the same job might have difficulty making ends meet on barely the minimum wage. Also, skilled and unskilled workers eat lunch separately. The supervisors and machine operators have a canteen that charges them for lunch (about 100 Nepalese rupees or 0.87 euros), while ordinary workers (like packers) and daily wage workers eat and drink under the bicycle stand.

Company workers receive a regular monthly salary and various incentives such as holiday pay, access to a provident fund, as well as a uniform, raincoat, and sweater; they can also participate in the yearly company excursion (which in 2013 consisted of a two-day trip to Pokhara). But the contract labor that is also essential to the operation of the factory is mostly undertaken by Tharus who work for piece rates on an irregular basis, carrying sacks of food weighing up to 100 kg on their heads from storage rooms to the transport trucks.

Determining the exact numbers of permanent, temporary, and daily wage workers proved difficult. At different times, and depending on whom I asked, I got different answers. For example, data provided by factory management suggested a constant trend of regularization over the past five years, as a result of which nearly 80 percent of all workers had permanent jobs. This data, however, did not account for the daily wage workers in the different factory units. Trade unionists estimated the number of permanent workers to be much lower. The Department of Labor indicated that 47 out of 125 registered workers were permanent. My own data from a random survey suggest that this proportion is realistic and confirm the trend toward regularization.[4] This trend would seem to contradict the grand narrative of greater global precarity (Standing 2011). In the next section, I highlight the role of the company's unions in bringing this situation about.

The Labor Law, the Unions, and Armed Police

The Nepali Labor Act of 1992 (amended in 1997) states that the worker "shall be kept on probation period unless he/she completes the continuous service period of one year and, based on his/her efficiency, sincerity, discipline, diligence toward works, punctuality, etc. in this period he/she shall be appointed permanently." But labor law is subject to different interpretations. It has "do side" (two sides), as "one hand gives, the other one takes." When Agrawal first opened, the labor act was not observed, and most workers had little idea of its provisions. All were working in the factory as *dainik jaladaris* (daily wage workers) for risible wages—roughly 33 Nepali rupees (0.29 euros) per day. But things have changed over the past two decades, and the law is now interpreted in a more worker-friendly way. Wages have increased, and workers have obtained permanent jobs and are represented by leaders who come from their own social strata. The company's unions played a crucial role in this transformation.

The two unions that historically played a role in the factory were Nepali Trade Union Congress (NTUC) and Akhil Nepal.[5] NTUC is affiliated with Nepali Congress—Nepal's "democrats"—and Akhil Nepal with the UCPN (Maoist). Representatives of the General Federation of Nepalese Trade Unions (GEFONT), which is affiliated with

Nepal's United Marxist Leninists, and of the Revolutionary Akhil Nepal, a unit formed by the more militant CPN Maoists, have never entered the company compound. Nepali Congress was historically the first union in the factory compound, while the Maoist union is regarded as the more radical union of the two.

Alarmed by the increasing conflict between the state and the Maoists, the Nepali Congress appeared on the shop floors of Agrawal around 1999/2000. According to some of the older workers, the formation of the Congress union within the factory followed a minor issue over the number of machine operators. Mohammed, a machine operator who is Muslim, recalled:

> Before, a machine operator had to look after just one machine, but later, according to the decision of the manager, a machine operator had to look after two. That was very difficult for a single operator. At that time, the union leaders were visiting the area. We had a meeting with them, and they said that they would raise their voices against management to get our demands heard. Then we started to agitate against them in 2000. Our demand was to make one machine operator run just one machine.

The owner fulfilled their demands and pressured them to resume work. But the group of workers insisted that a union be formed and began working again only after management accepted this condition. Management evidently viewed a Nepali Congress–led union not as a threat to the status quo but as a nonmilitant part of civil society that was manageable at a time of armed conflict between state and Maoist guerrillas.

However, only two months later the newly established union agitated more radically and submitted to the factory a letter that demanded further changes: permanent positions for those who had worked in the factory for more than 240 days; and services and facilities according to the law, such as a uniform, a bicycle parking area, a sleeping place, and a dining room, as well as a sweater for the cold season. These demands were by and large fulfilled, but the workers' appointment certificates were valid for only six months, and only 40 percent of workers got them.

The second wave of agitation followed soon afterward, as Mohammed remembered:

> Later, in 2003, we again submitted a demand letter for the increase of salaries and overtime. Previously, the factory used to pay us overtime at the same rate as our normal hourly rate. But according to the labor law, we should be paid 1.5 times our usual rate. Then we bought a book of labor law and we stopped being dependent on the leaders. We learned many things from that

book about labor law. Thus, later our demands were fulfilled, and we started working according to the rules of the government and we also started to get 1.5 times our usual rate for overtime work. We also started getting sweaters and raincoats after that. We also got the provision of a provident fund. The company opened a bank account for the provident fund. It also gave us a sleeping room, and an arrangement for food as well. There was the problem of water and toilet. It was bad for our health because the workers of the factory used to defecate outside the company compound. There were toilets only for staff. We raised our voices and we got toilets constructed, which were beneficial for us as well as for the factory.

The Nepali Congress union lost its grip on the factory in 2010 after its leadership organized a strike demanding an increase in the annual bonus and protesting management's decision to remove a small pocket from their uniforms—the latter, a rather trivial issue, being used by the union leaders to demonstrate their power to management. The strike went on for days until, on the sixth day, management persuaded the union leader to give up the strike. Feeling betrayed, the other unionists telephoned the Maoist party, whose local members convinced the Congress unionists to collectively change sides and join the Maoist union. There followed a meeting between the members of the local chambers of commerce, the Maoist party, and management, after which the general manager agreed to fulfill the union's demands and the factory resumed its operations.

Since the union's affiliation with the UCPN (Maoist), it has had to deal with two principal agents of the state security apparatus. First, throughout their demonstrations and protests, the Maoists had to fend off the local police, whom they regarded as a highly *bhrast* (corrupt) ally of the region's captains of industrial capital. In fact, several unionists claimed that the local industrialists used the local police as a protection racket. From 2012 onward, however, the police were basically quiescent in confronting the Maoist unionists. This was because parts of the nationwide armed police had been transformed into so-called "industrial flying squads" to protect industrial properties after armed groups carried out a series of kidnappings and murders of industrialists ("Agreement with Maoist Fighters" 2011). These new industrial flying squads replaced the local police in dealings with the unionists. From the Maoist union's perspective, the armed police were much less of a problem. They were considered to be less corrupt, and although they had formerly fought the Maoists on behalf of the state, now they were transformed into worker-friendly agents that allowed the Maoist union to become an effective voice for the company's workforce.

Improvements in Labor Conditions

Three themes were crucial to the factory-wide impact of Maoist activism: secure employment, guaranteed minimum wages, and a new form of union organization. The Agrawal workers frequently told me that working for the company was secure employment once you had a permanent position, and that Agrawal was a factory in which a temporary contract might realistically turn into a permanent one. Consider the following cases:

> K. Yadav is a Madheshi from a small village close to the factory. When he first started work at Agrawal in 2006, he was a daily wage worker in the rice mill. In 2011, after the Maoist union pressured the company, he became a permanent employee. He is now a member of the Maoist union.

> S. Magar, a local from a neighboring village, started in the Agrawal flour mill in December 2007. He worked for only twenty days as a daily wage laborer before being assigned to the packing department, where he put stickers on bags for two years. In 2010 he obtained a temporary contract as a machine helper in the flour mill. After the Maoist union pressured the company in 2012, he was given a permanent contract. He is now also the unit head of the Maoist trade union for the flour mill.

> L. Magar, another local and an ethnic Magar from a neighboring village who is in his midthirties, started working at Agrawal in 1999. He spent nine years as a daily wage laborer, working as a cleaner in the rice mill unit. The management then decided to give him a temporary contract for two years, whereupon he was promoted to assistant machine operator and helped run five different machines in the factory unit. Two years later he became an isthai worker doing the same job. He, too, is a member of the Maoist trade union, and he works for the union as a unit head representing the workers of his factory unit.

Common to all three employment histories was the Maoist union's involvement in the regularization of contract work: sixty-two of the most recent seventy-seven cases of regularization occurred with the help of the Maoist union. The majority of these were of Madheshis. To get a permanent job, a temporary worker needs to cultivate his Maoist unionist contacts, and Madheshi ethnicity seems to be a key factor.[6]

Permanent workers can count on receiving their pay on time and are, as management complains, very difficult to fire. That is true even when a worker is caught up in serious misdemeanors, as one manager illustrated with the following story: "There was one of our permanent oil mill workers who had tried to steal. He had put down

Table 1. Wage Ranges for Different Groups of Workers in the Flour Mill.

Group	Nepali Rupees	Euros
Supervisors	12,000–18,000	104–157
Machine Operators	12,000–18,000	104–157
Machine Helpers	9,200	80
Packers	9,200	80
Loaders	5,000–15,000	44–131

Source: Author's fieldwork.

a deposit for 10 kg of *dal* (pulses), but then went to the dal mill and took 20 kg. He tried to take it through the gate, but the security guard caught him, and he was reported to management. He then was suspended for seven days but was then taken back."

The Maoist union did not organize the paledars, who were nearly all Tharus, and their jobs were notoriously insecure. For them, redundancy was a very real threat. A manager confirmed this, telling me that "in the past there were a few cases when loaders tried to demonstrate their strength. In each case we fired them, and in one case we even fired seventy loaders at once." In their world of chronic precarity, no one gets a second chance—not even the son of one of the contractors, who was working as a loader in the factory when a security guard caught him bringing a flick-knife into the compound. He was immediately fired.

Meanwhile, wages in the factory have increased, as shown by the example of a foreman in the Saurabh oil mill who is from a village in the Indian state of Uttar Pradesh. He has a permanent contract and earns 12,000 Indian rupees per month—three times what he earned when he began work twenty years ago. This has allowed him to send his three children, who live back home in Uttar Pradesh, to private school. One of them now has a BSc in computer science. He rejected my claim that children of laborers will inevitably become laborers. His children would have middle-class careers.

All company workers in the factory are paid the current minimum wage of 8,000 Nepali rupees (70 euros) per month.[7] Wages in the flour mill are shown in Table 1.

Apart from the loaders, the range is from 8,000 Nepali rupees (70 euros) to 18,000 rupees (157 euros), and the differences are largely dependent on skill. All are above the legal minimum, in marked contrast to what is commonly reported from other parts of South Asia (e.g., Breman 2004; Parry 2014). Remarkably, workers were paid regardless of frequent power cuts that at times brought production to a halt. Workers had little to do during such enforced breaks, and management often complained about paying them for "just hanging around." But pay their wages it did, along with the fringe benefits to which permanent workers are entitled — largely because of the pressure exerted by the Maoist union. Since 2010, the principle that the union leaders should themselves be members of the workforce has been firmly established. Workers adamantly rejected the possibility that someone not employed at Agrawal could lead their union. The Maoist "in-charge" (leader) of the whole company, himself a skilled machine operator in one of its units, explained that "the laborers here are now very aware. They know about laws. They know that only a person who works in [the] industry can understand the workers' problems. That's why only workers themselves can become union leaders. Bringing in an outsider is not possible now."

In the past, things were different — as they are in many Indian factories (Ramaswamy 1977, 1981; Parry 2009). Under the Nepali Congress Party, the Agrawal labor leader had been a Nepalgunj banker without any experience of industrial work. Workers explained that in those days they themselves had been entirely ignorant of the labor laws and depended on an "educated" and literate outsider. Since the coming of the Maoist union, however, each factory unit is represented by a Maoist union head. The entire workforce of the company was represented by the Maoist in-charge, a man with a Muslim religious background who was also the district's labor in-charge of the UCPN (Maoist).

The new Maoist leadership was not exempt from criticism. An Indian contractor told me that the Maobadi are actually *khaobadi* (a local idiom used to express the idea that Maoists have become corrupt) or *paisa khane manchhe* (another slang expression for "corrupt people"). K. Yadav, a machine operator in the oil mill who had recently joined the Maoists, complained that the Maoist in-charge did not hold enough meetings and, Yadav claimed, siphoned money out of the annual excursion fund. Others were dissatisfied that the Maoists had agreed that workers should pay income tax. Although such payments remained relatively marginal and usually added up to no more than eighty Nepali rupees per month, many viewed the tax as an unfair burden that the working classes should not have to shoulder.

The Maoized Workplace

So far, I have argued that sweeping structural changes in the factory have been largely an outcome of Maoist union activism. I will now turn to changes in everyday working relations, with a focus on different types of work in the company's mills. I begin with a brief digression on issues of access to the factories. After an initial period in which the manager introduced me to the shop floors, I was able to move freely around the factory, observe the daily working routines, and interview workers and supervisors when they were free. Much of my time was spent on conducting a survey that helped me introduce myself and get to know workers better. I became particularly familiar with the work routines in the flour and oil mills.

One of my most striking initial impressions on the shop floors was that despite the Maoist unionists' everyday presence in the factories, and unlike the brick kiln workers I studied in Kailali in the aftermath of the Maoist People's War (see Hoffmann 2014a), none of the workers I engaged with used the well-known Maoist greeting *lal salam* (red salute). It became obvious that at this juncture in the post-conflict period (the brief period around the nationwide Constitution Assembly elections in November 2013), political affiliations were less clear-cut and visible. Understanding the subtler changes in the industrial labor regimes required long-term anthropological fieldwork. I began to frequently visit different workplaces inside Agrawal's company compound.

It was soon apparent that perceptions of work varied considerably between units and according to the type of work done. Workers from different shops spoke about *jahar* (poisonous) and *khataranāka* (dangerous) types of work. Nobody liked the idea of standing for long hours beside the big tank in the oil mill that filtered and purified the mustard oil and gave off pungent fumes that stung the eyes as if peeling onions all day. The job of the machine operator in that unit involved changing large filter bags through which the mustard oil was pumped. The operator worked eight-hour shifts without eye protection and often put in another four hours of overtime. Similarly, work in the company's herbal factory was considered extremely dangerous as it involved handling lethal chemicals. So, too, was working as a paledar: loaders had to be careful not to get hit by falling rice sacks when stacking them in the company storage rooms.

While spending more time in the oil and flour mills, however, I also discovered that much of the work was pretty easy, relaxed, and boring. It was spoken of as *sajilo kam* (easy work), *aram kam* (relaxed work), or *boring kam* (workers used the English word). Take, for example, the flour mill, located in a building consisting of several sections. Entering through the northern gate, one found oneself in the huge hall of the packing department, where sacks of rice were stacked. At a table by the entrance, a supervisor from Bihar monitored the work process from 6 a.m. to 6 p.m.; another, from the Nepal hills, was the monitor from 6 p.m. to 6 a.m. There was no computer; instead, everything was recorded in large red registers—one for workers' attendance, one for stock, and so forth. About twenty meters behind the supervisors' table, on a large metal construction, were two "vibro tanks" where the finished and processed flour was stored. Under the vibro tanks sat two groups of workers who worked in shifts from 8 a.m. to 4 p.m., 4 p.m. to noon, or noon to 8 a.m. Usually I counted three workers in the left packing group (one permanent, one temporary, and one daily wage worker), and four packers on the right side (one daily wage worker and three temporary workers). As with the supervisors at the entrance gate, their work was barely mechanized at all. The left packing group needed three workers: one to fill the sack of flour, one to put the sack on a modern electronic scale and use a scoop to bring it to the correct weight of exactly 50 kg, and one to take the sack off the scale and place it with the other sacks across the hall. The working group on the right consisted of one filler, one worker using archaic scales to measure the weight, and two sealers (one with a small sealing machine, and one with a hot sealing machine that seals the plastic sacks).

These workers regarded their work as *sajilo* (easy), though also monotonous and boring. The working group on the left filled, sealed, and stacked about three hundred bags per hour. Filling, sealing, and stacking one bag every twelve seconds left little time between bags to sit and chat. The same was true for the other working group, though at times a blockage in the pipes leading down from the vibro tank meant that workers had to move fast to remove enough flour from the tank to get the machine running again.

In contrast with the work of the packers, the work of the machine operators in the same mill was regarded as more *aram* (relaxed). This became apparent on several visits to the mill. For instance, when I first visited the machine operators in the "rolling room" on the second floor of the mill, which was usually full of dust, I was brought there by the Indian foreman, Yogendra Yadav, who then left me with a Madheshi Yadav machine helper who gave me a tour of the different floors. His job was to clean the machines on the second floor, but he had ample time to show me around. I then conducted a two-hour group interview with four of the workers—all good mutual friends who hailed from Bihar. No one bothered about the time, and only occasionally did one or another machine operator leave to look after his machine. A power cut occurred, and they all left to do maintenance work. It was easily done within two hours, after which they were off for another three hours. Things were not much different on my next visit to the mill. I interviewed three helpers, with the three machine operators listening eagerly. They soon tired of my inquiries, however, and left, leaving only one Bihari helper to answer my questions. In fact, they all disappeared for their lunch break shortly before midday. When I came back around 1 p.m., the foreman on the first floor was nearly asleep, and others were hanging around. I found the machine operators and helpers sitting together on sacks in the corner of the second floor. When asked how they would describe their work, they responded, "*aram kam.*" The rule, of course, was that no one could disappear from his work post, but the foreman rarely checked on tasks and often only shouted at the helpers to clean one of the machines, which got dusty quickly. He usually came past about once per hour to check how the work was going; otherwise, he left the workers alone.

Were these "relaxed" working environments simply related to the types of work that the labor engaged with? No, according to both workers and management. Madheshi workers praised the Maoist union for pressuring management to continue to pay the factory's permanent workforce at times of frequent electricity cuts, when they could roam around the factory after the machines were cleaned. And management often complained to me in interviews that the presence of Maoists on the shop floors meant that management had to keep paying salaries and had trouble imposing tighter work discipline on the workforce.

By hanging out at workplaces in the factory and at the Maoist union office in a nearby village, I learned more about why management was challenged to adopt the intensification of labor that neoliberal conditions have promoted elsewhere. According to my informants, every month the Maoist union took up three or four cases of excessive admonishment with management. I was told the story of a packer whose Indian supervisor had berated him for falling asleep in the packing room on the night shift. The next day, the packer complained to his unit's Maoist in-charge and he in turn complained to management, who then advised the supervisor to refrain from verbal attacks on the workers. The fact that complaints are now possible empowers workers and inhibits supervisors from overstepping their mark. In short, the Maoist union also protects its members from speedups in production.

However, such Maoist support was only extended to a certain ethnic segment of the workforce. Undoubtedly, far greater time discipline was required of the Tharu paledars, whose work was widely regarded as *mushkil* (difficult). Paledars carried heavy sacks on their heads from the storage rooms or the factory units to trucks waiting outside. To load them, they had to walk up a long wooden plank laid on an old rusty oil barrel to form a small bridge, which occasionally led to accidents. The work was heavy and exhausting, and they sweat profusely. To endure it, many of them drank highly concentrated alcohol on their breaks at the tea stall outside the factory gates.

Also revealing is that the everyday presence of the Maoist union in the factory had caused practices associated with *chuwa-choot* (untouchability) to disappear entirely from its shop floors. Hindu workers were no longer able to discriminate against the minority of Muslim company employees. Several Muslim workers told me that formerly they were not allowed to sit at the same bench as Hindu coworkers or eat with them. The story was told of an engineer called Mohammed, who, some twenty years back, had come to the factory to repair a machine in the flour mill. After not being allowed to sit in the canteen with his Indian colleagues, he had angrily left the company after only three days. That kind of discrimination had vanished upon the arrival of the Maoists. This also applied to spaces outside of the factory. For example, in 2001 Agrawal had rented a house to use as an office near a Shiva-Parvati temple in a nearby village. On the day it opened, the senior managers went to worship in the temple, but the *pujari* (priest) prevented the ordinary workers from witnessing the worship. They angrily challenged their exclusion, which the priest justified by saying he did not know who they were or to which castes they belonged. When the Maoist unionists heard about the priest's *rudhiwadi* (conservative) ways, they went to the temple and threatened him, with the result that he reopened the temple and let the workers in.

As a qualifying footnote to this, however, it needs to be said that not all workers in the permanent workforce appreciated the Maoist support on the shop floors. Those most in sympathy with the Maoist union were of Nepali origin and largely Madheshis. Indian workers were more guarded and would often privately accuse the Maoists of being self-interested khao-badi, a predictable reaction to one of the Maoist union's central demands—the appointment of "locals" to skilled jobs.[8]

Conclusion

According to Guy Standing (2011), the pressures of globalization have produced a new social class comprising all those engaged in insecure forms of labor, including temporary and part-time workers, subcontracted laborers, poor immigrants, and unemployed educated knowledge workers. This new global "precariat" is further marked not only by insecurity of employment and income, but also by the lack of a clearly defined worker identity. In many places, it is an angry, potentially violent social class that is prone to support right-wing political parties when public policy makes no effort to reintegrate it into society.

Jan Breman (2013) has critiqued Standing's picture by pointing out that in most parts of the world, precarity has been the condition of most workers throughout the history of urban industrial employment. I find that little of Standing's argument rings true in western Nepal, where the labor situation has become more rather than less secure over the last two decades, though not for all categories of worker. Today legal minimum wages are implemented, and workers organize themselves according to their own principles. I attribute these changes to union activism over the past decade and have highlighted the specific role that the Maoists have played in the transition to a post-conflict society. I further suggest that Maoist activism has also protected workers from the intensification of labor that neoliberal conditions have promoted elsewhere.

But in drawing attention to Maoist unionists' efforts to regularize contract labor, I do not wish to swell the chorus that praises radical left-wing parties as the saviors of the working classes. The Maoist union has been complicit in the entrenchment of new ethnic cleavages in the workplace, as the benefits of its activism are not felt among the Tharu paledars from outsider communities. This echoes what Feyzi Ismail and Apah Shah (2015) have noted about indigenous politics more generally: Nepal's Maoists, they argue on the basis of writings by senior Maoist leaders (Yami and Bhattarai 1996; Bhattarai 2004) as well as critical ethnographic work (Ogura 2007), have devoted "special emphasis to the case of Nepal's *Janajatis* (its ethnic minorities)" (Ismail and Shah 2015:118). I suggest that the ethnographic material presented in this chapter confirms that Maoist union politics in Nepal appears to mirror this shift from the politics of class to the politics of indigeneity.

Two themes emerge from the findings of this chapter. The first is that Maoist union policies may in some measure be contributing to intra-ethnic tension at workplaces. This raises the question of why the Maoist unionists remain seemingly uninterested in organizing casual labor to promote an ethnic cause. Is it because of the laborers' ethnicity (in that Tharus are not their support base)? Or is it because Tharus are casual labor and as such are difficult to organize? I can only speculate that the Maoist union leaders may have developed new forms of local patronage that will only further entrench ethnic grievances. Second, though regularization at Agrawal may not necessarily be representative of wider national trends, my data from factories nearby suggest at least a wider regional trend of regularizing contract workers. The latest statistical data indicate that in those factories where Maoist unions have been established (five out of eighteen factories), the proportion of regular workers (averaging 45 percent) is higher than that found in non-unionized factories (33 percent). In the following chapters, I will explore these themes further by looking more closely into the situation of the precarious contract workers (chapter 2), as well as by examining whether Nepal's Maoists had a similar impact on the regularization of labor within industries elsewhere in the mid-hills of the country (chapters 4 and 5).

Notes

This chapter is a revised version of "From Casual to Permanent Work: Maoist Unionists and the Regularization of Contract Labor in the Industries of Western Nepal," in Chris Hann and Jonathan Parry, ed., *Industrial Labor on the Margins of Capitalism: Precarity, Class and the Neoliberal Subject* (New York: Berghahn Books, 2018). I gratefully acknowledge permission to reprint this revised version.

1. In the Nepali context, the term "Marwari" refers to one of India's preeminent merchant castes, which originated in Rajasthan but has long-established and extremely important commercial interests in a great many Indian and Nepali towns.
2. The productive capacities of the factories on the company campus are as follows: flour mill, 100 metric tons per 24-hour day; oil mill, 10 tons per day; rice mill, 100 tons per day; pulses mill, 50 tons per day.
3. The legal status of the Indian workers was questionable. Under the India-Nepal Friendship Treaty of 1950, Indian and Nepali laborers were allowed to work in both countries, but the Labor Act of 1992 stipulates that foreigners (including Indians) are allowed to work in Nepal only with special permission granted by the local chief district officer. The Labor Act of 1992 furthermore states that any Indian worker who works for five years in Nepal must be replaced by a Nepali citizen after that period.
4. I conducted a survey with a sample of fifty of the company's workers.
5. For a more general account of the history of unionism in Nepal, see Hoffmann 2018a:126–129.
6. Like the permanent workers, the factory's temporary workers have jobs that are fairly secure due to Maoist patronage.

7. Loaders are not counted as company workers in the management's scheme of payment.
8. Such demands fit in with the UCPN (Maoist)'s broader distaste for Indian workers. Though the language against Indians softened in the post-insurgency period, senior Maoist leaders such as Baburam Bhatterai had previously railed against Indian influence in Nepal (Bhatterai 2003).

Chapter 2

FROM BONDED TO INDUSTRIAL LABOR IN A FOOD FACTORY

Introduction:
Discussions at the Tea Stall Next to the Factory

It is Sunday, 27 October, midday. I arrive on motorbike with my research assistant, Maddhu Chaudhary, at the factory compound, just in time to hear the *ghanti* (tridom) inside the factory compound being knocked twelve times to indicate the beginning of lunch break. Outside are two chai shops, one directly in front of the gate, the other behind. We drive to the second one, which is run by a shop owner who used to work at the factory and is the busier of the two. I came with the intention to interview the Muslim Mohammed, a machine operator from the factory compound. Mohammed is also the in-charge of the Akhil Maoist Union for the entire district, a local from the Banke district and informally the in-charge of the Maoist union inside the four factories of the compound. With the onset of lunch, about twenty Tharu paledars slowly exit the factory. A group of seven goes behind the shop and takes the pathway that is littered with plastic bottles of *sofie* (a hard liquor) and plastic packages of *surti* (chewing tobacco) to go fishing in a tiny river next to the factory compound. In two hours, they will return with fifteen fish in a bucket—but these can only be eaten at night when no one will see them. The owner of the factory forbids fish or meat inside and around the factory compound.

When we arrive, I see Sharuk Yadav, a Bihari *sardar* (contractor). He greets me warmly in Hindi and then asks Maddhu and me to sit down on a porch in the protective shade next to the factory wall. We sit there and begin to chat. First, I steer the discussion toward the issue of caste. Sharuk has his own theory on the subject. He tells Maddhu and me that there are only two castes in the world: "men and women." A Tharu paledar in the back shouts "Do nahi! Tin hai! Admi, aurat aur hijera" (Men, women, and third-gender), and then everyone laughs. Such "jokes" were partly meant to make fun of my sociological inquiries and partly to entertain the workforce. In general, the contractors at the factory often tried to make jokes with the workers to keep them entertained. Sometimes, however, workers chatted about mouse-hunting (most of the Tharu I know can name around seven different types of mice), or the paledars discussed different names for motorized vehicles and machines. *Childgadi*, for example, means "bird's car" and is a word used for "airplanes."[1]

This chapter focuses on how these workers have adapted to the new realities of an insecure capitalist labor market. It examines how the past shapes the uncertain labor experiences of the present, including resistance, and it reflects on the contemporary experience of precarious labor at industrial sites in western Nepal. It describes how former bonded laborers and their descendants have begun working as contract workers in a modern industrial food-processing factory through their connections with kin-related contractors. The chapter shows how one of the defining features of their new life in contract labor is its chronic precariousness. Undisguised forms of confrontation, such as open disregard for management instructions, are also part of their new reality in this uncertain labor market. Contract laborers are often strongly assertive in the face of managerial authority, and this assertiveness is shaped by a unique past. The chapter contributes to debates about bonded labor and its transformations in South Asia. It also offers a reflection on the limited impact of the Nepali Maoist revolution on precarious labor and on the ethnic dimensions of this segment of Nepali society. Finally, it contributes to discussions about industrialization and *Adivasi* (indigenous) communities in South Asia and beyond.

In the western lowlands of Nepal, bonded labor has an especially iconic importance. Over the past five decades, since the implementation of a state-sponsored malaria program in the 1960s, two main groups—the Pahadi and Tharu—have internally colonized the western lowland region, and their interactions have resulted in a highly unequal society. As a number of scholars have noted (e.g., Rankin 1999; Guneratne 2002; Fujikura 2007), when high-caste Pahadi outsiders began to migrate in large numbers to the lowland region, the local Tharu community experienced land loss and displacement as a result.

It was the literate Pahadi settlers who benefited most from these migration processes. In stark contrast, many of the illiterate Tharu were forced to become *kamaiya* (debt-bonded laborers), working on Pahadi agricultural estates in order to make a living. *Kamaiya* is a term that was made popular in the 1990s when nongovernmental organizations and human rights groups began to lobby the government on their behalf, ultimately leading to a ban on the bonded labor system in 2000.

The ethnographic case outlined in this chapter is based on ten months of anthropological field research undertaken between September 2013 and October 2014. By tracing the journey of former kamaiya laborers to a modern industrial factory, this chapter contributes to the literature on the transformation of the kamaiya system of bonded labor after its official abolition in 2000 (Chhetri 2005; Fujikura 2001, 2003, 2007; Hoffmann 2014a, 2014b, 2015; Maycock 2015, 2018).[2] While previous publications have highlighted how some of the former bonded laborers became labor unionists (Hoffmann 2014a) or turned to militant politics to make their claims heard (Fujikura 2007; Hoffmann 2015, 2018a), this chapter looks at how some of the former bonded laborers and their descendants have fared in an industrial setting in the post-Kamaiya period. Like their counterparts, whom the author encountered in a brick kiln in Kailali in the immediate aftermath of the Maoist revolution (Hoffmann 2014a, 2017), these former bonded laborers found themselves in a situation characterized by a mixture of severe exploitation and assertiveness. However, the underlying origins of their assertive behavior were different. In the case considered here, it was not the revolutionary past that served as a structural reference point to fuel their recalcitrance. Rather, their open disregard for managerial authority stemmed from their desire to avoid dangerous and difficult work, combined with vengeful sentiments that originate in the historical exploitation of low-caste Tharu by upper-caste employers.

More broadly, the case presented here is also an invitation to assess the impact of the Maoist revolution on an industrial labor workforce. In the previous chapter, I have suggested that, over the past few years, for a certain ethnic segment of the workforce in the area's food-processing industry, labor has become more rather than less secure due to the revolutionary context. For this ethnic group a minimum wage has been implemented, and—in contrast with the situation that is common elsewhere in the region—workers are now represented by leaders from their own social stratum. Yet those who previously worked as bonded laborers and are now engaged in precarious contract work remain largely excluded from any of the benefits of Maoist activism. It is little wonder, then, that despite some flickering nostalgia for their support of the Maoists during the insurgency period and its immediate aftermath, the Maoist Party has largely lost its appeal for many of the former bonded laborers working at the local industrial sites. In the context of a late post-conflict period such as the one I describe here, people are intentionally seeking a separation from the revolutionary past, and few may want to draw upon Maoism as a conceptual framework to resist industrialization. Rather, I suggest that the memories of the cruelty of bonded labor and the struggle to end that system have informed the consciousness underlying the frequent disregard of managerial directives in the workers' current industrial environment.

Finally, the argument presented in this chapter aligns with more recent anthropological work on the impact of industrialization on Adivasi communities in South Asia. Much of the literature on this theme has focused on how industrialization is often accompanied by historical processes of dispossession such as geographic displacement and the loss of the traditional livelihoods of Adivasis (Mosse 2005; Strümpell 2014b). The recent growth of extractive industries in predominantly Adivasi-inhabited areas in Jharkhand, Bihar, and Orissa has prompted scholars to examine related movements of resistance and Maoist insurgency, as well as the Indian state's military response (Padel and Das 2010; Shah 2010, 2011). More relevant for the purpose of this chapter is a discussion on the making and unmaking of an Adivasi working class in the Rourkela steel plant in Orissa, India, where Christian Strümpell (2014b) documents how an Adivasi identity was developed in the work environment. His account shows how Adivasis find themselves at the bottom of the industrial hierarchy in harsh working environments, and how this reinforces their sense of belonging to an Adivasi community exploited by higher-caste Odia, instead of forging a new working-class identity that transcends traditional distinctions of caste and tribe. In contrast, as I will explain more in detail throughout this chapter, the foregrounded ethnography highlights how the industrialization process reinforces a sense among former bonded laborers of belonging to a community yet prevents a broader Adivasi identity from emerging due to the union politics in the area.

Debt-Bonded Labor in the Past

To begin with, the western lowlands of Nepal were subject to a state-sponsored malaria eradication program in the 1960s in order to make the region more attractive for incoming settlers (Fujikura 2007). As a result of this government-led initiative, two distinct migration schemes emerged that would essentially form a highly unequal society. On the one hand, Pahadi settlers arriving from the northern hilly areas bought properties at cheap rates or acquired land through corrupt practices such as coercion, violence, and cheating. On the other hand, displaced groups of Tharu from the Dhang area arrived in the western lowlands to settle there, yet often remained illiterate. By developing the kamaiya system, new landlords—who predominantly consisted of Pahadis from the hilly regions of western Nepal—developed a sophisticated strategy to coerce the Tharu settlers into a form of bonded labor. Usually during the Tharu festival of Magghi Sanskrit in mid-January, Pahadi settlers began negotiating with the Tharu community about working on their farm. They usually created a contract that was supposed to last for a year, despite the Tharus' illiteracy. As exchange the Tharu workers would often obtain a certain amount of food compensation, which would help the Tharu worker's family survive over the year. However, in the case of an absence from work, landlords would charge a fine to the Tharu worker, and thus a new system of bonded labor was formed that resulted in lifelong indentured servitude. Debts could be paid off, and in some cases they were paid back. But in many cases they were not, and Pahadis emerged as landlords and Tharu workers turned into kamaiya.

The principal distinction in this system of bonded labor related to those working on large estates and those working on small estates (Rankin 1999). As Catherine Rankin has shown, those working on large estates were generally more prone to bind their labor using exploitative contracts than the small farmholders. Nevertheless, the issue of housing was equally important for the community of bonded laborers. Here, I suggest, is where the origins of the meaning of "labor camps" lie: Tharus used to work and live on the property of the landlord. Maybe it not surprising that landlords also considered Tharus as their property, as evident in the way they talked about their workers. The *ghar* (house) of the landlord varied according to his affluence, but in general the Tharu workers lived in very poor conditions on the estates of their landlords.

The Nepali government put an end to the practice of the kamaiya system in 2000. The decision to abolish this system came after a decade of agitation by a host of nongovernmental organizations that together constituted the kamaiya liberation movement. After the government resolved to end bonded labor in the western Terai region and threatened to fine landlords who retained such workers, many of the kamaiya became free men and women overnight. They began to form a landless proletariat, a section of which would go on to organize a Kamaiya-led movement, the Mukta Kamaiya Samaj (Freed Bonded Laborers Society). Throughout the second half of the People's War between Maoists and the state, this movement captured public land in urban areas and in rural community forests in the western Terai (lowland) region. As I have described elsewhere (Hoffmann 2018a), in Tikapur a local airport, parts of the university campus, and a high school compound were occupied and six settlements for ex-kamaiyas, known locally as *bastis* (slums), were established.

Maybe unsurprisingly, housing has been a crucial issue both in the time of the kamaiya system and in its aftermath; for example, the right to shelter was one of three core demands of the Mukta Kamaiya Samaj (the others were provision of food and cloth). Broadly, it can be said that in the period before the abolition of bonded labor there were some kamaiya who lived with their landlords and others who did not; after the liberation, many former bonded laborers lived in rehabilitation settlements. Such settlements were frequently visited by labor recruiters to solicit workers for construction and small-scale industries in the region, but they were also places from which labor unionists would begin to mobilize their campaigns. Of course, such labor camps were often remote from the worksite; many former bonded laborers also migrated seasonally to distant places in India or Nepal. But such camps frequently displayed a solidarity of action. For example, in the case of a labor dispute with a construction company over the late payment of wages, the workers would sometimes kidnap the contractor to collectively press for their compensation (see Hoffmann 2018a:139). Moreover, support for building houses in such camps was a political demand of the freed Kamaiya society, suggesting that there was a heightened emphasis on quality of housing in the camps.

Contractors and Contract Workers

Let us now turn to the contractors and contract workers at the Agrawal food company. Much of my ethnography comes from spending time with the paledar contract workers who load and unload bags of food, and with the contractors who organize them. I usually spent time with them at one of the tea stalls outside the factory gates, although I also visited some of the Tharu contractors' villages in the neighboring Bardiya district. A central feature in the life histories of all the contractors employed by Agrawal was that they had previously worked as paledars at the factory compound and were regarded as trusted employees. This is evident in the life histories of the two largest contractors at Agrawal, which are presented below.

Bishram Chaudhary, a Contractor from a Kamaiya Background

Bishram's life is strewn with tales of misfortune. When he was eight his family encountered financial difficulties, despite his eldest brother working in a nearby mill. Being *allare* (carefree), the elder brother cared little for the rest of the family, and Bishram was sent by his father to work as a cattle herder for a Brahman landlord. When, at age ten, Bishram saw the Brahman children going to school, he was inspired to enroll himself. His education was short-lived, however; after only fourteen months, he ran out of money. After leaving school, Bishram returned to his job as a cattle herder before going to work for his second-oldest brother. When he ran short of money again, he became a kamaiya with a landlord for a period of a year, during which time he met his wife. After finishing his yearlong contract (by now he was twenty years old), he left to work in construction in Mussoorie, India. But his family could not endure the cold winter there and soon returned to Nepal. Bishram briefly worked as a manual laborer on an irrigation project before a Tharu man he had befriended helped him get a mill job through a Bihari contractor. Bishram heard about Agrawal and began to work there as a paledar in 2000. After working for a couple of years with a flawless record, the management decided to promote Bishram to a contractor position along with his fellow Tharu worker and friend Tikaram.

Sharuk, an Educated Contractor

Sharuk is a Yadav from rural Bihar. Despite having been awarded his school-leaving certificate after grade ten, he could not find a job after graduating, and his family's finances were insufficient for him to pursue tertiary education. Instead, he left rural Bihar and worked for a year as a paledar with different contractors in eastern Nepal. This work brought him into contact with the manager of a factory; when the manager was transferred from eastern Nepal to begin a new role, he suggested Sharuk come along and work as a contractor for the newly established Agrawal company. Sharuk accepted this offer and has been working at the company for the last fourteen years. He is a humorous man and exhibits a certain degree of self-deprecation. Laughing, he relates how his workers call him "taklu" (the bald one) behind his back, referring to his receding hairline.

Each contractor at Agrawal is employed to monitor the loading and unloading of food items from trucks in different parts of the factory compound. For example, Bishram and his partner Tikaram had to ensure that there was sufficient labor to load and unload trucks at the flour mill. Similarly, Sharuk and his brother, who was also his partner, were responsible for managing labor at the lentil mill, while another contractor, Narayan, and his father were charged with supplying labor to the oil mill. The contractors' tasks inside the factories varied, but their main duties included waking up the contract labor force; planning the workday with management, which involved working out how many trucks would arrive on that day; organizing workers to restock food bags to ensure there was enough storage space inside the compound; and finding the labor to load and unload the trucks that came to the compound.

Nearly all the paledars were Tharu and hailed from the freed kamaiya settlements in Bardiya and Kailali districts. All of them were male, as management did not consider women to be physically strong enough to engage in the exhausting work of loading the trucks with food bags. Although most of the loaders came from poor families, there was some disparity in their class backgrounds. For example, Prabin was a young, tech-savvy bachelor's student who had been working at Agrawal for two years; at the end of April 2014, he left for Malaysia to work in the construction industry. Then there was Baburam, a twenty-five-year-old man, who had studied up to grade nine, always made insightful comments, and came to the factory just to earn extra income for his wife and children. One of the oldest was Hari Prasad Chaudhary, who had lost his land in unfortunate circumstances and had worked for a while as an illegal tiger poacher in a nearby Indian national park before coming to Agrawal.

Importantly, some of these older contract workers at Agrawal had also previously worked as kamaiya before the state abolished the system of bonded labor in 2000. In Bishram and Tikaram's working group, whose size varied between thirty and eighty workers depending on the company's demand for loaders, I counted six formerly bonded laborers. When interviewed, all of them insisted that their life as paledars at Agrawal were significantly better than their previous work as kamaiya. For example, Tilak Chaudhary explained to me that during his time as a kamaiya he worked as a goat herder, for which he was paid five sacks of paddy per year as well as a one-off payment of two sets of clothing and one basket of corn. Though his landlord was an absentee *pahadi* (hill dweller) who spent much of his time in Kathmandu and never scolded or beat him, Tilak insisted that he felt better working freely at Agrawal where he could make a good *phaida* (profit), at least during the season.

Not surprisingly, many of the younger workers judged the work as *mehnat* (hard work) whereas old timers of kamaiya origin regarded the work at Agrawal as *maza* (fun). By stressing this aspect of their work as paledars, they were not downplaying the physical hardship of the work, but rather were highlighting the pleasure they derived from socializing with the other paledars, many of whom were kin. This was because contractors recruited from Tharu villages through established networks of friends and family.

Chronic Precarity

Compared with the company's regular workforce who enjoy various forms of job security, including sick pay in addition to holiday pay, and are paid even when the power goes out, the casual loaders live a very precarious life. Their work schedule is not evenly regulated in eight-hour shifts, but instead depends on the number of trucks coming to the factory on a given day. As a result, shifts can be more than twelve hours long during harvesting seasons. Their payment is based on piece rates, and when workers are hired, the details of their wages often remain unclear; payment can depend on the "goodwill" of the contractor and the contractor's own financial situation. Hence, to a certain degree, casual workers in Agrawal remain bonded to their contractors through the practice of "payment in arrear," much like the contract labor force described by Jonathan Parry (2014) on Bhilai's construction sites.

However, the withholding of wages is only one side of the bonded labor relationship between casual workers and their contractors at Agrawal; the practice of handing out *peshghi* (advances) is another. Peshghi is given to workers before they begin working at the factory. This practice of binding labor through advances is well established and has been documented in other settings across South Asia (Breman 1996; De Neve 1999; Engelshoven 1999; Kapadia 1995). Compared with these other contexts, the size of the advances offered at Agrawal are small, usually amounting to about 4,000 NR per worker. Given that casual workers earn on average between 5,000 and 15,000 NR per month, an advance can be paid off comparatively quickly. Some workers disappear, leaving contractors to manage—and complain about—their yearly losses.

Another aspect of the precarious life of the loaders was obvious upon my first visit to the compound when I was shown around their dilapidated living quarters. After spending hours walking to and from trucks carrying rice sacks, the loaders retire to the dirty floor of a building where one room accommodates up to twenty men. I was shocked when I first encountered these conditions, and I was not the only one; new arrivals are usually just as surprised when they first experience the hard work in the compound and then encounter the dire living standards in the company dormitories. Only with time do they become accustomed to the working and living conditions in the company compound and begin to accept them, but not without a certain degree of pressure to do so by their relatives in the dormitories.

Paledar work is also considered *katarnak* (dangerous) compared with other jobs at the industrial estate. In addition to the threat posed by carrying heavy *boras* (sacks) of food on their heads, no one wears a helmet or gloves. In the oil mill, workers must pass through a dangerously narrow lane between the grinder machines, at the risk of becoming caught in their gears. During the loading and unloading of trucks, workers run up and down flimsy ladders; there is always a danger of slipping and twisting or breaking an ankle. This precise fate befell Kaluram, one of the workers in Bishram's group, during my time at the factory. However, the company's management only gets involved in cases involving larger accidents, so Bishram had to go to a local *guruwar* (shaman) to receive treatment for his injury. The most serious case I encountered was that of a paledar who was hit on the back by a food bag in the storage room. His back was severely injured, and at times doctors were unsure whether he would recover. In his case, the management paid for his treatment in a hospital; his family now survives on the income of a relative who has a permanent job in the factory.

The life of a contract worker is also extremely unhealthy. Most men develop a strong taste for *daru* (alcoholic beverage) while working at the factory. Drinking is part of the culture or custom of paledar work. On average the contract workers drink about two bottles of daru per day, with each bottle costing 40 NR. This amounts to approximately 2,400 NR per month, which represents a significant portion of their overall income. In addition, each Saturday (their day off), the contractors organize a small *mela* (fair), during which workers usually sit in the bushes behind the factory, drink daru, and eat pork or chicken prepared by one of the cooks from the contractor teams inside the company.

Unsurprisingly, paledar work is not unionized. The company does recognize two unions—one affiliated with the UCPN-Maoist Party and the other with the Nepali Congress—but these unions focus on the rights of permanent workers and providing stable work for temporary workers inside the food factories. Contracted paledars remain non-unionized, despite some efforts by the local Maoist authorities. During a trade fair in February 2014, the Maoist district labor in-charge took Bishram to one side and asked him whether the loader groups would like to join his union. Bishram's response was that contracted loaders were only brave when they were drunk and would shy away from joining the union. Meaningful unionism thus remains absent, as only part of the workforce belongs to a union.

The precariousness of the paledars' employment is also apparent in the length of time they work at the company compound. Many workers cannot endure the heavy labor and leave after just a few weeks. Yet the alternatives to this work are hardly more attractive; jobs in agriculture are held in even lower regard than loader work at the factory, and wages are lower. Many men try to make a living at the labor market at the nearby Tribuwan Chowk (a central square in Nepalgunj), where they hang around in the early hours in the hope of being offered short-term wage work.

Assertive Casual Workers

In my discussions with Agrawal management about the conditions in their factories, the common themes were the difficulty of training the Tharu contract labor force to comply with management rules and regulations, and the laborers' stubbornness and independence. For example, at one of my first meetings with the general manager, in September 2013, he had the following complaints: "Look, when one of the Tharu paledars decides to leave, it is very difficult to hold him back. Even if you offer him one lakh (100,000) rupees, he won't listen to you. When they make up their mind, there is nothing in the world that can change them. It's just like that!" When I came back to his office a few weeks later, shortly before the start of the Hindu festival of Dashain, he elaborated on his theory about the character of Tharu loaders, illustrated by the following ethnographic vignette:

> 10 October. I go to the factory at 10 a.m. and I find the general manager in his air-conditioned office in the staff building. However, unlike the past two days, he seems unsettled, and while he's staring at his laptop, his right foot

makes nervous movements. Curiously I inquire about the current situation in the factory. He begins by telling me that two days earlier, about a hundred loaders left the factory. In response, he called a crisis meeting with the contractors. He had announced previously that the factory would close over Dashain (12–14 October), yet the Tharu workers had returned to their villages four days early in order to celebrate the festival. During the crisis meeting, the manager talked with the three contractors. Two of them are from the Tharu community, while one is a Bihari. The contractors complained that the Tharu loaders did not listen to their commands. Against the will of the contractors, the paledars had left the company and returned to their villages, which were as far away as Kailali. This was not the first time this had happened; similar desertions had occurred during previous religious festivals. While we are sitting and chatting, he suddenly interrupts me and says, "Look, you see another three are leaving! Go to the window and look at the gate." Curious, I go to his office window and, sure enough, see three laborers leaving the company with rucksacks on their backs. I ask, "If it's such a big problem for you, why don't you just sack them?" The manager answers, "Look, we have done this for, like, twenty years. We started off with Biharis. It all worked well, they never left like the Tharu. But then we made a mistake. After the kamaiya got free, they came to ask for jobs. We let a good dozen of them work here, and they started to fight with the Biharis, not inside the compound but outside. As a result, the Biharis didn't want to work here anymore. I myself went several times to the contractor's house, but he didn't want to work here anymore. Even when we offered more money—no way! So, see, what we did is we hired more Tharu as loaders and unloaders! But they don't follow the rules. They have a simple food habit, and when they think they can leave, they just simply go. We sacked many of them in the past, but then we had a problem. They started to talk badly about us in the villages. Very badly— like, 'This company is not good and you have to work all the time!' And as a consequence, the villagers didn't want to work for us anymore! So now we compromised and let them do that—they run away and we try to negotiate. I mean, they have three days off but they simply go away before! They will never learn! And in the very end, we will replace them with machines! We will mechanize the heavy labor here! But, see, now the contractors will go to their houses and try to find them again. They go by bus and try to give them an advance between 2,000 and 5,000 NR to win them back to the factory. Then a few will show up again on Thursday, and then slowly we can start again. Meanwhile the company has to pay the costs for the permanent workers."

In other words, contract laborers can wander away from the factory to attend a festival when it suits them, and management cannot simply fire them because of fears that if the company gets a reputation for toughness, it will not be able to recruit replacements. But taking extended leave was not the only problem management faced when dealing with Tharu paledar contract laborers—violating the hygiene rules and regulations of the food factory was another, as I soon learned. In an interview, management stated: "They often spit on the factory floor. But we have told them that they are not allowed to spit. We have a rule now that punishes every spit with a fine of 500 NR. Still they continue to do so!"

Paledars also defied managerial rule in other ways. For example, they had a reputation for stopping work when they discovered mice in the factory units and trying to kill them with the iron hooks that were normally used to unload rice bags from the trucks. While such practices were said to be in decline, management always recounted such episodes in our discussions to emphasize how different the paledars were from the rest of the workforce. As the general manager once put it, "In this factory, the Tharu contract workers still have a lot to learn. It will take them a minimum of twenty years before they adapt to a modern industrial working culture."

While these acts of disobedience were usually targeted at the general management, the young Tharu loaders also occasionally defied their own contractors. I observed one such instance during the Hindu festival of Holi while the contractors were celebrating with their workforce in a neighboring factory. After the contractors gave ceremonial red vermilion powder to their workers, one of the laborers, known as Raj, got into a verbal dispute with the contractor Tikaram over a minor issue. Tikaram, sensing that his authority was being threatened, retaliated by throwing goat meat in Raj's face. In response, Raj took a stone in his hand and threatened to kill Tikaram then and there. Fearing for his life, Tikaram quickly apologized to Raj, making jokes to dispel the tension. Such acts of defiance against one's own sardar were rare, however, and only occurred when loaders were drunk enough to forget about their subordinate status and confront their employers. To sum up: at the Agrawal food factory, Tharu contract workers display an assertive attitude toward their employers. In fact, it appears as if management itself is in a precarious position in terms of the employment and punishment of labor. How has this sense of assertiveness emerged in workplaces such as the Agrawal factory and what are its roots? Has it been influenced by the broader post-conflict context (see Hoffmann 2018a), or is the attitude of the laborers related to their past and previous experiences of bonded labor?

Eigensinn in a Factory in Western Nepal

Much of the ethnographic data presented here is remarkably similar to that found in histories of labor elsewhere. For example, the German labor historian Alf Lüdtke (1993) has documented how in-

amaiya, while many others were from kamaiya families. As a result, many workers harbored bitterness toward high-caste outsiders such as their kamaiya landlords, bitterness that has more recently been redirected toward the loaders' company managers. Moreover, the loaders often expressed that in their freed kamaiya neighborhoods back in their natal villages, they felt a sense of unity and security vis-à-vis outsiders. The following ethnographic vignette from my fieldwork illustrates this emerging sentiment of assertiveness and wariness toward outsiders:

> October 2013, rural Banke district, Nepal. Sharuk Yadav and some of his contract workers were sitting on a porch in the shade of the high wall topped with barbed wire that surrounded the Agrawal factory. The work team was on a break from loading and unloading 100kg rice bags from a truck inside the factory. The team shared bidis and bottles of water as Sharuk entertained them with jokes about recent events and political issues. Some workers decided to treat themselves and each bought a 200ml bottle of hard liquor for 30 NR from the nearby tea stall; others bought *surti* (chewing tobacco); while a few used their time to go fishing in a nearby river. Suddenly, the relaxed atmosphere was shattered by a fierce tirade of insults. A drunken Tharu contract laborer was approaching the team, shouting at Sharuk, demanding that he give him the bus fare to return to his village. Sharuk refused on the grounds that he just hired him a couple of days before and had given him an advance of 4,000 NR to work for him. "Give me back my 4,000 and you can go back," he responded. Outraged, the worker shouted at him, "I'll give you 5,000 if you dare come to my village." Smarting at the insult, Sharuk picked up his shoes in his hands and threatened to beat the man. A relative of the Tharu worker jumped in, took the worker away, and fell on his knees, blowing kisses in the air, shouting "*Baba* [father], don't do that!" Then both walked away while Sharuk cursed the worker, calling him a *mahajod* (motherfucker).

This example illustrates that the Tharus' resistance to authority should be understood in light of their history of the bonded labor system. It was the feeling of security of belonging in a neighborhood comprising former bonded laborers that allowed the loader to challenge Sharuk, the outside contractor.

Third, recent political developments have also contributed to the emerging assertiveness among the paledars. To explain this, it is important to understand that, while there was previously strong support among Tharu workers for the UCPN-Maoist Party and even some identification with Maoist ideology (Hoffmann 2014b), by the time of my fieldwork (September 2013–July 2014) the political landscape had changed. By then the paledars appeared disenchanted with both the UCPN-Maoist Party and its splinter wing, the CPN-Maoist Party, led by Comrade Kiran. This became evident in a survey that I

dustrial workers in the Ruhr often had their own interpretatio factory rules and regulations, which led them to establish their practices at work that were often contrary to managerial instruc Lüdtke developed the concept of *Eigensinn* (stubborn self-reli to describe such behavior in order to narrate an everyday h of workers that went beyond the simple dichotomy of thei jugation versus their resistance. At the heart of Lüdtke's hist project was an attempt to reconstruct the workers' own spaces tonomy within their workplaces. Similarly, Dilip Subramanian highlights the autonomy of workers who assembled printed boards in a state-run telephone company in Bangalore, India. view, autonomy at work is the result of a specific managerial st that grants latitude to workers in order to preserve industri mony in the workplace. In much the same way, Agrawal's m ment allowed the loaders to engage in quasi-autonomous pr including wandering off from work at times of religious festiv cause management had developed a strong preference for ha in the workplace. At Agrawal, spaces of autonomy at work only exist because those in charge allowed them to emerge the region's prior history as a hotbed of Maoist guerrilla warfa emphasis on harmony was unsurprising.

It would be a mistake, however, to view workers' aut merely as an outcome of managerial strategy. Further quest clude: How did the loaders themselves turn into stubborn, a workers? Why did they prefer piece-rate work and openly management rather than aligning themselves with the co Maoist union? There are several possible answers. First and f it is necessary to reiterate that truck-loading was considere all, to be mehenat. Undoubtedly, it was difficult to endure th ous work for prolonged periods of time, and many paledars the visits to their natal villages during religious festivals a tunities to rest their exhausted bodies. Thus, the strenuous their work was one reason why they tried to carve out more in their work schedules. Other types of work in the factory less physically draining, and therefore those workers did no need to take unauthorized breaks to recover their strength.

Second, in the case of the loaders at the Agrawal comp heritage of bonded labor played an important part in the ing sense of autonomy at work. While loaders in the west had been primarily Bihari until the end of the abolition c labor, paledar work has since become a "closed occupatio largely limited to Tharus from the districts of Bardiya and I mentioned earlier, some of the paledars had previously

conducted in the aftermath of the elections, in which few of the loaders took part. Not because, as in Alpa Shah's famous example from Jharkhand (Shah 2007), they wished the state away, but because most of them lacked the required voter registration cards and, moreover, because a thirteen-day *bhandh* (strike) had been organized by the CPN-Maoist Party prior to the elections. Crucially, however, when asked how they would have voted had they had the chance, most loaders stated that they wanted the Tharuhat Autonomous Party to win. The support of poor Tharus for the Tharuhat Autonomous Party is significant and demonstrates that the Party was not just the vehicle of landlords. However, the reason for this vote swing was predictable. Prior to the elections, the Tharuhat Autonomous Party had promised to advocate for a Tharuhat state, in which Tharus would be included.[3] Thus, with Tharuhat politicians advocating for a future Tharuhat state, the practice of claiming rights and a sense of regional-ethnic belonging gained currency among the electorate.

Finally, the increased sense of assertiveness among loaders was also discursively constructed. Drawing on Michael Herzfeld's seminal work on cultural intimacy, Hans Steinmüller uses the notion of "communities of complicity" to point to "a space of intimate self-knowledge" created through the tension between official presentations and vernacular practice in local sociability. Such communities are formed by those "who share an awareness of intimate spaces that are marked by embarrassment, irony, and cynicism at their boundaries" (2010:548). Such intimacy was readily apparent among Tharu contract laborers. The fact that the Tharus are officially represented in the western lowlands of Nepal as a "backward" group—or, in the words of the manager, "a group of jungly people"—has created a tension within their own self-understanding and identity. There was a gnawing sense among the contract laborers that they were "backward" due to their lack of education, but there was also a corresponding reaction to this official representation. Assertiveness at work thus also had its roots in this contradictory discourse: the tension between official representation and local vernacular practice and sociability.

Conclusion

This chapter has offered a critical analysis of how people who formerly worked as bonded laborers have adapted to the new realities of a precarious capitalist labor market. It has demonstrated how former bonded laborers began working as contract laborers with the help of their kin-related contractors and ended up in a very insecure position at the bottom of the industrial hierarchy. I argued that their acts of defiance and resistance to control by contractors and managers represent a form of—in the words of German social historian Alf Lüdtke (1993)—Eigensinn that has its roots in their past experience as bonded laborers, not in the contemporary strength of the Maoist movement. The latter point complements an argument I have made in chapter 1—that the Maoist presence made a substantial difference for another category of workers. These workers were employed at the very same food-processing factory, but due to the intervention of Maoist unionists, they had managed to obtain permanent contracts. They were largely machine operators or packers, but not loaders, and they were Indians or, more often, Madheshis, not Tharu. I showed that the spirit of Eigensinn, which the Tharu have developed, related not only to the harsh working conditions in the factory but also to their stereotyping by management as unruly, "backward" Janajatis, as well as to the broader Maoist labor politics in industrial estates within the wider area.

From the worm's-eye view of the ethnographer, this chapter also illustrated how different ethnic groups experience industrial labor in Nepal. At first glance the story seems familiar. In the industrial area around Nepalgunj, members of an ethnic community end up doing the most back-breaking jobs within the factory and are judged by management to be unruly tribal people. Undoubtedly, this description evokes parallels to the historic descriptions of Chotanagpur "coolies" by colonial managers in neighboring India (Gosh 1982; Mohapatra 1985). Certainly, the few rare ethnographic descriptions of the "inclusion" of ethnic labor into industrial work processes suggest a similar picture. Alpa Shah (2006), for example, has demonstrated how ethnic laborers from Jharkhand did the most laborious work in a West Bengali brick factory. However, unlike in Strümpell's (2014b) description of the Rourkela steel plant in Orrisa I argue that a shared "Adivasi" identity that incorporates different ethnic communities has not yet emerged. This, I suggest, is ultimately a product of wider Maoist politics in the post-conflict period and the subsequent Maoist union activity in the factories of the area, which led to Maoist patronage of the Madheshi community. Hence, Agrawal management does not dare to openly criticize the Madheshi workers but rather vents its pent-up frustrations on the Tharu loaders, often in very ambivalent tones (workers are framed as "jungly" yet "hardworking," "stubborn" but "strong"). Paradoxically, I suggest, then, that the ethnic discrimination within the industrial estates is also a product of post-conflict Maoist politics. In the following chapter, I will further complexify this argument by looking at the role of religious rituals in cementing the division between permanent and contract labor in the factory examined.

Notes

1. The Tharu paledars had different names for motorized vehicles and machines: *childgadi* (bird's car) = airplane; *fatingwa* (grasshopper) = tractor; *dhakihawa gadi* (Tharu basket) = cement mixer; *ghetarwa* (small pig) = motorcycle; *mansari* (Mercedes) = truck.
2. The chapter also contributes to broader debates on the transformation of bonded to free-wage labor that go back at least to Max Weber's discussion of Polish workers who migrated to Germany's rapidly industrializing cities in the late nineteenth century.
3. The UCPN (Maoist) focused their electoral campaigning largely on the empowerment of other communities, such as Muslims and Madheshis. This contributed to the idea that Tharu independence was necessary, since Tharu loaders now regarded the Maoist parties and indeed the entire political establishment as *chorharu* (thieves).

Chapter 3

New Forms of Spirituality
in a Food Factory

Introduction

Agrawal Food Factory, Nepalgunj, 2013: Six weeks after I first met him at the tea stall outside a modern industrial food-processing factory near Nepalgunj, a Janajati man and paledar named Ram Chaudhary invited me to visit his natal village where he and other loaders hailed from. Shortly after, I embarked with my research assistant on a day visit to the neighborhood in the nearby Bardiya district where many former bonded laborers (*mukta kamaiya*) resided. We spent the day walking around the neighborhood, visiting different household members, and then had dinner with Ram and his family at his small mud hut in the evening. As is custom in such meetings, Ram offered us *dalbhat* (a Nepali dish) and *daru* (traditional alcoholic beverage) with all three of us getting slightly drunk as the evening progressed. In the middle of dinner, Ram told me a story. He said that a *boksi* (witch) lived in the Agrawal food-processing factory. Apparently, the witch resides in a broken sanitation building next to the dirty toilet area in the factory. My research assistant, a young Tharu who had grown up in Kathmandu, laughed heartily, teasing Ram by asking, "Well, have you seen her?" Serious, Ram countered, "No, I haven't, but some of my loader friends have seen her! She sometimes appears at night wearing a white dress, but when she turns around you can't see any flesh on her body!" Curious, I intervened and questioned further about her appearance and why the witch chose to reside in the factory. But Ram was keen to elaborate on the experience of residing with a witch in the same factory, stating that "usually we—the loaders—are afraid to go out of our labor compound in the factory at night. You know, women are not allowed to visit the factory overnight, and when we see a *boksi*, we get afraid."

Agrawal Food Factory, 2013: Four weeks into my fieldwork on industrial labor in western Nepal, I was having a chai with Bishram Chaudhary outside the fenced wall of a modern food-processing factory in western Nepal. That day, Bishram pointed out to me a rather unusual fact. A decade ago, the factory's management had shuttered the entrance to the factory that was facing west toward the highway and had built a new entrance gate that faced north. Inquiring why this apparently redundant operation had been performed, I learned that management at the time had been following the principles of Vastu Shastra, a kind of Indian design principle, similar to feng shui, that harnesses cosmic forces through the correct alignment of physical spaces and objects.

These two scenes have been carefully chosen to introduce this chapter. In it, I examine how the changing interactions in the new industrial world are conceived within local cosmologies. I take as a starting point the hint that Bishram was making that day and contextualize it. I explore the role of rituals within such industrial work environments, and the ways in which such practices support the social order. More specifically, I trace three religious rituals in the factory to examine the role of religious practices in propping up the industrial order: the geomancy of the managerial elite; the worship of a "machine god" by permanent employees; and the visits to ritual healers by contract workers to gain protection for their bodies and guard against risks. By focusing on such marginal practices, the chapter reveals a hierarchy of rituals that maps onto the hierarchy of workers in the factory. I argue that such a hierarchy of rituals not only reveals the ways that industrial elites make use of spiritual practices in their efforts to integrate a new and diverse labor force, but also illustrates how permanent and casual laborers appropriate spiritual ideas in the industrial context.

In doing so, the chapter aims to advance two different types of literature: a small set of literature on the importance of religious rituals in South Asian industries (see Cross 2012; Kumar 1988; De Neve 2000, 2005; Fernandes 1997; Parry 2007), as well as recent contributions that highlight the role of religious beliefs in ordering working lives in supposedly secular, modern industrial contexts in other countries (for Indonesia, see Rudnyckyj 2009, 2018; for Egypt, see

Makram-Ebeid 2018). This corpus of literature is largely inspired by a Marxist tradition of writing that views religion in a very functional way, often understanding religious rituals as either providing space for industrial owners to exercise some form of patronage over their workforces (De Neve 2000, 2005) or as a locus of resistance to modern industrial work regimes (Fernandes 1997). Building upon this critical anthropological work (Ingold 2001; Cross 2012), I aim to advance the current literature on the relationship between religion and industry by highlighting how different actors along the industrial hierarchy perform different type of religious rituals and develop a "technological intimacy" (Cross 2012:119) with their industrial environment.

Second, this chapter aims to advance a more recent corpus of literature on the divisions between permanent and contract work in industries (see Kesküla 2018; Kofti 2018; Mollona 2020; Hann and Parry 2018; Parry 2020; Sanchez 2016; Strümpell 2014a, 2018; Trevisani 2018, 2019). This literature has been helpful in pointing out the growing importance of the division between the "salariat" and the "precariat" in industrial settings. In this context, chapters 1 and 2 have highlighted how my informants distinguish between *isthai* (permanent employment) and *asthai kam* (temporary work) in the context of industries in western Nepal. This chapter advances these prior findings by exploring the role of religious rituals in stabilizing the social order in the factories examined.

Moreover, I view the emergence of new forms of spirituality in the industrial environment as related to two different factors. First, the religious rituals described—at least those at the top of the industrial hierarchy—are primarily a reaction to the uncertain industrial futures that emerged in the wake of the Maoist insurgency between 1996 and 2006. Second, these new forms of spirituality reflect a more general trend across South Asian industries and can be related to the rise of the religious project of the Hindu right throughout the wider region. I am not suggesting that South Asian industrial elites are transforming workforces into pious, obedient workers through religious reform. Rather, I suggest that religious ideas are becoming more prominent in the industrial sector in general, and that analyzing them is important to understanding how industrial elites appease a casual workforce and make workers more positively disposed toward their workplaces. One outcome of this process is that such elite articulations of religious identity may solidify existing divisions between permanent and contract workers.

Thus, I do not intend to conduct a Weberian analysis (2001) of the role of religious ideas in contemporary capitalism, nor do I entirely contest the recent work that claims that there is a new "spiritual economy" across Asia—broadly defined as the convergence of religious practices with business management ideas under the condition of a rapidly changing political economy (Rudnyckyj 2009). Indeed, many of the managers and industrial owners I interviewed acknowledged that they infuse their managerial techniques with religious ideas. However, as the ethnography foregrounded in this chapter illustrates, they also view the incorporation of religious practices as a gamble with fate. Religious practices may lead to better production rates and higher profits, but the outcome of their inclusion is always uncertain—success or failure is intimately related to one's own luck, fortune, and faith. This proposition echoes Giovanni da Col's (2007) call for a more serious anthropological engagement with the cosmological imaginations of luck, faith, and fate that underpin economies. Similarly, I suggest that religious beliefs and the way they inform industrial work should be taken more seriously in order to better understand how industrialists, managers, and workers all deal with the vagaries of notoriously uncertain industrial fortunes. Let me now begin to explore these dynamics by diving into a more general discussion of the importance of spirit beings in the region, before turning to the specific religious rituals made at the different levels of the industrial hierarchy.

Living with Spirit Beings

The regional literature recognizes the widespread belief among ordinary people in invisible "spirits" in both northern India (Parry 1994; Sax 2009) and Nepal (Gellner 1994; Walters 2001). For example, William Sax—writing about Gharwal in northern India—notes that "although the ghosts of deceased family members are rarely seen any more in Europe and North America, in Gharwal they are very much a part of life" (2009:165). In a similar way, Damian Walters recognizes that in "highland Nepal, spirits and people walk the same pathways. Ghosts and divinities inhabit the surrounding hills and forests" (2003:1). During the various stretches of fieldwork that I undertook in western Nepal, I also encountered the widespread belief of ordinary people in invisible spirits (see Hoffmann 2018a). It is important to emphasize that people distinguish between friendly and malicious spiritual beings. While the former are welcome "guests" in one's life, the latter are a common source of worry and concern. For example, throughout my time in Tikapur, in the Kailali district in the far western lowlands of Nepal, I discovered that members of the Tharu community often tried to avoid *pipal* trees in the forest as they were believed to host malicious spirits (Hoffmann 2018a:67). Another example were the many variants of a ghost story that was frequently told in villages, which told of a ghost that takes the human form of a friend and lures one to a forest before finally possessing one's own body. In short, such examples illustrate a more general belief in an environment imbued with the presence of spiritual beings.

To address the activities of malicious spiritual beings (for example, being possessed after crossing a place inhabited by a spirit), there were a number of ritual practitioners that were all believed to possess the ability to embody spiritual beings or ghosts. More specifically, such ritual practitioners—who people usually addressed with either the Nepali terms *dharma* or *jahkri*, or the Tharu term *guruwar* (shaman)—were said to have the ability to encounter and fight malicious spirits through ritual. To do this, the ritual specialists entered a heightened state of awareness, often accompanied by the beating of a drum or ritual chanting, and then began negotiating with the malicious spirits to leave a possessed body (see also Walters 2001). The people I encountered throughout my fieldwork frequently talked about the various forms of spiritual beings that influenced their everyday lives. In the following section, I will examine some of the beliefs I encountered inside the food-processing company discussed in the previous chapters.

The Practice of Vastu Shastra

Let me begin by turning to managerial practices and discourses surrounding Vastu Shastra at the Agrawal food company. As I mentioned in the ethnographic vignette at the beginning of this chapter, I heard about the application of Vastu Shastra to the factory from Bishram, the Tharu contractor working at Agrawal. As I soon learned, most of the workers at the Agrawal food company had little familiarity with the ideas, practices, and discourses of Vastu Shastra. Instead, many of my ethnographic insights on Vastu Shastra were gathered from spending time with the manager of the company, a Nepali Hindu. I spent the first two months visiting management on an almost daily basis, and after a good six weeks of fieldwork, they began to reveal more about their use of Vastu Shastra.

It is important to note that the application of Vastu Shastra to the Agrawal factory was not an isolated case. According to management, using Vastu Shastra principles was a new trend in running industrial factories within predominantly Hindu societies such as India or Nepal. For instance, the manager recounted to me several factories in Lucknow, Uttar Pradesh, and Mumbai where Vastu Shastra had been applied. Factory management emphasized that it was a modern practice and that it had only gained prominence in Nepal over the last decade, with homeowners in Kathmandu applying Vastu Shastra principles to the spatial arrangement of their homes.

A central feature in my discussions with management was their insistence that Vastu Shastra be regarded as a science, an old Hindu knowledge system that the owner and management had decided to apply to the factory at a time in 2008 when the company's profits were low and production fell short of expected targets. Vastu Shastra was regarded by management as the "science of directions," and they had redesigned the factory space according to the Vastu Purusha Mandala in order to create a perfectly balanced environment that would ensure the growth of health, wealth, and happiness. Like feng shui (Steinmüller 2013), Vastu Shastra connects astrological elements and cosmological meaning to the shapes and contours of the lived environment. To correctly apply it to the factory, management had invited a Vastu Shastra consultant from Mumbai to align the factory space with the "positive energies from the earth."

The Vastu consultant recommended various changes to the spatial arrangement of the factory. First, prior to the application of Vastu Shastra, the company's property was approximately in an "L" shape. However, according to the consultant, the "L" shape was far from ideal. As management explained, in Vastu Shastra all buildings should have either a circle or square shape to ensure the optimal flow of "earthly" energies. Thus, the factory's management decided to buy additional adjoining property and expand the factory's footprint to form a square. This was far from cheap, requiring an additional investment of around 30 to 40 lakh, but was done because the owner of the factory, a Marwari industrialist, desired to follow the recommendations of the Vastu consultant.

The second change to the spatial arrangement of the factory concerned the location of the building itself. As mentioned in the opening of this chapter, the main gate facing west directly toward the highway was closed and a new main gate was established at the northern border of the factory compound. This, according to management, was crucial for the success of the company—spaces that are oriented northward are considered to have a higher quality of life as everything is said to thrive in the north. Management explained this principle to me by drawing a simple map with the four directions and scribbling next to it: "north is excellent, south is bad, west is OK, and east is good."

Third, after relocating the entrance gate, management followed the Vastu consultant's recommendations and remodeled all the production units and the labor compound for the workers in a similar manner. This led to a new workflow in which raw materials were stored in the southern sections of the factory and then processed in the northern areas before leaving the factory via trucks through the new northern gate. Management was keen to point out that this new "south–north" workflow was key to establishing the success of the company. Along with this rearrangement of the factory workflow, management also decided to rebuild the workers' dormitories according to the Vastu principles and placed them in the eastern parts of the company compound, where management felt it would be most beneficial to labor. The sun rises in the east, and so east was considered to bring energy in the morning.

In everyday working lives this "science of directions" mattered little. For instance, regardless of their ethnicity, the workers knew little about Vastu Shastra but regarded it as a form of elite knowledge. In contrast, I learned over the course of my fieldwork that management had their own doubts about the application of Vastu Shastra to the factory's spaces. For instance, as one junior manager told me, the head manager might openly talk about Vastu Shastra but behind closed doors he did not believe in all of it. Undoubtedly, such comments from a junior manager to a foreign researcher may relate to a heightened reflexivity due to the researcher's position, but taken at face value, they do seem to suggest some doubt about the general usefulness of Vastu Shastra in the factory. Nevertheless, what all managers agreed upon, at least up front, was that "giving Vastu Shastra a try" was worth it—the factory's output and profitability had, after all, increased after making the changes recommended by the Vastu consultant.

The idea that "success" in running a factory is not only related to managerial strategy but also involves luck and faith is crucial to understanding the managerial tactics at the Agrawal food company. It shows that strategic leadership at Agrawal cannot be subsumed into more general neoliberal managerial techniques but was far more multifaceted. In recognizing the complexity of management's strategy, two tentative arguments can be made. First, I would like to suggest that part of the incorporation of supposedly ancient Hindu techniques such as Vastu Shastra into factory life is related to the managerial desire to position themselves to the company's lower-caste workforce as knowledgeable, pious patrons. On one hand, the factory's management remained skeptical in private about the usefulness of Vastu Shastra; on the other hand, their very public adherence to Vastu Shastra was an attempt to legitimize their own status in the factory hierarchy by implying to the workforce that they should be regarded as knowledgeable Hindus. Second, I do think that there is something more essential here at play as well. Part of the management might really believe in this practice because it signifies an expression of worship in which the devotees ask the deity for protection in order to make the factory function. In a world, such as western Nepal, where spiritual belief and enchantment are commonplace, such religious rituals to the gods are deeply familiar, and in the next section I will further elaborate on the everyday forms of religious rituals made by permanent machine workers to Vishwakarma, the god of the machines.

Religious Worship of the God of the Machines

Another practice that was related to the use of Vastu Shastra in the factory was the worship of the god Vishwakarma. This "tradition" was closely related to Vastu Shastra because Vishwakarma was assumed to be the original creator of the "science" of Vastu Shastra. Vishwakarma was a deity that was celebrated in both an annual festival and in everyday working life in the factory, as will be shown in the remainder of this section. Once per year, on 17 September, the factory's management held the festival of Vishwakarma. Though I have not witnessed it myself, according to the manager the festival was celebrated by holding a small ceremony in the factory compound, after which all the workers—whether permanent, temporary, or daily wage workers—received a free meal. An Indian machine operator from the oil mill described the annual festival as follows:

> The ceremony takes place in a yard next to the oil mill. That day a small statue of Vishwakarma is brought out and put in the middle of the yard. In front of the statue is a small bunch of mango wood that is burned. Around that, four pillars made of banana trees are made, and around that, a circle of flowers is arranged. The manager sits on the ground while the brahmin reads out the texts, and sometimes the manager makes an offering to the statue. The pandits sings but we don't know the songs. The laborers sit in the back and watch. At the end of the ceremony, they all get *prasad* (sweets) and a feast is held. The company spends around 5 lakh (approximately 5,000 euros) for the festival and every laborer has to voluntarily donate around 50 NR (approximately 50 euro cents) according to his financial status.

When I inquired about this festival outside of the factory, many people were not surprised. Vishwakarma is celebrated the same day across the country, and nearly all metallic materials are performed with a *puja* (worship). On that day, my research assistant was even doing puja to his motorbike. While the whole country celebrates Vishwakarma on the specific festival day in September, the mostly Indian machine operators in the Vikash flour mill worshipped Vishwakarma on a daily basis. "Vishwakarma hamare bagwan hai" (Vishwakarma is our god) is how a machine operator described their affiliation. Accordingly, Vishwakarma protects the machines and is their *rajak* (guardian). Vishwakarma is worshipped two times a day, each time at the beginning of the machine operators' shift. To conduct the ritual, a machine operator will take out an incense stick and swirl it five times in the air. Then he puts the incense stick in front of the small *mandir* (temple) of Vishwakarma on the first floor of the Vikash flour mill. It has a small picture of Vishwakarma inside. After, he will bow his head, bend over, and touch the "legs" of the machine. The leg of the machine, I was told, represents the extension of Vishwakarma's leg.

I was also told that Vishwakarma is celebrated daily because it protects the machines. This is not to say that Vishwakarma lives inside the machine (the machine operator laughed when asked this question). Rather, the god Vishwakarma is the guardian of the machine and protects it. "What happens when you forget to worship Vishwakarma?" I inquired further. Then, I was told, "we apologize five times—like 'maf karo, maf karo' [sorry, sorry]!" Yet the workers said that they worshipped Vishwakarma because it was religious tradition, rather than fearing his revenge when they were negligent.

It is not like Vishwakarma takes quick revenge when the ritual is forgotten. As a machine operator at the factory explained to me "It is our *kismat* [luck] that no accident has occurred here. The luck is already decided when you are born. We can't prevent accidents anyway." This posed a question to me: why was it that the machine operators really worshipped Vishwakarma and their machines? To explore this further, I will now discuss a bit more the materiality of the machines that are being worshipped.

Materializing Vishwakarma

The invocation of the Hindu deity Vishwakarma in the context of modern machine production may be less surprising when it is understood that these machines are primarily worshipped because they are made of metal. It is this materiality that is important and that distinguishes the machines from other industrial goods in the factory (such as the rice bags, which are not worshipped). Both the Nepali and Hindu word for metal is *dhatu* and refers to a variety of metals including gold, silver, and iron. But importantly, *dhatu* is not only used for metals—it also refers to semen and invokes reproductive powers.

Thus, when machine operators worship their metal machines, they are indirectly invoking the reproductive power of the Hindu deity Vishwakarma. This is unsurprising because metal is often a symbol of power in Nepal. For example, during a marriage ceremony gold ornaments are exchanged and given to wives, daughters, and sisters. Thus, Vishwakarma is a good candidate for the worshipping of machines because he is a potent deity.

Religious Rituals at the Margins

Compared with the public rituals that managers and permanent machine operators perform inside the factory compound, contract workers engage in their religious rituals to their animistic gods outside the factory walls—and often in secret. This is best illustrated by a story that Bishram Chaudhary told me:

> One day in the last month of summer, I was sleeping with my gang of contract laborers on the flat roof of the labor compound. The searing heat did not allow us to sleep inside the dusty labor compound. While sleeping on the roof, I woke up in the middle of night because I had a nightmare. Being awake, I realized I was afraid of having an accident in the factory. As a reaction to this dream, I decided to leave the company the next day and visit my home village in Bardiya, in order to conduct a ritual to satisfy our house god. The following day, I went to my home in Bardiya, bought milk, and offered it to our house god, before returning the next day to the factory. To avoid getting in trouble with management for leaving the factory to make a sacrifice at my home, I told my contractor partner Mangal to cover me for the work I had to do that day.

Bishram's story was by no means exceptional. Despite being officially Hindu, many of the Tharu workers maintained their indigenous religious beliefs and tried to appease their own village gods. This meant that when they felt the gods getting angry, they had to return to their home villages to appease these animist deities.

A second example of religious ritual among contract workers was revealed to me after two months of fieldwork. I learned that contract workers made frequent visits to a guruwa in cases of illness and minor injuries. For example, next to the Agrawal food factory was another food factory where a Tharu worked as a guard and day laborer. The workers in the area knew that he was believed to have *tantrik shakti* (spiritual powers) and visited him in case of minor incidents. The consensus was that it was more beneficial and cheaper to visit the Tharu guruwa next door because the company only paid for hospital visits in extreme cases. This guruwa was also frequently visited because Tharu workers generally—especially the older ones—believed that spiritual beings influenced and controlled the destiny of humans. The guruwa was said to have the ability to influence one's personal relations with spiritual beings through the appropriate rituals—often in which the guruwa embarked on a spiritual journey to fight with the demons that possessed the ill workers.

To understand why Tharus engaged in such sacrifices, whether to appease one's own house god or by making an offering to a guruwa, one must know a bit more about the wider cosmology of Tharu contract workers. At the risk of generalizing, it can be said that many of the contract workers continued to believe in spirits, a local custom that management tended to dismiss. According to Tharu cosmology, such spirits must be appeased regularly, for example by offering the blood of an animal (usually a chicken) or by offering milk. Against this background, then, it is not so surprising that such beliefs often interfered with factory work schedules. Yet walking home to conduct a sacrifice to appease a house god or visiting another factory to see a shaman were practices that the company's management dismissed out of hand. To management, such practices were considered "backward" for two reasons: first, management were wary that such customs interfered with the production schedule; second, they feared for the reputation of their company as it did not provide for health care (apart from severe cases), which was outsourced to contractors.

Limited Spiritual Economies

To some extent, Agrawal's modern food-processing factory resembled the Krakatau steel plant in Indonesia described by Daromir Rudnyckyj (2009, 2018). Building on Jean and John Comaroff's notion of "occult economies" (1999) and James Scott's "moral economy" (1987), Rudnyckyj innovated the concept of a "spiritual economy" to highlight the convergence of the religious resurgence and neoliberal transformation that occurred in the Indonesian context. In Rudnyckyj's account, religion was neither a "refuge" from nor a form of "resistance" to neoliberal reforms in Indonesia. Religion was also not a "retreat" into "magic and mystery" in response to global capitalism. Instead, he argues, religion and capitalism complemented each other to address the challenges of globalization. In his study, industrial elites mobilized Islamic virtues of self-discipline, accountability, and entrepreneurial action to create a "new type of subject, a worshipping worker, for whom labor was a matter of religious duty." Spiritual economies articulated how these practices were deployed to "remake the country's political economy, and.. [were] intented to elicit a type of subjectivity commensurable with neoliberal norms " (Rudnyckyj 2010:106). The situation in Nepalgunj was similar in the sense that there, too, an industrial elite resorted to a (Hindu) religious principle to make the factory function.

The difference from the situation described by Rudnyckyj was that the project of infusing religious values into the workplace was less successful in Nepalgunj than in the case of the Krakatau steel plant in Indonesia. Undoubtedly, for the owners of the Agrawal factory, Vastu Shastra signified a novel way to transform the company into a successful enterprise. But management, as we have seen, also had serious doubts about the effectiveness of Vastu Shastra and saw it more as a gamble with unknown outcomes. As a junior manager pointed out to me once: "Even our senior manager does not believe in Vastu Shastra at heart." Nevertheless, management implemented the "spiritual reforms" and recommendations of the pandit consultants who visited the factory and advised on its transformation. For the machine workers, engaging in the ritual to satisfy Vishwakarma was just one of the many religious practices they engaged in throughout the year. At Holi, for example, the entire factory drank *bhang lassi* (weed with curd), and it was the machine workers who attended the ceremonies of the pandits coming to the factory. Similarly, on other festival days, engaging in religious rituals was crucial for the permanent Indian machine workers to establish a company identity and a sense of belonging in the factory while away from home. Few of them could afford to spend substantial amounts on offerings when they had been living in Bihar, and thus religion served a community-building function that helped make the dull life in the factory more bearable.

The casual workers, however, did not embrace the spiritual reforms taking place in the factory. For them, Vastu Shastra had little meaning, and while they were present at the factory rituals to worship Hindu gods, few had any understanding of the details of the ceremonies. For them, the practices surrounding "their own" ethnic deities and their beliefs in witchcraft, ghosts, and shamans were far more important. But their forms of worship and expressing their religious ideas and practices could not be done on the shop floors. For example, Bishram chose to go home to appease the deity that was located there. He had to leave secretly because management would not want him to just take time off. As a result of the contract workers' continued engagement with their own religious practices and spiritual beliefs, management regarded them as being "backward." Too often the manager pointed out to me: "Look at these jungle people," referred to Adivasi beliefs in the supernatural world as "backward," and summoned Tharu workers to scold them for their misplaced piety and disruptive superstitions. As I showed in chapter 2, management often expressed that Tharu workers were behind in their development and needed a good two decades to "catch up" with modern industrial life. One senior manager in the food-processing company told me that "it would take twenty years for these workers to establish themselves in society." Management would sometimes refer to them as "jungle" people and criticize their habit of going hunting for mice during their work shifts. In addition, management believed that guruwas were things that Tharu believed in, things that just did not work. The irony, of course, lay in the fact that none of the management considered the ideas and practices of Vastu Shastra or Vishwakarma to be "backward." Moreover, while they publicly condemned Tharu shamanism, one senior manager told me that when his daughter was sick, he had gone to see a guruwa and her health had subsequently improved. Hence in comparison to the inscription of religious ideas, values, and practices in Indonesia, the case described may be best conceptualized as a limited form of a spiritual economy.

Conclusion: The Stability of Spiritual Economies

This chapter has engaged with religious practices in Agrawal's modern industrial food-processing factory. The ethnographic material put forward mapped specific religious practices onto different sections of the labor force to show how different groups in the industrial hierarchy engaged with religion in the workplace. More specifically, the ethnographic focus has been on managerial practices that are based on Vastu Shastra, the religious practices of permanent workers while on the job, as well as on the ways casual workers engage with their own indigenous religious ideas and practices. In drawing attention to the importance of Hindu rituals and beliefs to both managers and the upper strata of the local working classes, it is not my intention to swell the chorus of right-wing Hindu nationalists in India and Nepal who call for the "Hinduization" of the whole region. Yet the ethnographic case described shows that some orthodox Hindu industrialists in Nepal have indeed begun to ride the "saffron wave" (Blom Hansen 1999) by incorporating supposedly ancient Hindu "sciences" such as Vastu Shastra into the layout of their factories, or by allowing workers to worship the Hindu deity Vishwakarma—referred to as the "god of the machines." Central to my argument has been that such attempts to revive the supposedly glorious past of a lost Hindu knowledge should be read as an attempt by management to infuse the industrial workplace with a Hindu spirituality and a set of Hindu forms of worship that indigenous casual laborers were—so far—less able to associate with. Thus, managerial efforts to impose new forms of spirituality onto the factory body and its workers can be conceptualized as an attempt to integrate and unite a diverse workforce. More abstractly, this chapter suggests, then, a more general mechanism through which capital binds labor in the South Asian context: through the imposition of new forms of spirituality onto the work environment itself.

Of course, such efforts to impose a Hindu spirituality build upon older ideas, practices, and rituals in South Asian industries. Yet when compared to other such engagements with religious ideas and practices, two observations seem important. First, none of the new forms of religious ritual described in this chapter involved sacrifices. For example, Jonathan Parry's seminal ethnography on Bhilai (2020) reports on stories and rumors surrounding human sacrifices in the establishment of the Bhilai steel plant. Similarly, my previous work in Kailali district in far western Nepal documented rumors of a human sacrifice that was performed in the 1990s to appeal to the Hindu goddess Kali for the successful construction of the Chichapani Bridge (see Hoffmann 2018a).[1] Instead, none of the three religious rituals described in this chapter relate to endowing the factory's material body with the powers of gods such as Kali. Second, the religious practices described in this chapter are not only different from traditional practices but are also informed by the past, particularly by the more recent political history of Nepal. As I have documented in previous chapters and elsewhere (Hoffmann 2018a), the period after the insurgency was a particularly turbulent one, in which labor in specific urban pockets of Nepal became more assertive, at least until the dissolvement of the People's Liberation Army (PLA). The fact that management introduced Vastu Shastra at the height of the post-insurgency period indicates that this was also a way for management to deal with the uncertainties triggered by the Maoist insurgency and the post-conflict period. Strikingly, then, if the immediate post-conflict period can be said to have reconfigured labor relations (Hoffmann 2018a; Shakya 2018; Thapa 2019), it probably also reconfigured how industrial owners viewed their factory, namely as an "industrial body" that can be made more effective through the infusion of Vastu Shastra. For things to work in a factory in a post-conflict environment, managers must draw upon all kinds of registers, including the imposition of new religious ideas and practices. In this light, it is likely that other factories in Nepal also introduced similar practices to their shop floors in the immediate aftermath of the conflict.

These observations raise an important question: To what extent are the dynamics described in this chapter indicative of broader trends in the development of industrial capitalism in South Asia? Are we witnessing the rise of a new "spiritual economy," as suggested by anthropologist Daromir Rudnyckyj (2009) for Indonesia? The ethnography put forward suggests that while such "spiritual economies" may indeed be on the rise in the South Asian context, there remain at least two good reasons to expect that such spiritual economies will remain limited. First, the ethnographic material clearly shows that, despite their engagement with ideas and practices of geomancy, managers continue to doubt their effectiveness. Second, even when implemented, such attempts to transform an industrial workplace into what might be called a "Hindu workplace" are limited as indigenous labor remains unengaged by this new form of governmentality. It seems that the managerial tactic of seducing workers through new forms of spirituality in the workplace may have worked in the past, but in today's world—where millions of Nepali workers toil in distant workplaces in the Middle East and Malaysia (Zharkevich 2020)—such imposed religiosity may be less appealing to casual labor. There is thus a good reason to remain skeptical about the further rise of spiritual economies in the South Asian context.

Notes

1. See Hoffmann 2018a, 38, footnote 12: "Local legends tell of how the Indian contractors who built the suspension bridge at Chichapani sacrificed a kidnapped girl to the goddess Kali during the construction process, and how, when the bulldozers passed by the Ghora/Ghore lake, they were attacked by a swarm of snakes seeking to protect a local Tharu holy site."

PART II

Work at the Margins of Pokhara

Chapter 4

WORK, PRECARITY, AND MILITANT
UNIONISM IN AN INDUSTRIAL AREA

Introduction

In early February 2019, about a hundred members of Nepal's Maoist-affiliated union All Nepal Trade Union Federation (ANTUF) gathered in the early morning hours near the entrance gate to the industrial area in Pokhara. They had come to commemorate "martyrs" who died more than a decade ago in an encounter with Nepal's army. The local branch of the Maoist Party had previously installed a memorial to the martyrs inside the industrial area, visible to any visitor entering the gated terrain that was now guarded by armed police. The union members were patiently and silently following a small ceremony led by the Maoist district leader in-charge who told about the sacrifices made for the Party by the five martyrs, all of whom had worked in various industries in the industrial area. At the end of their short gathering, a minute of silence was held to honor their fallen comrades, and red vermilion powder was put on the gold-framed photograph of one of the martyrs which was placed at the base of the memorial statue. Then they all followed the district leader in-charge, Nirmal, to a large congress hall that was situated close by.

The district leader in-charge had invited me to the ceremony and given me permission to attend the union's internal meeting in order to assist me in my research on the current condition of Nepal's industrial working classes (see chapters 1–3). I was, however, not the only guest. Several high-level Maoist politicians were also attending the meeting in the congress hall, and at the beginning of the meeting, all of them briefly outlined their current assessment of the union as well as the activities and challenges that lay ahead to advance the cause of the working classes. After the usual rose-tinted political speeches, Nirmal began to give a lesson on the concept of the "social security fund"—a policy applying to all industries that the government of Nepal had developed together with the International Labor Organization (ILO) and passed into law three months prior. Nirmal began his presentation with a PowerPoint slide that displayed two comic characters signifying the struggle between labor and capital; he added that any conflict between the two would lead to necessary friction. Using this as a starting point to encourage his fellow unionists to apply the new labor law to all the industries in the compound, he then proceeded with a three-hour lecture that was only briefly interrupted by a snack break. Nearly all the unionists present—there were around twice as many men as women in attendance—stayed to hear the full lecture, and afterward a lively discussion ensued on the repercussions of the social security fund on their respective living situations and their specific industrial context. Ramesh, the secretary of the union, raised his hand and challenged Nirmal, his friend and superior: "Why would they apply it here? Even in Kathmandu, the industrialists have not done it yet! Only about a hundred factories have signed up for this plan and are willing to contribute to the social security fund!" Nirmal listened to this critical intervention and turned it to his favor by again reminding his fellow unionists that the social security fund policy would only be applied if "we hold together and keep our unity." Without the union, he reiterated, there would be no change as capitalists never change without the pressure of organized labor. The capitalists in question were those owners of the seventy-one different factories that had been set up inside the industrial area, most of them built over the last three decades.

This chapter examines how militant unionism has affected labor relations in the industries of the region that Nirmal was discussing. I show how, historically, the Maoist union operating in the industrial area had indeed made important inroads into the larger factories, and how they managed to challenge precarious labor regimes— above all in the years of *Andolan* (protest) immediately following the Maoist insurgency.[1] I briefly describe the regional historical and political context into which such forms of militant work-based activism must be situated. I then describe the labor relations inside the industrial area generally and then specifically within a modern noodle-processing factory. In this factory, the Maoist union has impressively managed to organize all the workers and succeeded in gaining permanent contracts for almost all of them—with the exception of the canteen workers, security guards, and a few subcontracted loaders. I argue that this instance of a mostly salaried workforce that enjoys various benefits, including the payout of a yearly bonus, remains a local exception and only relates to larger factories. Smaller factories inside the industrial region remain unaffected by the agitations of militant unionism. In these smaller factories, workers often do not earn the national minimum wage, nor do they have a permanent contract. They work as *asthai* (casual) laborers and are often afraid to challenge the factory owners for fear of losing their jobs.

I argue that the case of the large noodle factory complements my previous findings on the impact of Maoism in other lowland food-processing factories (see chapters 1 through 3). This research suggests that in some sectors in Nepal there is an increase in permanency that goes against the general trend toward precarity and insecurity within such industries around the world. Much of the ethnographic work on industry has tended to focus on cases of casualization while ignoring how more radical political formations have managed to change the conditions of the industrial working classes. I do not want to glorify such interventions but rather point out that they illustrate that the "imaginary horizon" of unionists remains alive. Unionists have not entirely failed to live up to their "revolutionary aspiration," as was argued by Andrew Sanchez and Eeva Keskülä (2019). Rather, unionists have had to confront the "knowable ground" of capitalism (Cross 2019) when applying their revolutionary ideals, and in that process have frequently become ensnared by bureaucratic procedures in no longer favorable political conditions. That is why, as I point out toward the end of the chapter, the militancy of the unions seems to be in decline and why people like Ramesh—a member of the militant union himself—expressed doubts about the implementation of laws supposedly favorable to the working classes.

The case presented here is significantly different from industrial sites in India (Cross 2014; Holmstroem 1984; Parry 1999; Sanchez 2016) for two primary reasons. First, unlike in the contexts described by those authors, the workers do not have to pay a bribe or commission to obtain a permanent job in the more desirable factories. This lack of bribes is hardly surprising given the specific political climate outside the factory gates. Managers are keenly aware that the acceptance of bribes in exchange for a job inside the factory might be used by the Maoist unions as a pretext to agitate their workforce. Maoist unionists, on the other hand, are now operating in the public spotlight; accepting bribes from their own union cadres would certainly discredit their labor movement. Second, the situation in the large factories in Nepal differs from industrial sites in India due to the broader influence on the labor market from wage-earning abroad, particularly in the Middle East and Malaysia. From the perspective of both managers and workers, life in small, industrialized places like Pokhara is also a life on the periphery of large industrial economies such as the Middle East and Malaysia (Bruslé 2010a, 2010b; Gardener 2012). As I will discuss in detail throughout the chapter, this affects how managers view working lives at home. For example, managers fear losing workers to jobs abroad, but they also sometimes use the international labor market to justify and legitimize inequalities at home. It is within this larger network of economic connections that the Maoist union's success in fighting for permanent employment for some workers in larger factories should be understood.

By largely focusing on food industries, this chapter also aims to contribute to two additional sets of literature: first, the emerging anthropology of modern food-processing industries around the world (see Dunn's [2004] work on baby-food industries in Poland, and Blanchette's [2018, 2020] work on industrial meat production in the midwestern USA); second, a small but growing anthropology of industrial labor in Nepal (Kondos 1991; Kondos, Kondos, and Ban 1991, 1992; Seddon, Blaikie, and Cameron 2002; Shakya 2018). I begin now by setting the context of the ethnography by outlining the broader political history of Nepal generally and in the Kaski district more specifically.

The Marginal Growth of Industries in Pokhara

Pokhara, a city located in the foothills of the Annapurna mountain range about 200 kilometers west of Kathmandu, was urbanized in the late twentieth century. In the early 1960s, it achieved worldwide recognition as many European and North American adherents of alternative cultural lifecycles saw it as the end of the "hippie trail" that led from London to Kathmandu via the famous "magic buses" (Adhikari and Seddon 2002:191). The hippies were soon followed by adventurous tourists, and later by more affluent nature-loving tourists. Over the last fifty years, the city has changed dramatically and grown rapidly. Currently, more than half a million people live in Pokhara, and the cityscape is marked by the ongoing construction boom. As in other cities in Nepal, the price of land has risen sharply and land in Pokhara today costs about twenty to forty times what it did fifteen years ago.[2]

Compared to the wider tourism industry in the city or the widespread labor migration to the Middle East and Malaysia, local industrial development has always played a marginal role in Nepal's overall economy. Unlike the garment industry in Kathmandu, which grew from small-scale entrepreneurial endeavors in the informal economy of the 1970s to a major industry in the 1990s (Shakya 2018), Pokhara's industrial growth occurred after the Nepali government began allocating land to planned industrial areas in the mid-1970s. However, the state's plan to entice Nepali industrialists to build up their industries inside these zones was often problematic. In the beginning, industrialists complained about the involvement of the royal family in choosing which companies would be allowed to operate in these new areas. One of the first companies to be established in Pokhara was Rara, which still runs a noodle factory inside the industrial area and whose brand is locally famous for sponsoring the city's soccer team. At present, the industrial area on the outskirts of the city is populated by many companies, which I will discuss further below.

Important for our discussion is the wider political context under which such a slow, local "industrial revolution" is taking place. It is worth mentioning that Pokhara, from its beginnings, had the reputation of a peaceful city. Unlike other places in Nepal (Adhikari 2014; Dhruba 2010; Hoffmann 2018a; Lawoti and Pahari 2010; Pettigrew 2015; Zharkevich 2019a) that saw major battles between state agents and the Maoist People's Army, Pokhara did not experience much violence during the insurgency period between 1996 and 2006. A few bombs were put in different locations around town, but otherwise the situation remained largely calm in the insurgency period. Surely, local tour operators and their guides had to pay *chanda* ("voluntary" donations) to the Maoists, and industrialists—as we will see below—also had to pay chanda in exchange for their operations being allowed to continue. But such practices of extortion were widespread throughout the conflict and happened in other parts of the country as well (see Dhruba 2010:191).

The peaceful reputation of Pokhara began to fray after the signing of the comprehensive peace agreement between the state and the Maoists in 2006. Many former soldiers of the Maoist's People's Liberation Army (PLA) came to the city and were given a camp near the bus station where they settled together with members of the Young Communist League (YCL), a Maoist outfit that at the time acted as a paramilitary wing of the party. With their trained soldiers nearby, the Maoists now had a certain leverage of power. The result was predictable: violence for those who did not follow the party line. More specifically, at the industrial area in Pokhara, there were at least two food industries where the Maoist union gained access through force. As a union member of GEFONT, the non-Maoist-associated United Marxist Leninist (UML) Party remembered the situation; the Maoists threatened both workers and unionists to switch to their union. Large segments of the old unions deserted and switched to the Maoists. Surely, some changed because of their ideological convictions. But others switched sides for fear of becoming embroiled in the violence that marked that period, as rival union leaders attested at the time of my fieldwork. For example, when asked about the violence, the local Maoist leader admitted that they had to learn to use non-violent methods; force had been their first choice in those days. The leader of GEFONT told me that he was beaten sixteen times by Maoists, and his construction union comrade had even been kidnapped by Maoists.

Everyone I interviewed agreed that the violence between unionists calmed down after the first Constituent Election in 2008, which the Maoist Party won by entering a coalition government. Before that, labor was extremely assertive. As the manager of a noodle factory inside the town's industrial area admitted to me: "At that time [2005–2008] the situation in the factory was so bad, even I did not want to go to my factory anymore. I simply could not take it. They [labor] formed action committees and never showed up to work. But they wanted to get paid all the same." After the dissolution of the People's Liberation Army in 2011, the Maoists also lost their "extra-power." Only with the recent merger of the UML and the Prachanda-led faction of the Maoist movement in 2018 has a more stable government emerged. However, this government has widely been described as showing authoritarian tendencies.

It is also worth mentioning that after the dissolving of the People's Army in 2011, the industrial area has been involved in the actions of two other militant outfits. In 2013, before the elections, the Chhetri Samaj called for a general *bandh* (strike) in town. The noodle factory that I will discuss below did not obey this demand and so activists of the Chhetri Samaj entered the factory and destroyed and looted several of its machines. Moreover, while doing fieldwork, I observed how the entire industrial area was closed after the newly formed revolutionary outfit led by Comrade Biplav—a former member and close associate of Maoist head leader Prachanda—called for a total bandh in the press for their imprisoned party comrades.[3] All the factories—except the dairy factories—closed that day as Biplav and his comrades were known and feared for their use of violence. They did attempt to put a pipe bomb at a roundabout close to where I lived, but the bomb was disarmed by the army who were called in after it was discovered.

The Industrial Area in Town

Factories began to locate to the industrial area in the early 1990s and have continued to do so over the following decades. Owners and managers gave a variety of reasons for locating to the area. First, land in the industrial area was cheap to rent. According to one manager of a dairy factory, the rent for one ropani (local unit of measurement) of land was between 2,000 and 3,000 NR per month. An accountant at a water-bottling plant even stated that the land for the whole factory area per year was about 8,000 NR. Compared with rental prices outside—where it is hard to find a large piece of land—the prices for rent inside the industrial area were about a sixth of the price. Second, the zone authorities offered constant electricity, although they could only deliver electricity during the daytime until a year ago. Third, the industrial area offered the security of an armed police camp that was set up a few years ago. The number of police was quadrupled last year to about 125 armed policemen.

From the industrialist's perspective, the advantages of establishing their factories in the industrial area were clear. Located close to the second largest city, it offered an attractive market and labor was abundant in the city. However, obtaining this cheap land was difficult as many industrialists wanted to reserve a piece for themselves. In the early days, two of the larger factories were established by two brothers from a family who are known to have had influential connections in politics. Now there is a waiting list to set up an enterprise inside the area. As one manager of a dairy factory told me, it was unimaginable that there were not some bribes involved in obtaining a place inside the industrial area. How large these bribes were and to which state organ they were given remained a mystery to me throughout my fieldwork, and I never did find out.

What was characteristic about this area, compared with the Special Economic Zones that are currently being set up throughout the country, was the absence of any multinational, international company. All the owners within the industrial area hailed from Nepali families. Most of them were high-caste Brahmins and Chhetris; I also encountered Newari industrialists and one Gurung factory owner (though he shared the ownership of his factory with two high-caste business partners).

There is also a clear relationship between the ownership of the factories and their market orientation. Most of the factories produced for the local market, but some of the larger ones that included a paper factory, a noodle factory, and a biscuit factory served the international market. It was these larger factories that were the only ones that were unionized. In town, three unions were active: a union close to the Nepali Congress Party, the Maoist-affiliated union ANTUF, and GEFONT. In three of the factories, Maoists and GEFONT were competing for the workforce,[4] while in the fourth factory—the largest of all—the Nepali Congress–associated union was representing the workers (see Table 2).

Several of the managers told me that while there was no union in their factory, workers belonged to political parties in the town and followed the general party lines. Some also complained about the New Communist Party government: "The government regards us as looters. But all we want is that the government does not intervene in our work". This was how the manager of an LPG gas factory described the situation to me. According to him, the government did a bad job in collecting taxes—both income and VAT—from the industries in the area and outside of it. He added: "How can we compete in a market where some competitor companies do not pay taxes? The government agents come, but they give them a tiny fraction of what they save on tax—1 or 2 lakh NR bribes and that's it. How is that fair?". In other words, despite the state-sponsored efforts to create industrial development inside the area, the state itself was corrupt and did not collect the fruits of its own labor for development.

Labor and the Workers in the Industrial Area

In most factories, labor recruitment seemed to follow a simple, familiar pattern. The owners who established the factories would often hire family members for management positions, and the laborers would be recruited from extended social networks in the owners' home villages. However, over time—and especially in the aftermath of the insurgency when international migration really took off—labor turnover also increased. Nearly all factory owners expressed to me their frustrations about the loss of laborers to the Middle East or Malaysia. The manager of a dairy factory, for example, recalled that he had lost at least eight workers in the previous eight months. Four of them had applied to go to the Middle East and had obtained visas. According to him, this was also the reason why many workers

Table 2. Sample Survey of Factories Inside the Industrial Area: Total Workforce, Gender Divisions, Degree of Casualization, and Union Membership

Factory 1	10 workers	7 men	3 women	No permanent	No union
Factory 2	9 workers	5 men	4 women	No permanent	No union
Factory 3	8–16 workers	All men	None	8 permanent, 8 contract	No union
Factory 4	17 workers	14 men	3 women	9 permanent, 8 contract	No union
Factory 5	20 workers	20 men	0 women	6 permanent, 14 contract	No union
Factory 6	27 workers	17 men	10 women	0 permanent, all contract	No union
Factory 7	6 workers	3 men	3 women	5	No union
Factory 8	16 workers	14 men	2 women	16	No union

Source: Author's fieldwork

refused permanent contracts—they wanted to keep their migration options open. Additionally, as the factory manager related to me, the workers were also leaving companies with low wages to go to factories with higher wages. "The industrial area is a sort of platform. Here people come, ask for work, and then go hunting for a better paying job or find a job abroad." This might be only half the story, as the gas manager added in another interview:

> The truth is that not all companies here pay the minimum wage.[5] We do. That's why laborers also come to our company and look for work. But they also leave for higher wages. Of course, losing labor due to migration has been an issue. But it has gone down in the last year. Labor has become more expensive. Before they earned like 10,000 NR, now they earn like 16,000 to 18,000 NR per month. Abroad you can expect a wage like 24,000 NR. So, you see, the difference is not that much anymore and that's why people consider staying here.

Inquiring further into this topic brought another important fact to light. According to many managers, workers left for the Middle East or Malaysia also because of the prestige as well as the ability to save more. They often blamed the wives of the workers as the ones who convinced them to go abroad. By going abroad, the workers could save a lot more—there was no time to spend it on items like mobiles or drinks with friends.

Hiring age and education standards have improved inside the area. Maybe thanks to an intensive campaign against child labor in the wider city, none of the factories I visited hired children, and in general most workers had at least some degree of schooling. Yet it is true that not all factories followed the labor laws that made it illegal to not pay the minimum wage, provident funds, or social security. Few of the managers I interviewed openly admitted to breaking the law, of course, but when I checked with the workers, I discovered that in several factories minimum wages were not paid. Managers also complained a lot about their ability to pay higher wages to the workers. As one manager in the noodle factory said to me:

> Look, it's like this. In India, the wages in Bihar are like 6,000, in Haryana it's 8,000, and in Delhi, it's 12,000 Indian Rupees. Ok, you factor in the conversion rate of 1.5, but still, it's cheaper to produce in India. And they come here and dump their cheap products. In the Middle East, the wages are even higher. So, we are trapped between these places. We need to pay labor something between 15,000 and 20,000 NR because of the unions and the new government's laws. But it also means that we have trouble staying competitive with Indian companies if the government does not bring in some anti-dumping policies at the border. And yes, we know that it's hard to survive in Nepal on 15,000 or 20,000 NR. But what to do? If we pay more, we can't compete unless there's a serious change in government policy towards price dumping from both the Chinese and the Indian side.

Most managers in the industrial area were keen to point out that caste was not an issue inside the industrial area. As the manager of the noodle factory put it: "Here everyone can come and work." When asked about the ethnic composition inside his factory, he added: "We don't have such data. And we don't care about caste. Everyone who is able can come and work here. But yes, the truth inside the industrial area is workers often come from ethnic groups such as *janajatis* [indigenous groups]. You'll encounter Magars, Gurungs, Rais, and other groups here." Although management was reluctant to give me data on ethnicity—and I have not been able to conduct a larger survey on the ethnic backgrounds of all the workers inside the industrial area due to its size—my own observations are congruent with this manager's statements. An estimated 30 percent of the workforce is from a higher-caste background, and an estimated 70 percent come from different ethnic backgrounds.

In terms of the gender divisions of the working classes inside the industrial area, I could observe that in some factories the workforces were predominantly women—these were in the noodle, biscuit, and water-bottling factories. Other factories, such as the metal industries, employed predominantly male workers. When asked why there were so few women in the metal factories, management often gave the expected answer: men can do hard work, and women are better for the light work such as in the noodle, biscuit, and water-bottling factories. Management also considered women to be easier to manage and assumed that they were cleaner than men, an important factor in the food and beverage industries. Importantly, management also often expressed that women were less expensive compared to men. It was common knowledge that women were usually paid less than men—both inside and outside the industrial area. For the factories I know best, the noodle and the water-bottling factories, I would like to add that the workers were mainly women who had a husband abroad, or single unmarried women. These women could be paid less, the rationale went, as their income was supported by a working husband or their family. In this way the domestic sphere contributed to the lower wages that women received in the industrial area.

Pokhara Instant Noodles Factory

The Pokhara Instant Noodles factory was established in 1991. It is one of the first factories in the industrial area and initially employed about thirty workers. Over the past three decades, the factory has grown into one of Nepal's largest food producers and employs more than three hundred workers. Its focus is on the production of noodles and biscuits. The workers from Pokhara Instant Noodles factory were largely from indigenous groups of Gurung and Magar, while the company's senior management were usually high castes. When asked, however, the company's management was keen to emphasize that this was not intentional, and that the company had the policy of employing whoever was willing to work hard for them. All the company's workers were permanent, the minimum wage was paid, and all of them were also part of one of the two unions that operated inside the factory: these were the UML-affiliated GEFONT and the Maoist-affiliated ANTUF. Like in the Agrawal food factory that I researched in Nepalgunj (chapters 1 through 3), the factory's union leaders were not outsiders but workers from the factory floor itself. The GEFONT union leader was a Magar and the ANTUF leader was a Brahmin.

Since its inception, the company has witnessed various forms of activism that management divided into different time periods. As one senior manager inside the Pokhara Instant Noodles factory put it: "The country faced great problems throughout the revolutionary period, but industries have still faced these challenges after the revolution ended. Or to put it simply: the revolution hurt the people, the aftermath has hurt the industries." According to another senior manager, the company's main problem during the revolutionary period was the extortion of money. Like elsewhere during the revolution (see Hoffmann 2018a; Shakya 2018), the Maoists called on the factory many times to make a donation.[6] The senior management saw itself in trouble. One senior manager said:

> On the one hand, we had to satisfy the demands of the Maoists. On the other, we had to satisfy the army. When the Maoists asked me for a donation—and at that time I was head of the zone's industrial association—I went to collect the donation from various industries and met with the Maoists in the jungle. After I delivered the cash, I went to the police. They asked, "Why didn't you inform us?" I told them an hour later—at that point the Maoists were already gone.

By carefully balancing his position, he managed to pull himself and the factory through that difficult time. However, all the senior managers and unionists I interviewed agreed that the real struggle began after the end of the insurgency. The period immediately after the end of the insurgency was particularly difficult—to the extent that even the senior manager and the other managers had wanted to stop going to work. What happened was that the Maoists began to quickly organize the factory. This was, according to the Maoist district leader in-charge, Nirmal, part of a broader strategy in the aftermath of the revolution. Maoists began to infiltrate industrial factories to challenge precarity by organizing workers and demanding higher wages. In the Pokhara Instant Noodles factory, this resulted in more than seventy out of two hundred workers joining so-called action committees set up by the Maoists. According to the same senior manager mentioned above, these workers often went to the action committees and did not show up for work. The next day they would come to him and demand to be paid for their absence. When asked whether the factory paid, the manager said, "Sometimes we did, sometimes we didn't—it was all horrible."

These types of activities only changed when the Maoists took power in 2008. At that time, the association of the zone—that the same senior manager was the head chairman of—asked senior Maoist leaders to stop their activities. As he remembered, he made the following request of the Prachanda-led government: "We do as you say. Even if you tell us to pay them for no work. But please control them." According to management, the Maoist senior leadership agreed, and the disruptions declined. Gradually, the less-militant GEFONT union won back members in the factory. This was in line with a more general decline in union activism inside the industrial area, a decline that could be measured by the number of political slogans that were painted on the walls of factories. During my fieldwork, union slogans were still visible, but the paintings were old and the number of slogans written on the walls had decreased.

The Maoists and GEFONT unionists were not the only ones who were active in the company. The senior managers also remembered one night when members of the Chhetri Samaj came early before the morning shift and vandalized their factory, destroying expensive machinery that cost the factory approximately 25 lakh NR. When talking about such incidents, the senior managers usually praised their own courage and boasted about their "level of experience to deal with difficult situations," even in times of conflict. The result of all this labor activism was that the company's management largely gave in to the demands of the unionists and promised the union members that they would follow the law. When the new labor act was published in 2016, the company finally decided to have all workers on the payroll and provide them with permanent contracts. Nowadays, management stresses that the company only faces problems "due to the egos of the union leaders." For example, when a union member was recently transferred to a different position within the company, he called for a strike and the company engaged in a long bureaucratic negotiation with his union. However, other factories in the industrial area did not enjoy such privileges, as I discovered in a nearby water-bottling plant where workers were not paid the minimum wage, had no permanent contracts, and were afraid to form a union.

The Work Process in the Factory

The Pokhara Instant Noodles factory located in the industrial area consisted of two factory sites and employed a total of 342 workers. Among them were 173 men and 169 women (the reason for having so many women was the 1 percent tax cut from the social security fund when a company hires more than a hundred women).[7] All the workers on the company's payroll were permanent, and the company followed the regulations of the Nepali labor law that stipulated that after a six-month probation period, all workers had to be given a permanent contract. The exceptions to this rule were the six workers who worked in the factory's canteen, as well as six security guards and twelve loaders. These positions were subcontracted by the company to outside contractors.

Most of the workers were between thirty and forty years old. The majority were married, and it was the company's explicit policy to hire women with children. This was because, according to management, they were more reliable and tended to stay longer than young unmarried women who often left the workplace after either an arranged or love marriage. Nearly all the workers were Hindu, and more than half of the workers were from ethnic communities including Magar, Gurung, Kumal, and Darai. The core of the workforce were locals who lived nearby. Unlike in other places, none of the workers had traveled from far away in search of work. In the factory's early days, the workers were hired on the basis of extended kin and friendship networks from nearby villages or localities, and many of the workers interviewed continued to have a personal connection to one of the managers within the factory.

The production site was located next to several other factories in the center of the industrial area. It ran 365 days a year, with a work schedule from 9 a.m. to 5 p.m. Only some of the senior machine operators arrived earlier at 8 a.m. to prepare the machines for the workday. Unlike in Nepalgunj timekeeping was not announced by security guards banging an iron stick with a hammer. Instead, each of the departments had its own clock—for instance, to keep track of quality controls for the processed noodle packages in the processing department. Workers generally arrived to work on time and used their own watches or, more often, their mobiles to keep time. The use of mobile phones inside the company was not allowed except for work purposes; nevertheless, many of the workers could be seen using their phones: sometimes a female employee on her expensive smartphone, sometimes a labeler who would not even hang up when the company's human resource manager was around.

As elsewhere in Nepal, the company does not produce all the elements that go into their packaged noodles. It is, as managers point out, only repackaging existing products bought from different places in Asia. For example, the soup in the noodle packages was bought in Singapore. The chemical paste to mix the noodles came from various companies in India and China that produce such mixtures. The company's technology was from Japan, though the equipment in the processing department was bought from China.

On any given day, when visiting the company, I often noticed groups of workers walking through the company yard at different times or hanging out in the large canteen inside the company compound. The reason for the abundant amount of idle time spent chatting or phoning was related to the company's work processes and the way it assigned labor to different tasks. The processing of a noodle started in the *maida* (flour) department. Here, two or three male workers were assigned to this task. In a dusty room coated in flour, the worker's task was to stack the room with flour sacks in the morning hours. After this was finished, the workers had to fill a machine with flour by opening the flour packages. This task took about three minutes, but the workers were given ten minutes to complete it. Every ten minutes they had a break, then spent ten minutes filling the machine. For much of the day, the three workers were idle, apparently bored, and sometimes they sat outside the dusty room, taking in the sun. It reminded me of the work schedule of brick burners inside a brick factory that could be similarly full of downtime (see Hoffmann 2018a:149–168).

The second step in the production of the noodles was the pumping of the flour by a machine into the second floor of the production hall via a giant tube. Here, two male, Brahmin machine operators and a female helper from the Magar community operated a machine that mixed the flour with a chemical paste acquired from India or China. The two machine operators traded shifts but made sure that there were always at least two people next to the machine in case of any problems. One time, for example, I was next to them when a red alert signal began to ring above the machine operator's toolset. Neither the operator nor the female helper seemed bothered. They just went to the tool board, pressed some buttons, and the flour began pumping again through the tube into the giant "mouth of the machine." "She was hungry," was how one of the machine operators explained this step to refill the mixing machine.

The mixture of flour and chemicals was then passed downstairs, where water was added to make a dough, which was then rolled out in various machines and finally cut. Two male machine operators dealt with this process. They had to be especially careful that the thin lines of noodle were cut correctly into eight different strips. The machine allowed for adjustments to the length and width of the noodle strips, and here the operator had to communicate over a good thirty meters with the two machine operators in the liquid department. Therefore, they used sign language to signal to each other about the quality of the noodle as it was cut, as well as any adjustments they had to make to the machines.

Afterward, the cut noodles were fried and passed through the "showering department," where they were dunked in "chicken aroma" or another of the flavors offered by the company. Here, the machine operators stood on a small pedestal and every now and then took a noodle sample from the assembly line. These machine operators were a male Brahmin and a female Dalit. They communicated in sign language with the operator at the cutting machine. They had gestures for four different states: not good, too high, too low, or make it broader. All four gestures were made by hand, and the machine operator would whistle to their colleague at the other end in case they did not see the signals being made. The section after the liquid department was overseen by a female supervisor. She and the head supervisor were often absent, but when present they were always ready for a chat with a foreign researcher interested in the production process of their company.

The next step was done by two women who sat in a yoga-like position on top of a machine next to the assembly line where they each used a large stick to rearrange the cut strips of noodle. This was hard work that required concentration. At first glance one wondered how long they could sit in this uncomfortable-looking position. But it turned out that the women worked in groups of three and each hour they traded spots. The third woman was a "spare," a concept that we also find later in the processing unit.

The processing department consisted of four assembly lines that looked like Frederick Taylor could have organized them. On each, one woman flipped the noodle, two women put the soup on top, and another woman corrected the soup. Then the noodles were passed through a machine for packaging, and some were removed for quality control by the male machine operators in the department. Finally, two women packed the packages into a cardboard box (about forty-five packages per box), and then another one taped the box and wrote with a pen a code such as "73D," which meant production day 73 and assembly line D. There was little room for workers to make mistakes, nor could someone put anything else in the packages — as I know sometimes happens from the stories of friends who have worked in other such industries. A complaint with the final product would lead to the immediate identification of the culprit on the assembly line. Such mistakes, however, were rare. Upon close inspection it turned out that although this department worked with spare workers, they often disappeared outside into the courtyard or went to the company's canteen.

The spares were tasked with putting the 20 kg boxes of processed soup on small wagons and taking them to the lift or to another door where a slide led directly into the factory storage halls. The elevator brought the packages downstairs where male loaders were stalking the halls until a company truck came to pick them up. Much of the market of the company was based in the lowlands, making production costs higher compared to other competitors in the region.

Conclusion: Nepal as an Exception to the General Trend of Growing Precarity?

According to the argument of Hann and Parry (2018), the claim that neoliberal ideology has become the "new common sense" of our times (Standing 2011, 2014) is not only questionable but also empirically wrong as there are a variety of conditions that create employment regimes based on flexible labor. In line with this argument, I have shown in previous chapters (chapters 1 through 3) that the modern food factories in the area around Nepalgunj have become more, rather than less, secure over the last thirty years, workers have achieved union representation, and for the most part the minimum wage is now being paid. Although I attributed such "progressive" tendencies to the rise of the Maoist movement in Nepal, I also pointed out that in the factories near Nepalgunj the Maoist unions favored the ethnic Madheshi residents over the "outsider" Tharu migrants. Class politics in Nepalgunj overlapped with ethnic politics, which I also attributed to the larger political context in the Banke district.

In this chapter, I explored the labor union activism in an industrial area in Pokhara. The ethnographic material shows striking similarities to the case of Nepalgunj. In the examined noodle factory, a similar process seems to have occurred. Before the arrival of the Maoist unionists on the factory floor after the end of the insurgency, the workers were organized by a UML-associated union. This union was less active in challenging precarious working conditions in the factory—maybe unsurprisingly, as the owner of the factory himself was a leading politician within the UML. Only with the arrival of the Maoist unionists did labor politics begin to change, and labor achieved many victories over the last decade, including the reorganization of nearly all the workers apart from the outsourced security guards, the canteen workers, and a few loaders. As this chapter has shown, both management and labor remember the times of revolution and protest quite vividly and are ready to talk about its impact on current working conditions.

This raises an important question: given that in both settings—Nepalgunj and Pokhara—the Maoist movement has indeed challenged precarity successfully and succeeded in making labor increasingly secure, should we now view Nepal as an outlier to the current trend of growing precarity in industries around the world (Hann and Parry 2018)? Were Nepal's unions reacting differently to the current "age of precarity" (Lazar and Sanchez 2019) because they were backed up by a powerful party and army during the revolution? More generally, even, when and how do specific conflict periods produce what Luke Sinwell and Siphiwe Mbatha (2016) call "insurgent trade unionists"? One possible answer suggests that Nepal indeed is an exception to the worldwide trend toward increasing precarity, and that, at least as far as large factories are concerned, this is largely due to the action of Maoist trade unions.

My claim requires three further qualifications. First, as the ethnographic material in this chapter has shown and as I will show in the next chapter, other factories inside the industrial area experienced little intervention by the Maoist unionists despite the precarious labor conditions that existed within them, or the occasional non-payment of minimum wages. This reality mirrored that of the town's hotel industry, where recent research (Baral 2018) suggested that only the larger hotels have been organized by unionists, while small hotels remain largely unorganized. Hence, Maoist activism remained limited to only larger sites of employment. Second, it is important to note that strong Maoist activism in industries does not automatically lead to an improvement in workers' lives but can also backfire. For example, Mallika Shakya's (2018) descriptions of Kathmandu's garment industry suggest that strong Maoist activism paradoxically contributed to the rapid decline of Nepal's formerly vibrant garment industry. This was because strong Maoist activism occurred in combination with state-led neoliberal reforms that together produced the "death" of one of Nepal's largest industries, leaving tens of thousands of workers unemployed in the streets of Kathmandu. Third, it is important to remember that the impact of Maoist unionism on the workforce is most likely short-lived. Workers are now agitating less frequently inside the companies discussed here and within the industrial area in general. The times of leaving the factory workplace to join a rally and demanding compensation for one's own absence are definitely over. Due to the changing political context, the firing of militant leaders, and the continuing animosity between unions, labor activism in the industrial area was limited to a few of the larger factories.

In essence, the ethnographic material shows that the Maoist unionists lost their main tool of influence—the threat of violence—and have faced damaging allegations of corruption. Some of their cadres have been fired from factories, and the broader labor union movement remains divided. The history of violence thereby plays an important role in understanding why, despite cooperation at the central level, labor activists in the two factions remain suspicious of each other. The result of this declining union activism is that only the large factories in the industrial area remain organized. There could be two reasons for this: larger factories are attractive to unions because they can organize many workers at the same time, and production in a capitalist mode has only been established recently in the country. The next chapter will explore these themes further by looking at the labor conditions in the water-bottling industry in and around Pokhara that emerged largely after the end of the revolutionary period.

Notes

1. See Hoffmann (2018a) for further accounts of militant activism in the post-conflict period.
2. In the context of Pokhara, this sharp rise in land prices was not unusual. Jagannath Adhikari and David Seddon report that the first major increase in land prices took place during the 1960s with an eighteen-fold increase between 1960 and 1970. From the 1970s until the turn of the century, land prices have increased by an estimated factor of five for each decade (2002:121).
3. For a more detailed description of the newly formed "revolutionary" Maoist party led by Comrade Biplav, see Spotlight Nepal (2017).
4. Following the unification of the CPN, UML, and CPN (Maoist Centre) in 2018, the UML-affiliated union, GEFONT, and the Maoist union were in the process of merging at the central level in Kathmandu. However, during the time of my fieldwork, both unions continued to operate separately in town.
5. At the time of fieldwork, the national minimum wage constituted 13,450 NR per month.
6. Shakya notes that the amount of such donations usually figured between a few thousand and several lakh Nepali Rupees (2018:114).
7. This gender ratio is similar to that which existed in Kathmandu's garment industry: Shakya reports that less than 50 percent of tailors in Nepal's garment industry were women (2018:121).

— Chapter 5 —

GENDERED DIVISIONS OF WORK
IN THE WATER-BOTTLING PLANTS

Introduction

In their book *Churning the Earth*, Aseem Shrivastava and Ashish Kothari (2012) address how India has handled its environmental and
natural resources, including the contemporary phenomenon of priva-
tizing key water resources. Through a focus on neoliberal reforms
and corporate-led development, the authors develop a narrative that
shows how water has been turned from a public good into a privately
owned asset that allows companies to earn huge profits. Accordingly,
India is the fastest-growing bottled-water market in the world, with
the number of bottles being sold tripling between 1999 and 2004.
The result is a severe drinking-water crisis in the country today, as
bottling plants for fizzy drinks have a profound effect on the avail-
ability of clean groundwater in many rural parts of the country. This
has sparked public protests against water-bottling plants, with the
protests against the Coca-Cola plants in Plachimada (Kerala), Med-
higanj (Uttar Pradesh), and Kala Dera (Rajasthan) being among the
best known.

While I am not aware of any protests against water-bottling plants
in Nepal, the narrative of *Churning the Earth* touches upon several
questions that are at the heart of this chapter: How is the increase of
water-bottling plants in Nepal related to the new urban middle-class
consumer culture? Who are the owners of the new water-bottling
plants that largely emerged in the aftermath of the Maoist insurgency? From which caste backgrounds do the owners hail? How is
work organized in the water-bottling plants, and from which commu-

nities do the workers hail? Have the unions been involved in organizing the workforces of water-bottling plants? Perhaps unsurprisingly, given the novelty of water-bottling plants in Nepal, the scholarship across the social sciences has left such questions unanswered. Accompanying this silence is a more general neglect of the food and beverage industry in the anthropology of labor. This chapter hopes to contribute to the closure of this knowledge gap by examining the new landscapes of work that have emerged in the water and food industries in Nepal.

In this chapter I aim to give an ethnographic description of the labor relations and informal work cultures that exist in the water-bottling plants in Pokhara and its rural Himalayan surroundings. I will begin the account with a broader discussion of how and why the residents of Pokhara have shifted their consumer preferences from tap to bottled water—a change that reflects a global trend, as outlined by Peter Gleick (2010). I will then discuss the history of water-bottling plants in the region before examining the organization of work in the plants around Pokhara. Here my emphasis is on the relationship between class, ethnicity, and gender in the water-bottling industries. By tracing the journey of *janajati* (indigenous) women into the factory spaces, the arguments presented in this chapter complement those in chapter 2, which discussed the impact of industrialization on janajati communities in the lowlands of the Tarai. I previously showed how janajati men from the Tharu community experience industrial work in the lowlands. This chapter explores how janajati women experience labor in industrial water-processing factories. In the last sections of this chapter, I discuss the role of unions in organizing labor and consider the reasons for the absence of strikes and other forms of mass protest in the water-bottling plants. Let me begin my discussion with a brief explanation of why locals have begun to drink water from one-liter bottles and twenty-liter jars rather than from the tap.

Developing a Taste for Processed Water: From the Tap to Water Bottles and Jars

According to a 2017 study by the German foundation Hans-Böckler-Stiftung, the per-person consumption of mineral water in Germany went up from 12.5 liters in 1970 to about 149 liters in 2017 (Stracke and Homann 2017:19). How does this growth (by a factor of twelve) in water consumption compare to Nepal? Such questions are difficult to answer, but on my second visit to a water-bottling plant, I had an interesting discussion with Girvesh, a young accountant, who ex-plained to me various reasons why people in Pokhara have begun to drink bottled water. First, according to him, drinking bottled water has become a status symbol, "a way to show that you belong to the middle class". Second, he emphasized the heightened awareness in the area about waterborne diseases. This view coincides with a study that found that "about one third of deaths of children below the age of five in the rural regions of Nepal were due to water borne dis-eases such as cholera, typhoid fever, dysentery, and gastro-enteritis" (Pradhan 2005:277). Unlike those in the study, according to Girvesh, the people in Pokhara generally take waterborne diseases more se-riously and know that the dry season between March and June is when they are most prevalent. Third, bottled water is in fashion and demand is rising because the government routinely fails to provide all houses with safe water, and even when it does provide water, it is not always safe. There is little surprise, then, that the growth in demand is such that Girvesh's factory cannot always fill its orders. Fourth, the increased demand for bottled water is related to market-ing skills and capacities by the small factories. Importantly, accord-ing to Girvesh, in Nepal there are no cultural roots for the idea that water can have a healing power—like with the holy water from such places as Lourdes in France. Wells and springs in Nepal are the sites of *bhuts* (ghosts) sometimes, but, according to him, no one believes in "the ghost in the bottle." Tap water is considered something new and modern, which can be seen in the foreign-language words that are used for brand names. The exception to this rule is the Soaltee brand of water—*soaltee* means "friend" in the Gurung language, suggesting that the water is safe and agreeable.

The Bottled-Water Industry in the Kaski District in Mid-Hill Nepal

According to the Nepal Bottled Water Association, around 75 per-cent of Nepal's water is supplied by approximately five hundred fifty privately owned water-bottling plants. These plants are spread around the country and employ twenty-six thousand workers (Kath-mandu Post 2020). Although the oldest water-bottling plant in the Kaski district has been in operation since 1998, most of the plants in the district were only built after the end of the armed conflict be-tween Maoists and the state. These factories primarily emerged due to an increased demand for bottled water from the growing urban middle-class population of Pokhara, the risk of water contamination due to high temperatures in the summer, and the lack of adequate water supply infrastructure in the region. But the growth of these factories was also indirectly linked to the Maoist insurgency; people were driven from their rural homes during the revolutionary period, and then outside investment was stalled by the insecure business climate. As a result of such political dynamics, at the time of my field research in winter 2018–2019, the water-bottling industry consisted of an estimated thirty factories in the Kaski district. Except for two, all such plants were built on private land, whose owners generally distinguished between two types of bottling plants: those that processed water from natural springs and those that obtained water by "drilling" from groundwater sources.

Like the brick kilns discussed in my previous work (Hoffmann 2014a), ownership of water-bottling plants was largely restricted to high-caste groups, with the notable exception of one water-bottling entrepreneur who hailed from the Gurung community, one of Nepal's indigenous groups. That factory ownership was composed of those with access to capital was predictable as the establishment of such a facility required, in addition to land, an estimated initial investment between 1.5 and 3 karoor NR (approximately 150,000 to 300,000 euros). The machinery alone cost 1 karoor. Of the entrepreneurs I interviewed, many afforded such investments by drawing from other businesses that they were involved with. For example, one water-bottling plant owner I met told me that he was previously involved in selling cars; others were farmers.[1]

The new water barons entered the highly profitable business as outsiders with no prior experience of this type of work. To set up their factories, different owners deployed different strategies. For example, the owner of Friendly Waters, who hailed from the Gurung ethnic community, studied tutorials on the internet about how to set up a factory. After a year of self-directed research, he ordered the equipment and material from China. He claimed to have set up the factory himself. Other, less tech-savvy, entrepreneurs hired experienced machine operators. In Dungal's factory, the owner and his younger brother bought the machine equipment from neighboring India and initially hired an Indian machine operator to set up the factory. After three months, this technician was replaced by a Nepali operator who is still called when severe problems with the machines occur. Similarly, in a water-bottling factory in a neighboring village, the owner occasionally hired a machine operator from Kathmandu when machines needed repair. His factory, however, had a broken machine that remained unrepaired as he deemed it not profitable to fix. At another water bottling company, Blue Waters, the owner bought the machinery from a dealer in Kathmandu and spent five days training the workers on how to use it.

After the factory was established, the owner had to obtain the quality certificate for the water being produced at the plant. At the factories I visited, these licenses were usually displayed in a visible place in the office. At Fresh Spring Waters, a factory inside the compound of the industrial area, the accountant proudly showed me the factory's licenses. The most important was the ISO certificate that the factory put on its bottle labels to show customers that their water was quality controlled. In Durlap's factory, the owner explained that several times each month, quality inspectors would appear on the factory floor. These inspectors came from the Department of Water Supply and tested the water. These tests concerned three areas — physical, chemical, and microbiological aspects of the water quality — and altogether there were twenty-seven different sub-groups of quality parameters that a factory was judged on.

The history of the bottling plants in the Kaski district is closely connected to how marketing strategies for bottled water have developed. As John Jewell (2014) has pointed out, "selling water is the largest marketing trick of the century." To advertise their product, the local companies have created brands over the last fifteen years that emphasize the pristine, clear, and "Himalayan" quality of their water. Often the bottle labels feature the company name as well as a logo that creates associations with fresh Himalayan water sources (for example, by depicting a Himalayan mountain). The company names are often in English. One of the recent marketing trends was started by an entrepreneur in the industrial area; while all bottles initially had a blue cap and often a blue label with white colors on it, he introduced a pink design that boosted sales. Pink, a color often used on Pokhara's houses, turned out to be a popular color for water-bottle packaging, and other brands have followed suit.

In the factories I visited, the workforces were composed of between twenty and thirty workers. Among these, fewer than a dozen worked on the production line. Importantly, almost all the workers on the production line were female and from indigenous backgrounds. The ratio of women to men on the shop floors was usually four to one. When I carefully asked managers why this was the case, twice the answer was a straightforward "because women are cheaper." In fact, the salaries of the men on the production lines were often 50 percent higher than those of the women working next to them. Nevertheless, women came to work for different reasons. At Blue Waters, for example, four out of eight female workers had a husband working abroad in the Middle East and needed the cash from the factory to make ends meet. Two were unmarried and two came from a farming background. In what follows, I will explore how this overlap of class, ethnicity, and gender played out in everyday life at a water-bottling factory.

Work in the Water-Bottling Plants

My initial contacts in the processed-water industry were factory managers or owners. In most cases it was the managers who I first encountered when visiting a factory. Few owners spent much time in the factory; many of them had other businesses apart from the water-bottling plant. Whether I visited small factories (Dungal's) or large ones (Fresh Spring Water), it proved difficult to talk freely with the workers. In small factories such as Dungal's, there was simply no extra space available for interviews. In factories that were a bit larger, CCTV cameras were common,[2] and my access was limited by careful managers who would follow me around the factory grounds.[3] Nevertheless, I was often permitted to observe a factory while it was operating normally. This helped me gain an understanding of the practices and discourses of the workspace, and I became particularly interested in how different assembly-line technologies helped shape "shop-floor cultures." To get a better understanding of how the workers conceptualized their own work, I made interview appointments with production-line workers and truck drivers to take place outside the confined, monitored spaces of their factories. What follows is a description of the two factories I got to know best: Dungal's and Himalayan Waterlands.

Dungal's Factory: A Water-Bottling Plant in the Rural Hinterlands of Pokhara

Dungal's water-bottling factory was in the remote mountainous area outside of Pokhara, in the Kaski district. Kaski is one of seventy-two districts in Nepal, and its rural countryside is home to various indigenous groups including Gurungs and Magars. The factory was established in 2008 by a high-caste businessman and erected on his own private property. The water-bottling factory used the spring on the property to produce two main products: water in twenty-liter jars and in one-liter bottles. As elsewhere in the region, the company sold its water to local distributors who then sold it to customers in rural villages and the nearby municipality. In general, the demand for water was high in the hot summer months from June to August, and in the cold winter months there was a significant decline in orders. This seasonality had significant effects on the intensity of the workday at different times of year. Informants told me that work in the winter was less busy than during the summer, when overtime was common.

Every production order began with a call to the manager's mobile or to his office inside the factory compound. Water retailers provided detailed specifications on how many card boxes (one card box held a dozen one-liter bottles), how many water jars they needed, and how many trucks they would send to pick up their order.[4] When the small pickup trucks arrived at the factory, the drivers would go into the manager's office and pay in cash for their order. Then they would go outside and help unload the empty twenty-liter jars. The unskilled laborers in the factory were all women, and they would take these jars into the "washing room" where they would clean them with a machine and a pipe. The jars were then put on an assembly line and cleaned again. At the end of the line, two men would take the washed bottles in fives and put them under five water taps. Once filled, the bottles were sealed and put back on the truck. The entire process from unloading the jars to refilling them was efficiently done and took about fifteen minutes per truck.

Unlike the twenty-liter jars, which were refilled on demand, the water bottles were fabricated according to the order and stacked in cardboard boxes in the "machine room." Once management decided to turn on the assembly line, the workers had different jobs to perform. There was one worker who put the bottles on the assembly line, where they were automatically rinsed, filled with water, and capped before exiting the transparent machine. On the other side of the assembly line, the bottles were quality controlled, labeled, and a plastic wrapper was put on the caps. A female worker performed each of these three roles: the "quality checker," the "labeler," and the "plastic-putter." Finally, a packaging machine put them into cardboard boxes of twelve, and these were stapled and stacked by two workers.

To save on production costs, management had purchased a special machine to produce its own plastic bottles. In a separate room, an operator produced the new plastic bottles by stacking "pre-forms" in the machine to heat. The heated pre-forms were then placed under another machine, a button was pressed, and the machine sucked the pre-forms up through a pipe and spilled them out the other end as manufactured bottles. This entire process was extremely loud, and the machine operator did not have any ear protection. Unlike the bottle itself, the bottle cap was not produced at the factory. It was bought in bulk on the internet, mainly from Chinese retail stores. At a cost of 5 NR per bottle, the production of management's own water bottles saved money for the company and was also a way to give "employment" to someone from the area, as the manager put it. This "water-bottle fabricator" position was a way to demonstrate patronage to the nearby community from which all the laborers were recruited.

The success of the factory depended on its speed and rhythm. From its beginning, the company's main problems were the frequent power cuts, which left the machines at a standstill. This was observed on my very first visit to a factory, when I saw all the laborers sitting in the courtyard with nothing to do. During such breaks they often chatted about local gossip from their village (for example, the price of a goat that someone purchased) and waited for the power to come back on. Due to the frequent line cuts, work was stalled and at times overtime was required to fulfill the outstanding orders. Management motivated workers by paying an extra 50 NR for overtime hours. In practice this meant that workers sometimes had to come early at 7 a.m. and work late into the evening. To avoid rapid worker turn-over, management carefully required all new hires to work for six to twelve months at the company. Unskilled laborers—who were all female in Dungal's factory—received 8,000 NR per month; skilled machine operators made 12,000 NR per month. When the company could not fill all its orders, it subcontracted other factories in the area to meet the demand.

Himalayan Waterland Factory: A Factory Located in an Old Villa in Town

The Himalayan Waterland factory was situated in a converted villa in northeastern Pokhara. From the main entrance a courtyard extended to a two-story mansion, the "factory." The factory was one of the businesses of the owner, who hailed from the Thakali community. Two rooms of the villa had been refitted to host the machines and equipment that processed the water. A room on the first floor held a set of large filters (two meters in height) that purified the water that was pumped up from groundwater sources. Next to the entrance of the villa was a room where the assembly line and machines that produced the bottled water were located. Adjacent to the courtyard was a garage in which twenty-liter jars could be cleaned and filled from water taps that were connected to the filtering system on the first floor of the villa. Each of these "shop floors" was not larger than thirty square meters in size.

The Himalayan Waterland factory was run by Sunil. He was from the Chetry community and lived inside the factory compound of the former villa. He was twenty-three years old and had just completed his BSc in management from a prestigious local college. Prior to working at Himalayan Waterland, Sunil had worked as a waiter in a restaurant that was owned by the same businessman who owned Himalayan Waterland. Through this prior work experience, Sunil obtained a job at Himalayan Waterland and began to work there for a salary of 23,000 NR per month. Apart from one male machine operator, the workforce that Sunil supervised were all female, and largely from janajati groups. They lived in rented rooms close to the converted villa, and all received 8,000 NR per month as well as an additional 50 NR for working overtime hours during the busy summer months. The machine operator in the factory received 15,000 NR. No one had a permanent contract; contracts were all made by oral agreement.

At Himalayan Waterland, workers worked in two rotating shifts: one shift was from 7 a.m. until 6 p.m.; the other one was from 9 a.m. to 5 p.m. The rationality behind the shift system was to always have enough manpower to sell water to trucks that were arriving at the company. The two different shift groups took breaks at different times: the first group worked from 7 to 9 a.m., had an hour break, then worked again from 10 a.m. to 1 p.m.; then they joined the other group for a lunch break and then more work from 2 to 6 p.m. The other group worked from 9 a.m. to 1 p.m., had a one-hour lunch break, and then worked from 2 to 5 p.m. These working times, however, were not always kept. For example, when I first arrived at the factory, workers were on lunch break from 11 a.m. to noon as they had to work longer to fulfill the demands of a customer.

The factory's heart was the assembly line. Workers in this room wore caps and rubber boots and had to stand at the assembly line the entire shift. Unlike Dungal's factory, which produced sixty bottles per minute, the Himalayan Waterland factory's assembly line could only process thirty-six bottles per minute. Seven people worked at the assembly line. Their jobs were fairly *sajilo* (easy): at the beginning of the assembly line was a worker who washed bottles and then put them on top of the assembly line; the bottles were then filled by a machine automatically, before being capped by a machine operator—Sunil. Then the assembly line transported the bottles to the other half of the room to a worker who checked the bottles for unwanted sediments against a white screen. Then the bottles were labeled by a worker, capped with a plastic cap, sealed at the end of the assembly line, and packed by two workers into cardboard boxes. The cardboard boxes with the processed water were stored in the next room.

Water Salesmen outside the Water-Bottling Factories

So far I have discussed owners, managers, and production-line workers in the water-bottling industry of the Kaski district. Let us now turn to the truck drivers who are crucial to transporting the bottles of processed water to customers in the nearby town or its rural hinterlands. As I mentioned, some of them are directly employed by the plant owners, while others work for a distribution company or as a self-employed entrepreneur. This distinction between those who work for water-bottling companies and those who are self-employed was reflected in the monthly income of a truck driver. Those who work for a company usually earn less than the minimum wage, about 12,000 NR per month. They usually work with a "helper" who may earn even less, around 8,000 NR to 10,000 NR per month. Those who own a truck, however, can make up to 50,000 NR per month.[5] Maybe unsurprisingly, then, becoming a self-employed truck driver is a desired job in the district.

Many drivers aspire and strive to get their own truck to escape the drudgery of working for a low salary at a water-processing company. Yet, as a driver told me, many also try and fail to establish their own business. Let us look at some of the career trajectories of the drivers I met.

DRIVER 1: Sanjay is twenty-seven years old and married with one child. He began working at the company Himalayan Rivers in 2009. He got the job through his nephew who already worked for the water-bottling company. When he began at the company, he worked as a driver. The salary was low and started at 6,000 NR; when he quit in 2017, he was earning 11,000 NR per month. Though the salary was low, he and his workmates never went to the union. The company's manager had told him that he would earn much more in the future when he became his own entrepreneur. Then, after working for eight years—during which he contemplated working abroad—he finally found uncles and other relatives that gave him a loan of 15 lakh. He had already saved 3 lakh. By taking the loan—which he took from different people at different interest rates between 20 and 30 percent—he was finally able to buy a truck. He bought one and worked together with his younger brother as a water dealer. His salary multiplied by five. He now earns 50,000 NR for the same job he did before.

DRIVER 2: Arun Adhikhari is thirty-nine years old. He has worked on the same line for eleven years. He got the job through his uncle who was a dealer for Blue Waters company. In his company, all eight cars are owned by the individual dealers. Before becoming a dealer, he went to school until receiving his certificate. Then he worked at Buddha Air for four years before living in Malaysia for four years. In Malaysia, he worked in a factory as quality control and made about 30,000 NR. He was able to save 4 lakh and returned to Nepal to become a water dealer. He bought a car for 12.5 lakh and was able to pay back his bank loan in five years. He is very happy with his job and makes a good income. He had an assistant for two years, but they cheated him and ran away with some money. In his company at Blue Waters, he is a bestseller and he sells about two hundred jars per day in the summer and around a hundred per day in winter. He buys the jars for 35 NR and sells them for 60 NR each, for a profit of 25 NR per jar. He works a lot—up to fifteen hours per day in the summer and around eight hours a day in the winter. In the summer he gets up at 6:30 a.m. to meet the demands of the market. Part of his job is also to look for new customers, and he prefers to sell to hotels and restaurants. On a good day, it takes only an hour to fill the bottles at the plant, sell them at the hotels in town, and return to the plant. His truck carries fifty-five bottles, and he always carries two bottles when selling. He is used to hard work and never worries about pain, occasionally taking painkillers, even when his doctor suggests that he should take a break.

DRIVER 3: Nabin Gurung is twenty-eight years old. He owned a goathouse before getting into the water business, and he has never been abroad. He had started working his line with his brother two months prior to our conversation. The Bolero jeep he drove was bought for 16.5 lakh and he needed to pay half from his savings and half using a bank loan. For this 8-lakh loan, he pays 18,500 NR in monthly interest to the bank, and he also pays about 500 NR every day for fuel. This means that he can hardly save anything and uses any extra money to pay back his credit. He needs to sell at least forty to fifty jars per day to break even and needs to work for around seven years to pay back the loan.

As I soon learned from trusted informants in the industry, water-processing companies are keen to help a driver become self-employed by providing a loan or asking banks to support the driver. They do this for a few reasons. First, when a driver uses his own car, companies can avoid the hassle in case of an accident. A serious accident or fatality can be a real problem for the company. Second, the owners assume that self-employed drivers are better employees than those on the payroll. They think indebted drivers will work harder to sell more bottles in order to repay their loan. Companies have also begun giving credit to drivers in order to increase competition, meaning more indebted drivers. Third, this incentivizing of the profit motive among the drivers not only leads to higher sales in town but also helps promote the brand of the factory.[6]

The work itself is highly gendered. I never encountered any woman who worked as a driver for a water-bottling factory in the Kaski district. Being a driver is a male profession, and drivers usually work with a trusted helper. Their day starts early in the morning when they drive to a water-bottling company to pick up the cardboard boxes containing twelve 1-liter bottles and the 20-liter jars. The loading of the bottles often involves some waiting, especially when there is a cut in the power.[7] Once the processed water bottles and jars are loaded, the drivers go to visit different hotels, shops, and middle-class homes in the nearby town and the rural villages to deliver their goods. Therefore, most drivers travel in regular circuits, often at breakneck speeds. Most would deny that they have a certain sense of territoriality over their circuit, but sometimes there are disputes between drivers of competing companies. The hardest part of the job is delivering the bottles and jars. For instance, they might have to carry filled jars up four floors in a hotel.

The incentives for "working-class" men to work as drivers for a water-bottling plant are obvious. Though working for a water company pays less than the minimum wage, the job seems to offer a long-term career trajectory. By transitioning from employee to self-made entrepreneur, the workers hope to earn more than they can from other alternatives. Like brick-molders (Hoffmann 2014a, 2017), they can work at their convenience and alongside relatives or friends. As they are often forced to admit, however, many workers try and fail to make this transition from employee to self-made entrepreneur.

Unions and Water-Bottling Plants

In a small village outside of Pokhara, there are four water-bottling plants. Upon entering the village in early January 2019, I spotted several Maoist slogans painted on the walls of one of the factories. At the Mountain Waters factory, there were two slogans: "Shanti ra Sambhidhan sunishchit gar" (Make sure of peace and the constitution) and "Pratikrantikaary shaDyantra banda gar" (Stop the counterrevolutionary conspiracy). Another one painted in yellow read: "Rastriya sarbabhaumikata bhaugolik akhaNDataa ra swaadhinataako rakshaa garyau" (National sovereignty should protect geographical integrity and independence). The painting of Maoist slogans on houses, factories, and walls was common throughout the revolutionary period and its aftermath. But according to local villagers, such slogans were relics of the past; they had been written in the immediate aftermath of the Maoist insurgency, but nobody I interviewed could remember an exact date when they appeared.

The villagers' observation of vanishing Maoist labor activism in the area aligns with the current politics of labor in the local water-bottling industry. Despite Maoist unions' organizing the local food industry in the industrial area of the town (see chapter 4), the local water-bottling industry has been spared such party activism, and unions remain unheard of. In fact, the workers in the water-bottling industry who I interviewed claimed that they did not participate in any union activities. I learned through an acquaintance in a local union that one non-Maoist union had tried to organize a water-bottling plant in town, but workers had rejected this interference. The local union informant told me, "the women there were too afraid of losing their jobs." When asked, one female worker from the respective factory confirmed the unionist's theory, telling me, "I can't go to union meetings, I have to work. Who will pay the bills if I lose this job?"

Undoubtedly, the lack of participation in union activities also stems from larger structural factors. First, none of the factories had more than a dozen workers on the production line, and such small groups were not very appealing to unions. Second, many of the factories were relatively new and were dispersed across the city and its rural outskirts, which made them harder for unionists to organize. Third, given the almost "family business" character of many of the factories, workers often felt a certain loyalty to the owner of their factory.

The exception to this general lack of union activity were the two factories in the industrial area, where, according to local informants, the situation of labor was apparently "slightly better." In fact, an informant from one of these factories claimed: "We pay the minimum wage because unions check here. They are present in several other factories in the industrial area and sometimes they come to check whether we comply with the law. We do, and so they are happy and leave after checking." The fact that these companies in the industrial area that were in proximity to union activism did, in fact, pay the minimum wage suggests another case of what I have previously called the "invisible hand of Mao" (Hoffmann 2018a:13). The presence of labor mobilizers in an industrial region often leads to different business practices among entrepreneurs. The confined space of the industrial area is a zone where labor law is generally followed, unlike the unregulated world beyond its gates.

Conclusion

In this chapter, I expanded my discussion of the situation of labor in industrial environments in contemporary Nepal and presented the argument that in post-insurgency Nepal a new water-bottling industry emerged in the shadows of Pokhara's urban growth. I further showed that the ownership of the new local water-bottling industry is to a large extent controlled by high-caste members of the upper tier of local society. Labor in such new working environments is divided mainly along the lines of gender and ethnicity, as many of the workers in the new water-bottling plants are women from janajati communities. The chapter has explored the situation of labor and the working processes in two such water-bottling plants, which are marked by idle time during the off-season in winter and busy overtime schedules in the hot summer months. I further showed that, unlike in the food-processing factories examined in previous chapters, the water-bottling plants were largely unaffected by the vibrant union activism that surrounded them.

How, then, should we interpret the fact that the Maoist unions organized the food-processing factories but shied away from organizing the water-bottling plants? Here, it is important to remember that the water-bottling industry was relatively new, developing mostly after the conflict. This may partly explain why unions have not yet emerged in this sector of the local economy. But it is also important that many of these new water-bottling plants were employing only a small number of workers and operating either in converted town houses or in places outside the town that were difficult to reach. The

Maoist unions, as we have seen in previous chapters, were mainly focused on organizing large factories for a number of reasons; it was not only more practical but also allowed the unions to effectively demonstrate their strength by using the organized factories as showcase projects for the Maoist leadership at the local union scene. By nurturing the public image that the Maoist union has "power" through organizing large factories, the party wing of the Maoists hoped to enlarge its constituency.

The situation described in this chapter—together with the previous chapters—helps us better understand the situation of labor in the food-processing and water-bottling industries on the margins of two major Nepali cities. But the urban growth in the last two years has also been accompanied by the growth of a sizable construction industry. Moreover, as sand is a key ingredient in the concrete used in new buildings, a sand-mining industry has emerged along the rivers next to many urban centers in the country. In the following chapters, we will further explore the situation of labor in such industries; the interaction between class, caste, ethnicity, and gender; and the ways in which the broader political economic context has inflected upon labor in such emerging industries.

Notes

1. Most water-bottling factory owners I interviewed claimed that investments could be earned back within two years of starting a factory. To become profitable quickly, many used a tactic of undercutting competitors in price in the initial years, which sometimes led to disputes among factory owners. This caused some of the established factory owners to form a new association to fix the price for a bottle and save them from the entry of new competitors in the market.
2. Video surveillance of the workers was available in most beverage-bottling plants. From the managers' point of view, such devices were necessary to ensure the quality of the water but also to ensure the quality of the work. For this purpose, managers' offices often had one or more monitors that allowed them to overlook the factory floor from behind their office desk.
3. For predictable reasons, filming was generally not allowed in the factories; the footage could be sold to a competitor, or it could be distributed on social media in a way that did not correspond to the marketing strategies of management.
4. As the management explained, there was little profit in the filling of water bottles. Water bottles were sold at the price of 11 to 12 NR per bottle to retailers who then sold it for between 20 and 25 NR to shops in town and nearby local markets. But bottles had to be purchased at the price of 5.5 NR per bottle. According to management, these margins were considered small: "We make only 5 NR per bottle."
5. Some also do side business, such as delivering milk, to pay off their loans.
6. Most drivers are self-employed.
7. In the past, the power could be cut for up to five hours, during which the workers could only wait.

— Chapter 6 —

CLASS, ETHNICITY, AND LABOR MOBILIZATION IN THE CONSTRUCTION INDUSTRY

Introduction

Manoj Magar, a labor contractor from the Magar ethnic community, and his team of four male Tharu workers had been working on the spacious middle-class home on the outskirts of Pokhara for two months before I visited them on a cold November morning in 2018. They had already managed to construct the rough structure of the two-story house. I met Manoj through an acquaintance, and when I told him that I wanted to study labor in town, he offered to show me his construction project. We went to visit the house and he introduced me to the workers. Two of his Tharu *mistriharu* (mason workers) chatted with me about their history of debt-bonded labor in the western lowlands of Nepal. Then Manoj took me on a tour of the house. When we entered, I passed an empty room on the left that only had a single mattress on the floor that was shared by four workers. On an improvised washing line, some pieces of cloth had been hung to dry in the air that blew into the room from two open windows. I asked who slept in there, and Manoj responded, "The workers." I was surprised—until then I had never considered that construction workers might sleep at their work sites. Manoj, sensing my discomfort with the bare conditions of the room, told me that having laborers at the house was necessary to protect the tools from roaming *chorharu* (thieves).[1] When I later asked the workers what they thought about their sleeping conditions, they did not think it was a bad deal. "We get to sleep here and don't have to spend money on accommodation. In that way we can earn more, and Manoj Magar even pays us more to stay here," was how a young Tharu *mistri* (mason) described it. "Hami jaha kam garchhau, yehi sutch-hau" (Where we work, we sleep), added his coworker.

Fundamental to the rapid development of the city are people in the local construction industry like Manoj and his workers. Based on seven months of fieldwork undertaken between October 2018 and April 2019, and a return trip in January 2019, this chapter investigates the character of the local construction industry, its daily labor markets, and the everyday sociality that develops at construction sites.[2] By concentrating on the class differentiation within the construction industry of the city, this chapter aims to highlight how the class situation of developers differs from their workers. I argue that developers (who often engage in both manual and managerial work) and manual laborers (e.g., masons, helpers) often live in two different economic worlds, and thereby constitute two different segments of class. Furthermore, this chapter sheds light on the differences of locality, ethnicity, and gender that exist among the manual laborers themselves. This means that middle-class developers—who largely hail from the Bahun (Brahmin), Chhetri, Gurung, Newar, and Magar communities in Nepal, or come from India—increasingly recruit workers from India, from the Tharu or Madeshi communities of the lowland region, or from Magar communities in villages in Rolpa and Rukkum in Nepal. They do so not only because of the stereotypes attached to such communities (for example, many contractors consider Tharus as "hardworking"), but also because the migrants from the southern parts of Nepal or from India are less expensive than the local labor force that prefers to work abroad in distant places like the Middle East or Malaysia. I argue that this mix of local and migrant workers has not been able to unite politically and seriously challenge their employers because years of post-revolutionary unionization efforts in the construction industry have largely benefited only the developers. The chapter concludes that this process of dual economic stratification mirrors broader trends across Nepal that I began to outline in previous chapters.

Recent research (Liechty 2003; Shakya 2018) suggests that class has become the dominant principle of self-identification and the most important determinant of life chances in Nepal—at least in Kathmandu, the capital and largest city. Perhaps unsurprisingly, outside of the capital the importance of class consciousness over traditional caste and ethnic identities has developed at a slower pace. For example, my previous work in the far-western lowland region of Nepal illustrated how the boundaries of the emerging working class are still defined by ethnicity (Hoffmann 2018a). Moreover, recent research on Nepali labor migrants in the Middle East suggests that ethnic and caste identities become less important while they are abroad (see Bruslé 2010a, 2010b; Gardener 2012). My own ethnography on construction labor situates itself in these debates by showing how in Nepal's second-largest city, class consciousness has begun to largely trump caste and ethnicity, though at different levels of the class hierarchy.

The situation of the working class in the construction industry of Pokhara also invites comparison with the construction industries in other countries (see Breman 1994, Parry 2014, Picherit 2012, Raj and Axelby 2019, and Van de Loop 1996 for India; see Thiel 2010, 2012a, 2012b, Pink et al. 2012, Waldinger 2005, and Woodward 2002 for the UK). It becomes clear that, like in India or the UK, contractors in Nepal's construction economy rely heavily on ethnic and local networks to fill their labor needs. Yet, unlike the case of the Indian construction economy, as described by anthropologist Jonathan Parry (2014), the contractors in Pokhara rely less on the labor of local women. This is because much of the ordinary workforce in contractor teams are long-term migrants from the country's south or from neighboring India, and such migrants are usually unmarried or leave their wives in their home villages. As a result, only a few local women work at construction sites.

Urban Development and the Growth of the Construction Industry

Pokhara is Nepal's second-largest municipality, located in the picturesque foothills of the beautiful Annapurna Himalaya mountain range. Over the past sixty years, immigration and tourism have considerably changed the social geography of the city and its rural hinterland. In the late 1960s the town remained a predominantly rural area except for a single line of shops in the old market area that established the town's commercial center (Adhikari and Seddon 2002:50). During the 1970s and 1980s, however, the city experienced rapid growth after it was recognized in 1972 as the regional headquarters of the Western Development region (2002:75). The city rapidly became a major administrative center, which fueled commercial activity that in turn attracted migrants from surrounding villages. At the same time, the city was becoming a major tourist destination; by 1990 the average number of annual visitors was estimated to be over sixty thousand (Adhikari and Seddon 1991). In 1998 the number of annual tourists had grown to one hundred thousand.

During the armed conflict between the Maoist People's Liberation Army and state agents that lasted from 1996 until 2006, the town became a destination for refugees fleeing from the conflict raging in the western hills. To expand its numbers, the Maoist People's Liberation Army recruited children and young teenagers to fight, causing many fearful parents to move their families to urban centers such as Pokhara where they felt more secure (Dhruba 2010; Adhikari 2014; Lawoti and Pahari 2010; Pettigrew 2015). The population continued to grow throughout the 2000s as more and more people left their rural villages for cities like Pokhara, hoping to give their children access to better education and life prospects. As a result, by 2011 the city had swelled to 313,841 inhabitants. The disastrous earthquakes of April 2015 (see Nelson 2015) had little impact on the demographics of the city; the city itself experienced little damage, and only a few refugees from the afflicted areas made their way to Pokhara in the immediate aftermath.

Pokhara's rapid urbanization was accompanied by the growth of a considerable construction industry in town. Jagannath Adhikari and David Seddon report that there were five construction companies operating in town between 1969 and 1973 (2002:236). By 1999, there were 328 construction companies worth a total of 52.4 million NR (2002:242), rivaling the local food industry, which had a total value of 49 million NR in the same year. In its brief history of around fifty years, the local construction industry has developed a complex structure; the larger companies—which the state classifies as either A-, B-, or C-class—usually have their headquarters in Kathmandu but run a branch office in Pokhara.[3] However, D-class companies and those that are outside the purview of the state are a large majority of the companies situated in town. At the time of my fieldwork, 331 companies were registered at the city's municipality office as D-class. As elsewhere in Nepal, initially the construction labor hailed from India, but over the years Nepalis have taken up various jobs in the industry, including working as contractors, masons, and helpers.

These changes did not go unnoticed by the middle-class residents of Pokhara. During my fieldwork, I met numerous hotel owners, restaurant managers, and owners of local trekking agencies, all of whom shared a common perspective on the emerging construction industry in town. Nearly everyone I met thought that the construction industry was comprised mainly of Indians or people from the Tarai lowland. Construction workers were often referred to as *bhaiyas* or *dhotis*,[4] though there was a growing sense that such terms were derogative and should not be used anymore. For example, I overheard Swarel, a young Brahmin restaurant manager in the tourist area near the lake, admonish a tourist from India for asking whether the workers at a nearby construction site were referred to as dhotis or bhaiyas. Swarel quickly corrected the tourist, saying that such words should not be used anymore. The Maoist revolution had changed perceptions about the Madheshis from the lowland region who were previously looked down upon (see also Adhikari 2014).

Two elements in the discourse of middle-class residents about construction workers raised my interest. First, many of the town's middle-class residents claimed that people generally did not want to work in the local construction industry but preferred to go abroad to work hard in places like the Middle East and Malaysia. This was because construction work was considered to have little *ijjat* (honor), and, as the same restaurant manager put it, "people want to work hard elsewhere and then come back to show off." Such claims were not unique to Pokhara and were frequently voiced in national newspapers. For example, a 2018 *Kathmandu Post* article titled "Indian Construction Workers Coming to Nepal in Droves" lamented that despite growing investment in infrastructure projects in Nepal, few Nepalis took up the opportunity to work in construction.[5] Accordingly, the problem was said to be a lack of technical and skill training for Nepalis. For many middle-class locals, however, it was much more a question of culture. "It is not what you do here. You do not want to be seen at the construction sites," was how another trusted middle-class informant from the Chhetri community framed it.

The second interesting element about the way middle-class residents talked about the local construction industry was how they thought the industry to be highly spatialized. Like the construction industry in London (see Thiel 2010, 2012a, 2012b), middle-class residents often knew where in town to find specific kinds of contractors and workers. Two places stood out: the roundabout at Srijana Chowk where a day labor market could be found, and in Ram Krishna Tole where many of the Indian migrant population had settled.

The Character of Construction Labor

Despite being one of the largest employers after agriculture, the construction industry in Nepal remains at the periphery of scholarly attention (for exceptions, see Hoffmann 2014b; Hirslund 2021).

Moreover, since the 2018 merger of the UCPN (Maoist) Party and the United Marxist Leninist (UML) Party into the Nepal Communist Party, the construction sector has been a focal point of post-earthquake governance.[6] There has been a national recognition that the sector sustains the livelihoods of many Nepalis. While debt-bonded labor has been banned in Nepal, similar conditions have arisen in the form of delayed payments by contractors to construction workers—a reality that former Maoist insurgents and guerrillas-turned-politicians tend to overlook in their discussions of the working class (see Hoffmann 2018a). The construction industry is heavily subcontracted on both public- and private-sector building sites. Like in other industries (see Shakya 2018; Hoffmann 2018a), the construction industry used to be dominated by Indian contractors who have gradually been replaced by Nepali newcomers. It is largely male dominated, with women often only doing the most backbreaking and difficult jobs (Hoffmann 2018a). Like other workplaces in Nepal (ILO 2005; Dhakal 2009), the construction industry suffers from various forms of gender inequality, particularly the persistence of a gender pay-gap and various forms of sexual harassment. Yet, as recent studies show, sexual harassment might be more prevalent in the garment (ILO 2005) and carpet industries (Dhakal 2009). Nepali newspapers often complain about the death of Nepali construction workers abroad in places like Qatar or Malaysia, but rarely comment on the working conditions and dangers associated with construction work in Nepal. For example, the media almost never make a fuss about the fact that, except on public road projects, construction workers rarely wear helmets or gloves. The fact that every year in the Kaski district alone, two or three workers fall from house roofs—often by slipping off the bamboo ladders used for scaffolding—also goes largely unmentioned by the media.[7]

The health of the local construction industry is strongly linked to the political stability of the country and is also scheduled around certain key events in the annual calendar. Thus, unsurprisingly, during the Maoist uprising between 1996 and 2006, and in the wake of the earthquake and the subsequent "Indian blockade," orders for housing construction were in decline. It was only after the end of the Indian blockade that the industry picked up again. In addition, the state of the construction industry is affected by certain key annual events: government budget announcements are accompanied by short-term increases in the price of steel, which is used in house pillars. This usually results in fewer orders for new houses. The health of the construction industry is also linked to labor migration to the

Middle East and Malaysia, as returning migrants often use their savings to invest in the construction of a new house or the formation of a small business.

Most of the smaller construction projects in town were complex subcontracts. In material terms, there were large differences between the incomes of the site managers and smaller differences between the wages of the workers within a work team. At the lowest end of the wage scale in 2018 were the unskilled workers, earning about 700 NR (about five euros) for men and about 500 NR for women per day, which is about two-thirds of what a precarious day laborer could make in the labor markets in the city.[8] In the middle of the wage scale were skilled bricklayers or experienced foremen, whose earnings were about 900 to 1,000 NR per day. At the upper end of the wage scale were people like Sandeep, an experienced wood carpenter whose earnings averaged about 1,200 NR per day (31,200 NR per month)—comparable to the monthly wage of a mid-level hotel manager in town.

Considering that most workers worked about six days a week, the average monthly income was between 18,200 NR and 23,400 NR for unskilled work and about 26,000 NR for skilled work. As workers were hard to find, especially those with qualifications, it was perhaps not surprising that some of them received advances before joining a work team in Pokhara.[9] Kamal, for example, usually promised an advance of 20,000 NR (sometimes up to 50,000 NR) to his painters, whom he recruited from the Bara district in the lowlands. But he was also reluctant to pay advances, and usually only did so when the worker was seriously short of money, such as when a family member became ill and needed hospital treatment. Others, like Manoj Magar, did not distribute advances. They were proud of their ability to pay largely on time, which built trust between contractor and worker.

In contrast to India (Parry 2014)[10] or the lowlands of Nepal (Hoffmann 2018), where women make up 30 percent of the construction workforce, relatively few women worked on Pokhara's construction sites. Of the few women I met on the sites, most were either related or married to another worker. In interviews, site managers openly admitted that they deliberately avoided hiring women, but for different reasons. Manoj, for example, had previously hired local women from nearby villages, but the contact between these local women and the Tharu men led to too much *phohari kura* (dirty talk) on the site, which the homeowners and builders sometimes complained about. Therefore, he now avoided hiring women in order to keep the site focused on work rather than on socializing. One builder, Joginder Acharya, a

Brahmin who rose from electrician to builder, said he avoided hiring women because his company often worked at night. Night work was crucial to his company as he often had several projects underway and was under pressure to complete them all on schedule. Especially the *dhalai* (the pouring of concrete) was work done at night. In Joginder's view, women were completely unsuitable because working at night could lead to sexual relationships between male and female workers. He had no problem with work flirtations that developed into a marriage, but he feared the extramarital relationships that might result from night work, especially because he wanted to avoid being an involuntary witness to such "connections." Accordingly, rumors about sexual relationships forming on his worksites were bad for business as having a good reputation was fundamental to obtaining new projects. Such patriarchal ideas not only are found in the construction industry but have been documented in other sectors such as the carpet (Dhakal 2009) and textile (ILO 2005) industries.

Most of the workers in Pokhara's construction industry were Hindus. Only the marble tilers in the city had the reputation of being mostly Muslim. However, religion played only a minor role in everyday life on a construction site. The two most important religious practices on-site were the *jag halne puja* (worship of the foundation) and the *dhoka puja* (worship of the establishment of the main door). The former occurred when the foundation of a house was laid; the latter was observed to keep evil spirits outside the house and to provide security for its future inhabitants. But such rituals were usually more important to the owners of the house than to the contractors and workers who built it.

The Contractors

The principal distinction among contractors in Pokhara was between the Indians and Nepalis. Until a few years ago, nearly all plastering and tiling was given to Indian contractors, largely coming from Bihar, who almost always brought their Indian workforces with them. Yet, over the years, this monopoly has been reduced by the entry of Nepali contractors into the market. As I was told in interviews with the staff of the Department of Planning for the municipality and with the head of the local chapter of the Contractor Association Nepal (CAN), these Nepali contractors typically hailed from one of three common backgrounds. First, many were self-made men who had worked themselves up the construction hierarchy, often from humble peasant origins. Second, others were the sons of contractors, although these constituted only about 10 percent of the contractors. For example, the head of the CAN is from an established construction family. Third, there were some who had previously studied civil engineering and then started their own construction companies in town.

Importantly, as I learned through interviews with contractors, in the early days of the industry it was possible to climb up the labor hierarchy in a predictable way; those who were determined could start as a laborer, then become *mistri* (mason), then sometimes *naike* (supervisor), and finally *thekedar* (contractor). To illustrate this process, let us look at the different career trajectories of three contractors I met during my fieldwork.

Manoj Magar: A Local Building Contractor

Manoj Magar is forty years old and from a village in the Makawanpur district. He came to Pokhara when he was eighteen. He worked for one year as an unskilled laborer, then for three years as a mason, and then for seven years as a supervisor at building sites. He then became a thekedar as he knew how to organize people. He now works as a thekedar and has an average of three or four projects going at the same time. He always recruits his labor from the Dhang district, mostly from the Tharu communities. About nineteen people work for him. Some live in a camp at the construction site; for others Manoj rented an apartment in the center of Leknath. Unlike his *bhanja* (nephew) who also works as a thekedar in Pokhara and owns a motorbike, Manoj does not own a motorbike or a car. He has a rather simple lifestyle and is proud that he can live for the whole year from two months of work.

Narinder Yadav: A Painter Contractor

Narinder Yadav, thirty-four years old, is from the Bara district in the lowlands of Nepal. When I met him, he had just returned from the Chhath festival (after Tihar) in the Bara district.[11] He left Bara when he was twenty-two and moved to Pokhara with his brother. He began working in construction: two years as a laborer, three years as a mistri, and then seven years as a thekedar. He initially struggled and had to work for only 60 NR per day. Later he made the transition from mistri to thekedar without much capital investment. At that time, it was between 50,000 NR and 1 lakh to start one's own business. For this he relied on his savings and did not need to take out a loan. He is now earning a lot and has managed to establish his own paint shop in town where his younger brother looks after the business. Narinder exclusively hires laborers from his home village. He has bought land in Pokhara, bought a car, and built a two-story house back in his village.

Joginder Acharya: A Brahmin Contractor and Builder

Joginder Acharya, forty years old, used to work as a teacher in a primary school and earned 3,000 NR. That was nineteen years ago. He thought that the salary was too little to sustain himself and his family and began looking for other jobs. He went to Pokhara's Industrial Development Zone and asked for a job. But they told him he needed to have a skill. He trained as an electrician for six months and then began to do electrical work in different hotels, including a five-star hotel in town. He worked like this for fifteen years, and while working he learned more about the construction industry and managed to gain contacts, including many builders, laborers, and homeowners. He developed many relationships in the industry and then started his own construction business without much investment. The first two or three projects were well-built but earned little profit. This was just to show that he was able to build houses properly. After that his business increased and he now has about thirty-five laborers. His first son is studying civil engineering and his second son is in private school. He bought land in Pokhara and built his own house. He is still referred to as *bijuli ko thekedar* (electricity fixer) in the industry and works as a thekedar for entire projects.

Each of the three contractors who were interviewed emphasized that they made it in the construction industry on their own terms. They each agreed that when they had entered the industry, little investment capital was needed to set up a company. Social capital had been critical, however, and their building trusted relationships with potential homeowners and maintaining a spotless reputation as a hard worker over the years had been key to their success. This type of upward mobility in the construction industry, however, is no longer possible. It has become much more difficult to climb up the labor hierarchy and advance from worker to contractor. Many workers try, but few succeed due to two main factors. First, the cost of labor and tools has substantially increased over the last twenty years. As a result, more capital is needed to set up one's own company. Second, in contrast to earlier years, contractors now need to obtain a license from the local state for building houses. Although the local builder license costs 10,000 NR, the D-class license also requires one to have a tipper or tractor, a level machine, a cement mixer, and an office, as well as to employ an administrative officer and a civil engineer on the payroll.

Becoming a contractor has also become riskier as homeowners might pay late—for example, in cases where financial investments are tied to labor migrations to the Middle East or Malaysia. Financial promises to a contractor might not be fulfilled for other unforeseen reasons as well. To cope with this unpredictability and to minimize the risk of bankruptcy, contractors usually have several projects going at the same time. This allows them to have some cash resources on hand to keep paying their laborers, who would otherwise return home to their natal villages in the southern lowlands or India.

Nevertheless, those who do stay afloat in the business can make a good living, and they usually have a middle-class lifestyle. The contractor Kamal, for example, started by earning only 60 NR per day, but now has a company with twenty people, owns a house in Pokhara, and drives his own car, a symbolic marker for successful *dhani manchhe* (rich people). Because of high import taxes on cars of up to three times the original price, few people in Nepal can afford such a luxury. He is not the only one; other contractors lead equally luxurious lifestyles with yearly earnings around five to ten times that of a mason. However, many contractors also struggle and fall back down the class ladder.

Caste and ethnicity continue to play an important role in this process of class formation. Data obtained from the municipality on the caste and ethnic backgrounds of D-class companies shows that nearly two-thirds of contractors are from Brahmin or Chhetri backgrounds. After them are the Gurung, Magar, and Newari—ethnic groups from Pokhara's neighboring regions—who have also made recent inroads into the city's construction industry. Those who are hardly represented in the ranks of contractors are local, low-caste groups, as well as the indigenous communities from the southern lowlands, including the Tharus and Madheshis. These are the same groups that, together with the already established stream of migrants from Indian states such as Bihar, form the working classes of Pokhara.

The Day Labor Chowk

Srijana chowk was a road crossing in the center of Pokhara. It was a well-known place in the city, and many of the middle-class hotel managers knew they could find daily laborers for hire there. Although the numbers varied, between forty and fifty workers gathered at the chowk each day. It was not uncommon for the first workers to arrive around 6 a.m., although most of the workers arrived later, between 7 and 8 a.m. The chowk was usually at its busiest between 8 and 9 a.m., with workers often hanging around in small groups. By 10 a.m. most of them had found a job, and it became difficult for the casual observer to notice that there were day laborers looking for work among the normal bustle of the crossing. Almost all the workers who came here were Nepali, but not all of them were always looking for work. A few were already drunk in the early hours of the morning and came just to hang out or to meet with worker friends.

Almost all the workers at the chowk could find some work as loaders on construction sites across the city. But to get such a job requires lots of waiting. Many just stood around, surveying the scene or gossiping with friends. Those who owned a smartphone passed the time playing games. Engaging in their own practices of "time-pass" (Jeffrey 2010), the workers played well-known mobile videogames like "Candy Crush Saga," "Call Break," or "Marriage" to ease the boredom of their uncertain work schedules.[12]

In contrast to the daily labor market in Nepalgunj where I witnessed the participation of women and even sometimes *Hijras*, in Pokhara I encountered nearly only men at the chowk. In fact, on all my visits to the chowk I only saw a single woman looking for work. Workers who had been there for a long time, however, remembered a woman who once came every day to the road crossing looking for work. But she, as the veteran workers would usually add, was the mother of a small child, and her husband was known as a notorious drunkard. They surmised that she did not come looking for work voluntarily, but that her impoverished situation forced her to.

The day laborers of Srijana chowk shared certain characteristics with the laborers in markets in other countries, such as India and Japan (see Parry 2014 for labor markets in the east Indian city of Bhilai, or Gill 2001 for Yoseba labor markets in Japan). Many came to the labor market expecting to be paid daily, and many pressed for immediate payment. Many were proud to finish their work late in the afternoon. Sometimes they would finish their work after only a few hours and would be allowed to return home. When I asked the day laborers about *eklopan* (loneliness) while waiting and referred to the fictional literature about construction workers by the Indian author Aman Sethi (2011), the workers often contradicted me. They told me that many of them knew each other and would often spend the waiting time together. This feeling of community knew no caste barriers from the workers' point of view—at the daily labor market, everyone was considered equal and caste did not matter. But this was hardly surprising; in these labor systems, networks are vital for survival. On their own a worker might find a new employer, but if they made friends with other workers, their chances increased.

When I interviewed contractors about day labor markets, many of them saw the day laborers as stubborn, undisciplined, and uncooperative toward authority, and they hesitated to hire them. Those who did often expressed that using day labor was only ever a last resort. Nevertheless, due to the booming construction industry in the city, few workers seemed to have problems finding work if they wanted it. Many of them indicated that it was easy for them to find work in the city. Around two hundred trucks came to the market every day to pick up workers, or they passed through the city and the surrounding area looking for people with various skills, especially loading and unloading materials. While not everyone could find work every day, many said they could.

Because of this high demand, the workers did not have to compete or undercut their wages. The general rule in the labor market was that whomever the employer chose got the job—no haggling or self-promotion at the expense of another. In contrast to the daily labor market in Bhilai (Parry 2014:1262), wages in the construction industry did not vary according to the time of day. Workers were paid per ton (1,000 kilograms), and on average a loader could expect to be paid 120 NR per ton of goods lifted, but prices sometimes varied according to negotiations with employers or how far the workers had to carry the load. Some of the workers who claimed that they could do masonry or painting work charged higher prices than they would normally receive. For example, a bricklayer or skilled painter could charge 1,200 NR per day.

Ethnicity and Gender at Work

The previous sections explored how it has become more difficult to climb the labor hierarchy of Pokhara's construction industry, and how caste and ethnicity continue to inform the composition of the builder class in the city. They have also outlined how caste and ethnicity played a minor role in the thinking of the day laborers at the bottom of the hierarchy, and how a kind of casual solidarity existed among them. This section further explores how ethnic and gender hierarchies are experienced at the construction sites in the city. As several authors have found for the Indian context (Holmstroem 1984; Breman 1996; and Harriss-White 2003), labor contractors usually recruit from their kinship networks, often resulting in "well-guarded barriers to entry into even the most unenviable informal sector occupations" (Parry 2014:1245). In line with such findings, I will argue that Pokhara's construction industry also has a "closed shop character" (Breman 1996:257) as recruitment patterns continue to be based largely on ethnic and kinship ties that restrict horizontal mobility.

As mentioned, many of the workers at the construction sites in Pokhara hailed from the Tharu ethnic communities in the western lowlands of Nepal, from Madheshi communities in the eastern lowlands of Nepal, or from the north Indian state of Bihar. All of them experience the same socioeconomic conditions that force them to seek out a living as male labor migrants in cities far from their homes. They usually live in houses rented by the contractors, or on the construction sites. Both *sutne thau* (sleeping places) are usually equipped with only the most basic necessities, and, as I mentioned in the introductory vignette, sleeping on-site can be rough in the cold winter months from November to February, so it is often the junior workers who do this.

Among the different contractors, I did most of my fieldwork with Manoj Magar, the contractor mentioned earlier in this chapter. At the time of fieldwork, he was running several building projects in town, including the construction of a villa, a small kitchen building next to a kindergarten, and an office building project. Manoj recruited exclusively Tharu workers, who all hailed from villages in Dhang, and had rented rooms in at the outskirts of the city to host such workers. Some of them also slept on-site. Each morning, he gave orders to the workers, telling them which of his construction sites they should go to. They would ride on their bicycles to the different worksites, where they usually worked until 5 p.m. before returning to their rented houses. Their working day was fairly regular, lasting from 8 a.m. until 5 p.m., but in the cold winter months, work started later, around 9 a.m. In the monsoon season, he would lay off part of his workforce.

As the construction of a building requires a variety of specialists (electricians, plumbers, plasterers), Manoj subcontracted parts of the work process to other smaller companies; the painting, window installations, and plumbing were assigned to external building companies. The main jobs that Manoj's team did while building the house included building the foundation of the house; fixing the columns; and plastering the new floors, which is referred to as the *dhalai* (the pouring of concrete). While the dhalai used to be a lengthy operation that required lots of laborers, modern machines made it now much easier and less labor intensive to set up. Instead of long lines of laborers passing *karai* (shallow metal basins) up various floors, a cement truck was ordered that pumps the concrete up through a pipe.

Most of the work on normal building projects Manoj conducted himself together with his workforce. For that he relied above all on his two most skilled workers—Baburam Tharu and Dinesh Tharu— two masons from a village in Dhang. Both were in their midthirties and had worked for Manoj for more than four years, following him from one building site to the next and rarely going back to their villages—apart from the festivals of Magghi and Tihar. To keep them satisfied, Manoj provided them—and the two helpers who also hailed from the same village—with *masu* (meat) twice a week. For Dinesh, who smoked, Manoj also occasionally provided a free pack of cigarettes.

Everyone usually referred to Manoj Magar as *thekedar saheb* (contractor sir), and he was known for his quiet and stable demeanor. Much of the sociality at his various construction sites consisted of quiet working, interrupted only by an occasional joke and laughter to keep the workday more interesting. Often such jokes related to stereotypes with regards to ethnicity. For example, when Baburam drank too much, his colleague Dinesh would tease him the next day and say "Chaudha bottle chaudhary, ek bottle yadav, ani pach bottle pundit" (Fourteen bottles for the Tharu, one bottle for the Yadav, and five for the priest), indicating that Tharus are associated with heavy drinking. When the two helpers on Manoj Magar's team disappeared for two days and went off drinking after being paid, Manoj scolded them upon their return. He referred to them as "twake ra jiri" (drunker and spice). By this he was referring to the stereotype that Tharus are drinkers with short statures. This was meant somewhat ironically, however, as Tharus are also called *jiri* for their small, but powerful, physiques. Workers did not dare to use ethnic stereotypes in front of Manoj, but sometimes one of the helpers referred to Manoj as *lide* (stupid) behind his back.

The reason why such teasing rarely turned into a serious fight might lie in the fact that the workers were generally satisfied with working for Manoj Magar. Baburam compared working in the construction industry to his childhood experience as a kamaiya (debt-bonded laborer) in Dhang, telling me: "Being a kamaiya and working for a landlord was what we used to do. This was what our parents did before us. But after the *mukti ko din* [the day the bonded laborers were freed], we left, and now things are much better. I work here freely as a mason and earn my own money."

Another aspect of working in Pokhara's construction industry, although rarely discussed openly, was the exclusion or financial disadvantaging and harassment of women. As previously mentioned, relatively few women worked in the construction industry. When they did, they usually did the same simple jobs as their male colleagues but were usually paid much less. This form of exploitation by male contractors was mostly rationalized by sexist discourses describing women as being less "strong" than men. Some of the contractors even refused to hire women at all, as I mentioned previously. But at the few construction sites where women did work, I sometimes observed various forms of joking and teasing of a sexual nature between male workers and unmarried young women working as helpers. For example, at the construction site of Joginder Acharya, there were two Magar masons working, Harke and Indra, with a female helper named Sunita. They were working on the second floor of a building while I observed from a floor above. When Harke needed the iron rods to lift the pillar at the construction site, he asked Sunita to bring him the rods, saying "Gal lyau ra tyaha hala" (Bring the iron rod and put it there). Then he went downstairs, and shouted from the lower floor to Sunita: "Gal halyau?" (Did you put the iron rod?) Sunita responded, "hale" (I put). Then Indra asked Sunita, "Majja ayo?" (Was it fun?) In response, Sunita turned red, said "shhhh," and kept working silently.

I learned through interviews with union officers that women working in the construction industry were rather reserved and afraid of being teased sexually by men. To avoid conversations slipping into fohori kura, they usually tried to keep a formal distance from their male colleagues by referring to them with fictive kin-names such as *dhai* (big brother) or *bhai* (little brother). Such terms are supposed to signal a familial, platonic relationship. While the sexual undertone of many workplace jokes may be interpreted by some women as liberating from their usual family or social environments (see Shah 2006), sexual jokes can quickly turn into coercive, sexual relationships that are not freely entered (Parry 2014). A sad example is the case of a local female construction worker who was the victim of a gang rape by a team of Indian plasterers at a construction site in Pokhara in the 2010s. This story was told to me by a GEFONT trade unionist, and he emphasized the double injustice that the female victim experienced; not only was the worker the victim of rape, but when she went to the police after the incident, no inflicted physical abuse such as a bruise could be proven and the case was dropped.

But such extreme cases of sexual abuse have become less frequent, according to the same trade unionist. It is of course difficult to prove such suspicions, but according to the same informant, there were at least three reasons for the decrease in sexual harassment. First, he saw the increase in the use of social media as a shield for women that would deter male colleagues from sexual acts. Second, the trade unionist emphasized the educational efforts being made in the city by female Province Assembly member Mina Gurung, who worked to fight discrimination against women.[13] Third, the same informant also saw potential in the awareness campaigns of his own union denouncing sexual harassment. To what extent the unionist was correct in his statements and that there really had been a decrease in sexual harassment is difficult to assess because such cases were often not publicly discussed. It is possible that these trade union discourses could even be worsening the position of women in the construction industry, because, as Jonathan Parry (2014) has observed, such discourses can also be used to legitimize and trivialize sexual violence in the workplace.

The Role of the Unions in the City's Construction Industry

To further understand how the life-worlds of the builders differ from those of the ordinary workers, it is necessary to know something of the interventions of the labor unions into the city's construction economy. At the time of my fieldwork, three labor unions operated in the city: GEFONT, the Maoist-affiliated All Nepal Trade Union Federation (ANTUF), and a union associated with the Nepali Congress Party. Despite efforts to unify all three unions at the central level in Kathmandu, in town each of them had their own separate union office located close to the city's main bus station. However, as I learned through my interviews with contractors, workers, and unionists, only the ANTUF and GEFONT had historically played a role in the city's construction economy. Contractors such as Manoj Magar remembered how ANTUF was particularly aggressive in organizing labor in the aftermath of the Maoist revolutionary period by collecting *chanda* (voluntary donations) from contractors and asking workers from construction sites to join protest demonstrations in town. However, ANTUF's activities in the construction economy declined in the post-conflict years when they shifted the focus of their union activities toward organizing labor in the town's industrial area.

This decline of ANTUF in the construction economy has strong parallels with the post-revolutionary union landscapes in other parts of Nepal, such as Tikapur (see Hoffmann 2018:123–148). The space left by ANTUF has been filled by their rival union, GEFONT. In fact, throughout my fieldwork, when asked who represented them, nearly all construction workers in town were aware of GEFONT and pointed out that it was the union that best understood the "issues" in the construction economy. Through repeated visits to the GEFONT office during my fieldwork, I learned that the union supported the workers in the city's construction economy at various levels. First, GEFONT provided a minimum-security net to all its members, including financial support in the case of a severe accident or illness. For example, in 2017 three people died in the Kaski district through workplace-related accidents (e.g., one worker fell off a bamboo scaffolding while working on a house). Second, the union sometimes provided free health checkups for the workers. Third, the union had established a local wing to specifically support the women working in the construction industry.

To what extent were such union activities helpful to those working in the local construction industry? To understand this better, it is useful to have some idea of how the union arbitration process works. As I soon learned, the union had a three-step procedure to turn a complaint into a legal case. After a dispute at work occurred, laborers would either call the union or simply walk into the office to file a complaint. After this, the CUPPEC (Central Union of Painters, Plumbers, Electro and Constructions workers) unionists would send a letter to the contractor or the respective homeowner, depending on the nature of the complaint. As a response, the latter would either call or visit the union office to provide clarity about the incident. If they did not make contact within a short time period, the unionists would then either send a letter or visit the construction site where the dispute occurred, find the subject of the complaint, and attempt to arbitrate the case. If the accused and accuser managed to agree on a settlement, the union would drop the case after it was paid its respective fees. In cases where no agreement could be reached, the unionists would file a court case. This, however, did not occur very often. Senior unionists only remembered one larger case in the last five years that went to the Kaski district court. The reason that so few of the complaints made it to district court was straightforward: the union had a financial interest in successfully arbitrating disputes as it received between 3 and 8 percent of any settlement amount.

In the union office, I was permitted to look at the legal cases filed on behalf of the union. While the number of cases arbitrated was high, with approximately 150 complaints registered per year, to my surprise I learned that many of the cases not only were between labor contractors and workers but also included disputes between home-owners and contractors. For example, the contractor Kamal told me that in one case of a six-month-late payment, he had used the union to pressure the homeowner who owed him money. I also noticed that there were very few cases filed by women workers against contractors. This was not surprising as both male and female unionists had told me that women in the construction industry were generally afraid of filing a complaint against their contractor for fear of losing their job.

Why was the union frequently representing the contractors rather than the laborers? Examining the rise and the fall of the Nepali garment industry in Kathmandu, anthropologist Mallika Shakya (2018:121) argues that "leaders of the mainstream unions seemed to have taken up opportunities offered by neoliberal democracy to consolidate their own power." In her case, the mainstream union was a GEFONT union whose leaders remained indifferent to the fate of garment workers in the wake of their industry's steep decline in the 2000s (2018:122). This echoes what Massimiliano Mollona (2009b) has noted about recent trends in labor unions more generally: unions, he argues, can be distinguished between "community" and "business" unions. The former work on "behalf" of the working classes; the latter work at the "behest" of the working classes. The ethnographic material presented in this chapter suggests that the construction unions in Pokhara have begun this shift from the politics of class to neoliberal business politics in which the primary interest is raising cash for the union itself rather than addressing the plight of the working classes.

Conclusion

Long gone are the days when the familiar idiom "Nepal ma siyo pani bandaina" (Nepal does not even make sewing needles) accurately described the situation in the country. Instead, Nepal is currently a hive of activity and urbanizing at a faster rate than other countries in South Asia including India, Pakistan, and Bangladesh (see UN 2010).[14] This chapter has shed light on the class differences between contractors and workers operating in Pokhara's construction economy. We have seen how the upward social mobility for laborers has decreased over the years. The figure of the "worker-turned-contractor" is now largely a relic of the past as the cost of starting a construction company has soared, putting it out of reach for most of those toiling at the bottom of the labor hierarchy. As a result of this process, the town's construction economy is now largely dominated by players that achieved the transformation from worker to contractor in the early years, when social rather than financial capital was most important. While I encountered contractors from a variety of different caste and ethnic backgrounds, the business continues to be dominated by upper-caste males, as well as contractors from the Gurung and Magar indigenous communities. Hardly any low-caste people or those from the indigenous groups of the lowlands have become contractors in Pokhara. In terms of their class position, all the contractors identified as middle class, both in terms of a principle of self-identification as well as where they saw themselves in the overall societal hierarchy.

But the success of a labor contractor in town is as much a matter of seniority as of having the ability to quickly mobilize a reliable workforce. Labor contractors in the house construction industry often undertake multiple projects simultaneously and require both skilled and unskilled workers to fulfill the demands of homeowners. To mobilize labor, contractors not only have to compete with job offers from construction companies in the Middle East (Gardener 2010) and Malaysia, but they must also find what many of them describe as "easy-to-handle" workers. This has caused many of the contractors to increasingly recruit from local low-caste communities, Tharu or Madheshi indigenous communities from the southern lowlands, or even from India. Many contractors viewed Tharu labor as their preferred workforce as they had the reputation of being especially honest and mehenat (hardworking). As the ethnographic material has shown, while local women do take up some of the most back-breaking jobs on the construction sites, contractors often refrain from employing women due to the fear of distraction and trouble that might result from their presence at a worksite. These ethnic and gender dynamics of inclusion and exclusion also had their impact on the everyday work culture.

Looking at the role of labor unions in the process of class formation in the city's construction economy, the ethnographic material suggests that despite the rhetoric of working-class solidarity, union activities largely benefited the builders rather than those working as laborers. This paradox emerged because unions not only represented laborers but also took up the role of police sheriff in the house construction economy. Whenever a homeowner did not pay a contractor, the latter could turn to the unions to ask for their support in winning the promised cash. I noted how many of the applications to the union were in fact requests by contractors to assist in cases of non-payment. To an extent, such assistance also benefits laborers as it helps construction companies to stay afloat and prevents bankruptcy. Moreover, the union—through its assistance program—provided some basic security for everyday laborers; all workers in the construction industry can expect some financial help in the case of severe illnesses or accidents, males receive a minimum wage, and construction workers have moved on to become unionists. But the biggest winners of the union activities proved to be the labor contractors and the unions themselves. Undoubtedly, one could argue that such shortcomings make a different kind of activism necessary to improve the situation of labor. But given the current political climate, in which the Maoist movement has merged with the UML Party to form the new Nepal Communist Party (NCP), such a scenario seems unlikely.

As a final remark, I would like to conclude that what we are witnessing in Nepal is a more general process of economic bifurcation among the urban working classes. As previous chapters have shown, the upper segment of Nepal's working class seem to enjoy the benefits of trade unionism while unions largely ignore the lower segments of Nepal's working classes. In other words, formerly militant activism seems to have become ensnared by the bureaucratization and standardization of the labor unions. In chapter 7, I will further explore the themes of class formation and class politics in the context of the informal sand mining that is taking place in the rivers close to the city.

Notes

1. For this "security service," the contractor paid his four workers a meagre 3,000 NR extra per month, which they had to divide among themselves.
2. A great deal of my ethnography in this chapter comes from interviews with contractors at their homes, as well as from making frequent visits to small-scale construction sites and the daily labor market.
3. The Nepali government classifies construction companies according to the following scheme: A-class companies are those that deal with projects worth more than 10 karoor NR, B-class at least 6 karoor NR, C-class at least 2 karoor NR, and D-class are smaller than 2 karoor NR.

4. Though *bhaiya* (meaning "brother" in Hindi) is often used in a friendly manner, when used aggressively it was considered an insult. The term *dhoti* refers to someone wearing a loincloth and was considered a disrespectful way of greeting someone.
5. See Chandra Karki, "Indian Construction Workers Coming to Nepal in Droves," *Kathmandu Post*, 21 January 2018, https://kathmandupost.com/money/2018/01/21/indian-construction-workers-coming-to-nepal-in-droves, accessed 30 January 2019.
6. In a late January interview with the chairman of Pokhara's Contractor Association Nepal (CAN), I was told that there are approximately fifteen thousand to seventeen thousand contractors currently operating in Nepal.
7. Conversation with chairman of CUPPEC in Pokhara.
8. At government-sponsored construction sites, the rates for labor were 740 NR for unskilled labor and about 980 NR for skilled labor. Often contractors paid more to skilled masons, around 1,200 NR, to avoid them leaving for places abroad in the Middle East or Malaysia where wages for skilled workers were assumed to be higher.
9. Contractors also frequently worried that their most skilled workers would leave their team and go to work in the Middle East or Malaysia. In fact, in an interview with the head of the local CAN, I was told that many of the more skilled contractors in town had left to work abroad. Hence, the distribution of advances to skilled workers may also be related to such uneven developments between different countries.
10. According to Jonathan Parry, "in India, up to a third or even half of those who work on construction sites are women" (2014:1252).
11. Chhath is an annual religious festival to commemorate the sun and Shashti devi (Chhathi Maiya).
12. "Call Break" and "Marriage" are popular mobile card games.
13. See also https://english.onlinekhabar.com/role-of-media-important-for-change-province-minister-pun.html.
14. The UN estimated the growth rate of urban areas in Nepal to be 6.4 percent per year (2010:3).

— Chapter 7 —

MAFIA, LABOR, AND SHAMANISM
IN A SAND MINE

Introduction

In early December 2018, I met a group of four workers near a sand mine along the Sethi River in the mid-hills of Nepal. The workers were in the process of removing stones from the river, which were sold as building material to local construction companies. One of the workers had driven a tractor into the depths of the river and the other three were busy lifting larger stones with the help of an iron bar and loading them onto the truck bed of the tractor. The water reached them between their knees and upper body, and larger stones that could not be removed from the river were broken into pieces with a huge sledgehammer to make them ready for the tractor. After a while of quietly watching the work, I began to strike up a conversation. As it turned out, all four of the workers belonged to the ethnic community of the Magar and had been doing the hard, dangerous work of sand and river mining for years. That day, the group had broken enough rocks to load five trucks before they finished their work at 3 p.m.

Toward the end of their workday, I met Sajit, the mine's contractor. He wrote invoices and handed out coupons to the truck drivers who transported the stones to local construction sites. Since contractors for river and sand mines were usually called "dons" — mafia-like figures — in the Nepalese press, I began to inquire about Sajit's background. As it soon turned out, Sajit was the son of a wealthy farmer from the Chhetri community in the area and had enjoyed a rather privileged childhood. After school, he met a fellow student from an equally privileged farming family in college, and together they entered the sand-mining business. This first foray into the business was very successful, and they had earned back their initial investment of 3 lakh NR (300,000NR) within two weeks of the start of the mining season. They had made more than 32 lakh NR by the end of their first season.

Despite his early success in the industry, Sajit initially had other plans for his future. He wanted to use his earnings for a trip to Europe, but he did not meet the visa requirements. Instead, he enrolled for university studies. After graduating, he returned to the construction industry and founded a company that became involved in the building of several large infrastructure projects in the region, including the construction of roads. With his company, Sajit has managed to get the local authorities to award him the contract to extract sand and river stones three times throughout his career over the past twenty years. When he talked to me about this, he made it clear to me that in the past, to win such a large contract, you needed *goondas* (local strongmen), and with sand mining becoming more capital intensive over the last decade, one also needed a "background group of investors" to ensure that the tender contract could be obtained successfully. When asked about the profitability of sand mining, he told me that for an investment of 10 lakh, an investor could expect a return of 20 to 30 lakh for a mining season that would begin after the monsoon rains, when the river water brings down new sand from the mountains.

This chapter offers a descriptive analysis of the working worlds of sand miners along a river near Pokhara. I argue that the sand mines in the region are effectively mafia run, but those who work in them do not resent their mafioso employers and instead view them as patrons who provide much-needed employment. The chapter highlights workers' understanding of sand-mine work, which ranges from viewing sand-mine work as a springboard to a better job in faraway countries, to more negative renderings of sand mines as dangerous places where one risks losing one's own life. It further shows that workers mediate this tension between their attempts to achieve their "big dreams" of upward socioeconomic mobility and their fears of accidents by engaging in shamanistic practices.

I argue that the case of the sand mine complements my previous findings on the impact of Maoism in a nearby urban industrial area (see chapters 4 and 5) as well as in modern food-processing factories in the lowlands (see chapters 1 through 3). In line with more recent work on Maoism in Nepal that highlighted the micro-sociological changes triggered by the Maoist revolution (see Pettigrew 2015; Shakya 2018; Snellinger 2018; Zharkevich 2019a), this prior research suggests that in some sectors of Nepal's economy, Maoist ideology has inflected upon both the everyday textures and the organization of work. More specifically, I showed how radical political formations managed to change the conditions of work for the industrial working classes. In this chapter, I further expand on the dialectic between political ideology and labor through a focus on the everyday work of sand miners in the mid-hills. As I point out toward the end of the chapter, the current economic situation of the sand workers cannot be understood without considering the broader political developments of the country.

The ethnographic case presented here stands in line with recent scholarly findings that demonstrate how, in different parts of the globe, criminal groups have become involved in the supply of sand (Rege 2016; Rege and Lavorgna 2017; Beiser 2018; Marschke et al. 2020). More specifically, it makes two distinct contributions to an emerging discourse surrounding the emergence of a "mafia-raj" (Michelutti et al. 2018) in the South Asian context. First, in line with other recent scholarship (Martin and Michelutti 2017; Michelutti et al. 2018; Hoque and Michelutti 2018; and Harriss-White and Michelutti 2020), this chapter shows how the organization of the "sand mafia" in Nepal is a relatively decentralized, network-like structure between business owners, politicians, and criminals. Drawing on Ashraf Hoque and Lucia Michelutti's (2018) most recent work on "political jugaad," I not only explain the emergence of such network-like structures in the Nepali context but also present the case of a former sand miner from the Dalit community who turned into a sand-mine contractor due to his capacities to play such networks to his own advances through a creative "political jugaad" (Hoque and Michelutti 2018:991): the art of getting by through developing social connections to influential business owners and criminal-like organizations. "The art of bossing," a phrase used and described by Michelutti et al. (2018), thus reveals itself as a quintessential tool to achieve upward social mobility.

Second, the case presented also confirms more recent scholarship on the "mafia-raj" in India that demonstrates that "mafia-like" work in South Asia is not necessarily violent. While in some Indian cases, mafia-like work is accompanied by violence (see Beiser 2018; Guardian 2018; Weinstein 2008; Witsoe 2012), in other cases it is not; this is particularly true in cases where a specific form of organized crime has gained a monopoly over the extraction of resources in compliance with the state. The chapter maintains that for the ethnography presented, we witness a case of a mafia-like organization involved in the extraction of sand without the use of extreme violence, but rather through tactics of fear and intimidation. For the workers in the sand mine, the potential for violence is just as important as violence itself. In cases of a delayed payment by a truck driver to a sand miner, for example, the latter will often prefer to keep silent for fear of the don and will not engage the local unions that claim to have organized large parts of the town's informal economy.

This chapter builds upon my empirical and theoretical findings of Nepal's emerging industrial working class as laid out in the previous chapters of this book. This chapter adds to them by focusing on the experience of work in a sand mine and demonstrates how uncertainties are often dealt with through shamanistic practices. By doing so, the chapter also contributes to a well-established literature on "occult economies" (Comaroff and Comaroff 2000). Some of the discussions surrounding magic stones found in the rivers relate to an emerging literature on Hinduism, magic stones, and riverscapes (see Van der Geer et al. 2008, Walters 2020). I begin now by discussing the context of the ethnography by outlining the broader emergency of mafia-like structures in Nepal against the backdrop of the country's more recent history of rapid political change.

The Maoist Revolution and the Emergence of Mafia-Like Assemblages in Nepal

According to a broad corpus of anthropological and sociological literature, the growth of extortion practices in Nepal was particularly intensive in the period of the Maoist revolutionary period between 1996 and 2006 (see Dhruba 2010:191). Both Maoist rebels as well as shadowy figures pretending to be Maoists began to contact local businesses in order to extort money from business owners. The demand for such payments was justified by the rebels as they framed them often as "contributions" to their revolutionary project. In exchange, the Maoists—and those pretending to be Maoists—promised the industrialists and business owners to spare them from violent attacks on their private property. As a result of such social dynamics, a "market of protection" emerged that was somewhat novel though certainly not an unknown criminal phenomenon. Already in the early 1990s, the established political parties in Nepal asked for *chanda* (volunteer donations) from business owners and sometimes even enforced such "political" demands with violence. Throughout the revolutionary period, however, extortion practices increased to an alarming scale, with many business owners from various industries such as the tourism, food and beverage, or *yarsagumba* trade complaining about the new "violent entrepreneurs" (Volkov 2002) who had "captured" the political-economic landscape of the country.

But much of what is known about this period in Nepal only reflects broader trends, as many shop owners who were blackmailed never went to the police and thus incidents remained underreported for fear of violence. One of the consequences of this broader social dynamic, however, was the emergence of a discourse of a moral decay immediately following the Maoist revolution: a public discourse emerged that complained about the "culture of impunity" across the country that facilitated the spread of criminal outfits and leveraged politized crime. One telling example was that in 2009 the government published a list of 109 armed groups said to be active in Nepal (Thapa 2017:108). Many of these groups were not politically motivated but used the lack of state power to their own advantage to gain financial benefits by extorting and blackmailing businesses.[1]

The post-revolutionary period, and its "culture of impunity," has certainly provided a fertile ground for the growth of "violent entrepreneurs" across the country. Undoubtedly, from my own observations in three different urban areas where I undertook fieldwork since 2008, the Maoists' own activities of extortion seem to have been curbed significantly after the Party climbed to power in 2008 and after its subsequent efforts in transforming its party into a more established model of party organization. This observation may remain impressionist, but the fact is that in the period since 2006, public media has shown time and again the "varieties of mafia" that have emerged in different parts of Nepal's economy: particularly in the wealthy timber-smuggling mafia (Bampton and Cammaert 2007:30), illegal gold-smuggling rackets (Kathmandu Post 2019), and illegal sand extraction along the rivers of the country (Kathmandu Post 2017).

In the context of Pokhara, the history of such mafia-like networks remains void in official accounts of the city. Shortly after my arrival in town in October 2018, however, I discovered that residents in the town often referred to a variety of youth gangs or the "dons" in the adjacent sand mines when asked about the history of violent entrepreneurs in the post-conflict period of the city. The former were remembered by their "name": for example, the most notoriously dangerous youth gangs in town were known as the "LG group," "Archal

Bot," or the "Buddha Guys." They were known to work for political parties in the region and extort money from certain business groups. Their activities, however, became less visible over the years because the town's superintendent of police (SP) arrested the leader of the LG group in 2014, and because "Tanke," another notorious criminal throughout the insurgency, was killed by Maoists. Tanke had made the mistake of trying to keep landless groups from squatting on land he wanted to sell. When the Maoists found out, they shot him dead.

The second group of people, often referred to when asked about mafia-like organizations in the city, were private contractors who operated sand mines along the river that cut through the city. These contractors were often referred to as "boss," "hakim," "mafioso," or "don." For example, in an article about sand mining near Pokhara that appeared in the Kathmandu Post in 2014 read: "Currently, mining of sand and gravel is under way at as many as 35 sites and almost all of them are operated by so-called dons who get the tender in their names by any means necessary" (Kathmandu Post 2014). Similarly, bosses of sand mines were also referred to as mafia-like figures in everyday conversations. I heard this first from a local hotel manager in town who claimed that sand mining was an industry that was controlled by mafia-like dons who competed for the annual contracts that were awarded by the municipality.

Determining the organization of this local "sand mafia" proved difficult. At different times, and depending on whom I asked, I got different answers. The most established wisdom among key informants, however, was that the sand mafia consisted of a loose and decentralized network of private contractors, investor groups, youth gangs, and politicians. It may in some measure resemble what Lucia Michelutti describes as a "mafia assemblage" for the context of Indian sand mining (2020:168).[2] But I hasten to add that the exact connections between the different parties are difficult to pin down as informants remained often obscure about it. What can be said, however, is that in order to win an annual contract from the local state authorities, private contractors needed influential contacts in politics as well as to temporarily hire one of the abovementioned violent youth gangs—so-called goondas—to shy away from other private contractors in their bid for the contract. I even know of one case where a leader of a youth gang become himself a private contractor and exploited a mine for a period of one year.

But equally important for our discussion is that violence associated with sand mining has decreased in the recent past for two reasons. First, my ethnographic material suggests that the investor groups involved in sand mining seem to have established themselves in the area, and with the price for a tender contract to exploit a sand mine skyrocketing, the competition has diminished. Second, the newly minted Communist Party of Nepal—which merged from the UML and UCPN (Maoist)—has delegated the handout of tender contracts from the District Development Committee to the local municipality, and thereby obtained an upper hand in controlling the violence associated with sand mining. In the next section, I begin to explore these dynamics more in depth with an ethnographic vignette of my first encounter with the don who runs the sand mine I know best.

Meeting Hari Jee, the Boss

Four months after starting my fieldwork in Pokhara, I met the don of the sand mine, whom everyone called "Hari Jee." We met in the parking lot of the sand mine, and he gave me a short tour of the mine before we went to one of the nearby "hotels" to discuss my questions. Right at our first meeting, I noticed that Hari did not fit the typical stereotype of a mafia boss. He did not come to the sand mine in a big SUV jeep but came to the mine on a "Scootie." Compared to Sajit, whom I mentioned in the ethnographic vignette at the beginning of this chapter, Hari was also relatively young. When I asked him about his age and family background, it turned out that Hari was only thirty-one years old, had worked in the mine himself as a sand worker, and came from a Dalit family. After a few more questions, it turned out that Hari had finished school with a two-plus degree and had also worked as a truck driver in the mine before he was awarded the contract for sand mining twice in a row by the local state authorities.

In our meeting, Hari also told me exactly how the market for sand had developed in recent years and how demand had increased due to the construction boom in Pokhara. In the past, as he explained, you needed "money and muscle" to win the tender contract from the District Development Committee. In the past, he was forced to work with local goonda groups to influence the chances in his favor. Today, as he emphasized in our conversation, money and muscle power were less important. The new Nepalese Communist Party had carried out a local reform, and now contracts were only handled at the municipal level. The new government had introduced a computerized awarding procedure where bidders could apply via the internet for the sand-mining contract. The result was that the new government was able to reduce the violence in the sand mines because it was no longer immediately obvious which contractors had applied for the mining contract. In our conversation, Hari evaluated the introduction of this computerized tendering procedure as positive, because now he neither had to hire nor pay goondas to intimidate his opponents.

Hari managed to get the contract in 2017 with the help of around forty to forty-five investors. While the municipality put up 4 karoor 30 lakh as a minimum bid, Hari secured the contract through a bid of 6 karoor 30 lakh. Half of this amount came from a local bank, which operated as a silent investor. Around ten to fifteen *kaniwallas* (sand miners) were themselves operating as partners by investing in the contract. He estimated that the mine would make 10 percent profit per year. Last year, however, it made a good 80 percent profit. Thus, investing in the mine could be a risky game with an uncertain outcome. Hari was proud to provide employment to several hundreds of people working at the mine. As he put it: "This is our Saudi Arabia! No need to go abroad—you'll make at least 50,000 a month and some make even 1 lakh per month." While this was true, he understated many of the younger workers' desire to go abroad for work. He also emphasized that they celebrated a workers' day on 1 May, a day when several politicians would come to the mine. In a way, as he put it, the mine was like the "green card" system in the United States. Only those who lived around the mine—mainly from formerly landless communities—were allowed to work there, and working was a privilege as it provided three times the income opportunity as the other factories around town.

The workers themselves did not despise dons such as Hari, as I would learn from our conversations. For example, on 15 November 2018, I met a sand worker (Mr. Nepali—also from a Dalit background) who was sitting under an umbrella with his son and daughter-in-law in the sand mine. He had just returned from Sudan where he worked as a machine operator in a factory and earned about 65,000 NR per month. When I asked why the workers did not try to get the contract themselves, he said that Hari had goondas and things had gotten worse in the past years: "I know them because Hari jee and his goondas are locals, but I'm not afraid of them, because I know them and they are close to Ram Ghat. Even though Hari jee invites us to also invest in the mine and become shareholders, I will not do it. I have made money in Sudan, but it's all about trust. I was thinking about investing one lakh [approx. 1,000 euros], but I won't do it. I don't know if he will give my money back, let alone any share of the profits." However, Deepak Gurung, a sand miner in his midforties, said that he was afraid of Hari jee and his goondas, who he accused of being drug addicts. According to him, a ten-year-old girl was raped by a drug-addicted goonda in 2018. Deepak was an outsider in Pokhara, having come to the sand mine from his faraway village. He was afraid that the locals could call on the goondas at any time to kick him out of the sand mine. He was willing to fight to the death to keep his job, which he needed to feed his pregnant wife and two-year-old daughter. So far nothing serious had happened, but he was so scared of the goondas that he avoided calling the labor union for help if he had a dispute with the truck drivers over payment.

Working in the Sand Mine

Ram Ghat was one of five sand mines in the vicinity of Pokhara. According to local estimates, it was the largest sand mine in the area, and the mine employed several hundred workers.[3] Like the work in Nepal's brick kilns (see Hoffmann 2018a), work in the sand mine was seasonal for most of the workers, as the heavy monsoon rains flooded the sand mine in the summer, making sand mining a dangerous job. Hence, only few workers worked during the monsoon season as there was the danger of drowning in the torrential river that crossed the sand mine. In addition to the workers, there were also religious followers who visited the sand mine for two reasons: first, in large groups with family and friends to cremate deceased relatives in the riverbed and participate in Hinduist death rituals; and second, in smaller groups of close family members who visited the sand mine with a priest to perform rituals to honor deceased relatives.

At the top of the hierarchy of the sand mine was a private contractor, who leased the mine from the municipality for a period of one year. In order to obtain the lease from the municipality, a contractor had to hand in an estimated price for the lease beforehand. Importantly, prices for the purchase of an annual lease had gone up dramatically over the last couple of years prior to my arrival in the field in late 2018. Maybe unsurprisingly, nearly all workers I met in the sand mine had an accurate idea of the latest price for a lease. This amounted to about 7 karoor NR. Less known to most workers were the profits made by a variety of different contractors/lease-holders over the past years. One who knew was Deepak Gurung, who estimated the expected turnover of the mine per year at about twice the amount of investment. To estimate this number, Deepak had counted the number of trucks leaving the mine on various days. This observation matches with what several contractors interviewed had indicated as the profit rate, and some of my most trusted informants in the field compared such a profitable business with profits in the local pharmaceutical industry. Yet, despite this obvious form of exploitation, the sand-mining scheme and the activities of Hari and his "background investors" did not create a moral outcry among the workers in the mine. When confronted with the profit rates, most workers expressed just simply that they were glad that Hari Jee did share a part of his profit with them. That's probably not very surprising, as Nepalese are used to such forms of exploitation, which becomes obvious when you consider that even a loan from friends or family members is usually charged between 18 percent and 25 percent interest annually, sometimes even as high as 60 percent.

The tekkedar (contractor) did not employ the workers directly with monthly wages but tolerated the development of the mine by residents who pay 2,500 NR to the tekkedar for each load of sand for a truck. The work hierarchy in the mine itself was divided into two parts: first, there are the kaniwallas. These were usually local inhabitants from about 180 different families from the immediate neighborhood. Many of them were landless before they moved near the sand mine. Only residents from the neighborhood had permission to open a clearly defined area of the mine—a *kani*—and dig there for sand. Kaniwallas usually worked in pairs, often as married couples or with family members. The second part of the hierarchy consisted of the so-called *bogne manche*: porters who transported the sand from the kani to the trucks, carrying the loads on their heads. This very hard work was done mainly by male long-distant labor migrants, often from the Magar ethnic group or from remote villages.[4] The majority of mine workers were adults, and a significant portion of them were women, often with Magar or Gurung backgrounds. Sometimes, during the holidays, one could also see some children in the mine. Not all these children are workers—some just play near their parents; others, like Basalt's fourteen-year-old brother, skip school, while some are taught by their parents how to do the mine work.

Work in the mine started early; although there were no fixed working hours, the first kaniwallas were in the mine by six in the morning. Gradually the sand mine would fill with workers, each on their own schedule. Krishna Dungel Dhai, for example, was a sixty-five-year-old worker who had been mining sand at Ram Ghat for over fifty-five years. He usually worked for three hours in the morning from 7 a.m. until 10 a.m. and then an equally long shift in the afternoon.

Others worked more, but seven to eight hours a day was average. Kaniwallas usually dug in the earth at their demarcated space with a shovel and then shoveled the sand onto an inclined filter net so that stones remained on one side of the net while the sand was filtered to the other. As soon as enough sand had been accumulated behind the filter, the carriers took the sand and the stones to a parking lot at the entrance of the ghats, where the sand was sold and packed onto waiting trucks.

The price for the sand was determined by the contractor. A so-called tip—the rear loading area of a truck—was sold for 5,500 NR to truck drivers who delivered it to construction companies and resold it for about 7,000 NR per load. From the sale of one truckload, the contractor kept about 2,500 NR, and the remaining 3,000 NR was divided between kaniwallas and porters. Most carriers earned between 1,100 and 1,300 NR per truckload. This meant that they had to haul between forty and fifty loads of sand from the mine to the truck. The price for *gittis* (stones) was different: stones were sold for 3,500 NR per truckload, while the contractor kept about 1,500 NR per load, leaving the kaniwallas and carriers with an estimated 2,000 NR to share in a distribution similar to that of the sand.

Carrying the loads of sand from the mine to the trucks was hard work. Carriers carried either 65 or 50 kg of sand in a *thunse* (basket), which they carried on their foreheads on a *namlo* (headscarf). When they carried the basket from the mine to the trucks, they had to climb about 40 meters uphill. The steps to the ghats were often worn out—so much so that I almost slid into the mine during a visit. A few of the porters were women; they used smaller baskets and had to go up and down the hill seventy times to fill the tip of a truck.

It varies depending on capacity, but usually a kaniwalla or *bogne walla (carrier)* team sold about one to one and a half tips per day. Famous in the ghats, however, was a well-known carrier whom everyone called "ek laghe" (a lakh). This kaniwalla was famous for carrying up to three truckloads of sand to the parking lot every day, thus making about three times the income as the other workers. Kaniwallas and bogne walla usually made about 30,000 to 35,000 NR per month (note Krishna made only about 15,000 to 18,000 NR per month, but he was sixty-five years old and had worked there for more than fifty-five years), which was higher than the pay of a public teacher in Nepal (23,000 NR), and was considered locally as middle-class income.

In terms of ethnic and caste composition, the sand mine at Rham Ghat was a mixed place. I encountered miners from Chettry, Magar,

Gurung, Tamang, Rai, and Dalits (for example, Nepali (trad shoe-maker), *pariyar* (tailor), BK (*bisho karma* = blacksmith) communities. Many of the sand miners were also related. For example, I met a Magar family who had at least seven plots in the mine, and when they visited each other during breaks they would usually speak in the Magar language. There was a Tamang family who had two plots of land and who spoke in their own Tamang language. Not even my research assistant—who was very skilled in local Nepali languages—could understand them. Strikingly, however, there were no people from the lowlands working in the mine. Minority ethnic groups and Dalits formed the main part of the workforce at the sand mine, and despite some use of local dialects, the lingua franca in the mine was Nepali. Compared to the construction industry, sand mining had a decisive advantage for the workers: they were paid directly by Hari Jee on the day, rather than having to wait to receive their wages. To ensure this, Hari Jee had set up a token system. Each truck received a token when it arrived at the mine. This token was then given to the appropriate carrier after the truck was loaded, who then passed it to the kaniwalla family who mined the sand. The family was then able to exchange the token daily for cash at a fixed rate.

Leisure, Dangers, and Magic Stones in the Sand Mine

At first glance, sand mining in Ram Ghat appears as a banal and secular type of work. Both types of workers, sand miners and sand carriers, usually start around 6 a.m. and work about four hours. This is followed by a rest, and then most workers return to put in another three hours from 2 p.m. to 5 p.m. In between there are "snack breaks," usually around 10 a.m. and again in the afternoon, at three different sites within the sand mine where different working groups meet and exchange daily gossip. As I mentioned earlier, the working process is rather simple; sand is dug out and thrown through a filter net, which workers buy for an estimated 2,000 NR. Everyone works to their own capacity, and during breaks, workers sit at their own kani or visit their neighbors to chat and catch up. At times, kaniwallas exchange their metal nets; sometimes the workers, including the women, smoke a cigarette. Every ten minutes, a plane flies over Ram Ghat, making a loud noise and making it difficult for the workers to understand each other. Amid all this, there are usually people who roam the area looking for jobs as sand carriers. In the parking lot is where most of the social activity takes place. There are three types of sand that cost the same: for the *dhalai*, for plastering, and for building walls. Here, when a truck arrives, different workers try to convince the driver that their sand is the type and quality that they need. For example, people would come to the parking lot and yell at the driver "Mero balua hernus" (Look at my sand) or "Mero balua lai janus" (Take my sand).

But work here is also dangerous, as I learned when I did an interview with Deepak Gurung in his kani in the mine. During the interview, his two-year-old daughter began to play with a bone that she found. Seeing her, Deepak snatched the bone and tossed it away, pondering aloud what kind of animal it had come from. Sitting behind us, Basanta, a young member of the ethnic Tamang community, laughed and said: "She took a human bone—it was a human bone. What other bones are you expecting here in Ram Ghat?" Deepak was more concerned about his daughter. She had sand in her right eye and Deepak blew some air on her face and told her she was fine. My research assistant later confided to me that he felt uncomfortable during this episode. Apparently, young children can go blind when they get sand in their eyes. According to my research assistant, sand miners like Deepak would explain blindness as an attack from ghosts in the area, when it was actually their own carelessness that produced such tragedies. But a child being blinded was only one of the hazards at Ram Ghat. There were others, as Deepak noted: "Some people drown in Ram Ghat throughout the monsoon months when the water is rising and the sand has to be fetched from the emerging sandbanks. Then people have to cross the river sometimes with the water up to their necks." But most people do not work in the summer months, so drownings were infrequent.

Unlike in the brick factory where I conducted fieldwork (see Hoffmann 2018a), only a few of the workers drank alcohol to sustain the physically exhausting daily grind. Moreover, only a few of the workers smoked cannabis, contradicting the popular local stereotype that people hailing from the Gurung ethnic community were known for this habit. But those who did take intoxicants were easily recognizable and usually found in a few certain places around the mine. For example, several times I encountered unemployed carriers already drunk in the early morning; another time I met a small group of workers peacefully smoking ganja on the top of the hill overlooking the sand mine. One of them was passed out and lay in the cool grass beneath the late November sun.

During their leisure time, sand miners undertook different activities. The father of Ramesh Pun Magar—whose family has several plots in the mine—would go fishing in the lake near Lakeside in Pokhara. This was because, as he put it, "over there the fish are still fresh, but inside the mine people cremate bodies, the fish eat the remains, and the fish end up tasting bad." His son, Ramesh Pun Magar, who had been to Malaysia and Saudi Arabia and now worked as a kaniwalla inside the mine, watched Manchester United play soccer on his mobile phone. Another carrier I met sat on the hill and played an electronic card game on his mobile. And a young kaniwalla from the Tamang community—who had worked at a BMW supplier factory in Saudi Arabia—loved to watch professional wrestling on his mobile. To my surprise, I learned that he knew older wrestling superstars such as Hulk Hogan and the Undertaker, but his favorites were Tony Ramos and John Cena.[5]

Sometimes workers used their work breaks to tell each other stories about stones found in the mine. Two of these stories were told to me by Ramesh's father, who worked in the sand mine as a kaniwalla. In the first story, a kaniwalla found a valuable blue and white stone in the mine and sold it for about 1 lakh in the tourist area of the city. The other story was about a magic stone that a carrier found in the mine. This stone leaked water when it was touched. The carrier passed it on to another merchant to sell it at Lakeside, but he disappeared and was never seen again. Legendary miners were another frequently discussed topic among the workers. For example, the two people everyone knew were "junga dhai" (mustache brother), who worked in the sand mine for fifty-five years, and "ek lakhe," the carrier who could carry so much that he was earning a lakh a month. People doubted that ek lakhe could really make that much money.

The work in the sand mine also produced its own shadow economy. Some of the workers in the mine developed an entrepreneurial spirit and began to sell products to the other sand miners. For example, the tea-walla sold tea, boiled vegetables, and chow mein to the workers. Cooked vegetables were especially popular with the workers—not surprisingly, as they only cost 20 NR. Workers started ordering early in the morning, and by 8 a.m. the tea and vegetables were often sold out. Another business that emerged from the sand mine was invented by a member of the Rai community who sat almost every day under a black umbrella on the hill above the parking lot where he made and sold bamboo baskets to the porters. His innovation was that he specialized in modifying existing baskets by adding a second, reinforcing layer of bamboo (which he obtains from a village). He sold these baskets to other miners for 250 NR.

One important observation was that when I asked whether workers went on hikes in the nearby mountains in their spare time, I was usually met with astonished laughter. "We don't do that," they said. "But it's free," I sometimes replied. Such middle-class activities, however, did not occur here. This was surprising to me, as many employees of Tarai-based companies came here for annual company excursions (see chapter 1). However, the workers had apparently never thought of doing so.

Dreams of Working Elsewhere in Faraway Countries

Many of the younger workers at the Ram Ghat sand mine had previously worked abroad, mainly in the Middle East and Malaysia. This was not surprising—as previously mentioned, labor migration from Nepal to these countries has increased enormously in the years since the Maoist revolution.[6] What is important for our discussion, however, is what role the work in the sand mine has played in facilitating this labor migration. Two short ethnographic vignettes will explain how I became acquainted with the migration plans of workers in the sand mine.

I first met Sunnita during the Tihar Festival in November 2018, when there were significantly fewer workers in the sand mine. She worked as a kaniwalla in the sand mine, but she had a bachelor's degree in management. She previously worked as a teacher but quit the job and followed in her parents' footsteps by starting to work in the sand mine. When I met Sunnita, she was carrying a heavy basket of sand up the hill to the trucks. She asked me where I came from and then told me that she wanted to go to Europe to work in agriculture in southern Spain or Portugal. She had found a staffing agency that said they would get her work in Europe for 9 lakh (around 8000 euros), which she planned to partly finance by working in the sand mine. Hearing this, my research assistant immediately intervened and advised her against this trip. According to him, Sunnita ran the risk of making a big financial mistake; she would most likely only earn as much in Europe as she would in the sand mine, but taking out a loan for the trip would cause her massive debt and high-interest payments. But despite his warnings, Sunnita was resolute in her decision to leave, stating, "Here we cannot improve our lives, and there is little ijjat [honor] in this work." She had already paid 2,000 euros to the recruitment agency and did not want to risk losing this investment. Even after a long discussion, she wanted to leave because that was her "big dream."

The day after hearing about Sunnita's dream, Basanta explained to me his plans to go abroad for work. According to him the work as a bogne manche (carrier) was hard and sometimes infrequent, leading to periods of unemployment. Before coming to the mine, he had worked in a small shop in his village, but the rent was increased and he left. Along with his younger brother, Basanta had taken a cheap twelve-hour bus trip from his hometown to the mine, looking for work. Apparently, he had married early at eighteen, and now, at twenty-eight, he only had one goal: working in the mine for five months would allow him to earn 30,000 to 35,000 NR per month. With this money, he wanted to join a group of friends from his village who were going to work as security guards in Dubai or the Middle East. The staffing agency that organizes the travel and employment in Dubai and the necessary papers would charge him between 1.2 and 2 lakh. When I went through the numbers and carefully suggested to him that it probably made more sense financially to stay in the sand mine, he insisted on his desire to migrate abroad. He judged the life of a sand carrier as "egdam garo" (very hard work) and saw little hope for upward mobility. After working for three months in Dubai, he might get promoted and earn something like 60,000 NR (around 500 euros per month, but food and accommodation are paid for by the company). But Basanta acknowledged that this scenario was possible only "if things go well."

Other workers in the mine who also wanted to migrate to other countries made similar arguments to those of Sunnita and Basanta. Working in the sand mine was very strenuous and there was little hope of any new career openings. However, some of my informants pointed out that not everyone who worked abroad really did the work they said they did. As Ram Bahadur, a forty-five-year-old worker, remarked over a tea with me during his work break: "Nobody knows what kind of job you were doing in the Middle East or Malaysia. That's why nobody looks down on you when you come back, and you can tell people that you worked all kinds of jobs."

Some of the former labor migrants had doubts about working abroad again. For example, Pun Magar finished grade ten in his home village, then got a three-year work visa for Malaysia and paid the recruitment agency 80,000 NR. He went there and worked for one year at different branches of 7-Eleven, then changed to work as a cashier. He earned 20,000 NR and received overtime pay from the recruitment agency that the 7-Eleven store owners never paid him.

Nevertheless, he extended the deadline by another year, and then moved back to Nepal. A while later, he again went to Saudi Arabia and paid 60,000 NR to the personnel agency and worked there as a loader for loading and unloading trucks in a dairy factory. He worked there for two years and earned 20,000 NR per month—with overtime, sometimes 25,000 NR per month. Since he earned very little at both jobs, he returned to work at the Ram Ghat sand mine. When asked whether he would return to Malaysia, he said he was thinking about it. The job here was hard and seasonal, but the other job was not much better either. He told me, "The money here is good, but the work is hard. In Malaysia, the work is easier, but the income is low."

Others did not plan to go abroad at all and were happy to work at the sand mine. Take the Chetry boy, for example, who worked for Pun Magar. His previous career was a catastrophe: he used to work in a hotel on Lakeside where he worked for twenty hours a day earning 10,000 NR (10 a.m. until 5 p.m. as a housekeeper, 6 p.m. to 10 p.m. as a waiter, and then late nights as a security guard). He started working as a carrier in the sand mine and earned nearly triple as much. Or take Pun Magar's neighbor Santosh who had been in the mine for fifteen years, or Krishna Dungel Bhai, who had been sand mining for fifty-five years. They viewed their work as *swatantra* (freedom). They said they felt free in the mine and that is why they liked their job. This attitude reminded me of the mukta kamaiya whom I encountered in the brick kilns in the far-western lowlands in 2008 who also viewed their work as "free" because there was little control and one could make their own schedule (Hoffmann 2014a).

Shamanistic Practices to Cope with the Uncertainties of Sand Mining

So far, I have shown how sand mining in the region is embedded in broader political developments and described how sand mining is experienced by its workforce both in terms of work and leisure. We have seen that for some of the younger workers, sand mining provides a platform to save earnings before leaving for faraway workplaces in the Middle East or Malaysia, in the hope for better-paid employment. The fact that sand mining allows for many to earn an income of nearly double than that in the local manufacturing industry is key to understanding its popularity. But as I also already mentioned, sand mining is not only physically exhausting but also a dangerous type of work: workers risk either being buried in a sandpit or drowning in the river throughout the monsoon season. How, then, do workers cope with the uncertainties associated with sand mining? To understand this better, I begin with a brief digression by focusing on the wider "occult economy" in town.

After a few months of fieldwork in the sand mine, I realized that some of the workers who planned to leave the sand-mining business and move abroad were visiting the local *jhākri* (shamans) to figure out an auspicious day for their departure. This, I was told by my informants, would help make the labor migration journey to a faraway place more economically successful.

But sand miners not only visited jhākris to figure out auspicious days for their labor sojourns. They also visited shamanic healers to cope with various types of health issues. Take Ram Magar, a fifty-year-old worker in the mine: when I interviewed him, he told me a story that took place a few years ago. At that time, Ram Magar was concerned about his health as his right foot had swollen up. He went to visit a nearby hospital but none of the doctors could help him. Thus, Ram Magar went to see various jhākri in the region and finally found one who was able to heal his foot after recognizing that Ram Magar had been attacked by a *masan*, a demonic spirit who according to Hindu belief is known to be "the lord of the cremation ground" (Sax 2009:67). In Ram Magar's view, the fact that he was attacked by a demonic spirit made sense because sand mining took place at Ram Ghat, which was the city's largest Hindu cremation site. As a result, sand mining occurred in a place that was locally believed to be haunted by evil spirits.

Among those workers who did believe in ghosts and malevolent spirits roaming the mine, I encountered a further distinction between bhuts (ghosts) and the prets, which are often referred to as masans. According to my informants, both occur after the body of a person who died unnaturally (for example, suicide by hanging) was cremated near the river. Moreover, some of my informants further distinguished between tal masans—who occurred after an untimely death that happened on land—and jal masans, who tended to appear after a person has died in the river. But then there were those who did acknowledge the existence of such natural beings but quickly added that they were not afraid of them. A telling example was an elderly female sand miner from the Magar community who expressed to me: "We are not afraid of ghosts because we are many here." In her view, the fact that the sand mine was populated by several hundreds of workers prevented the ghosts from attacking them. Moreover, of those workers encountered who did believe in ghosts,

I heard often the story of a female worker who was possessed by a malevolent ghost and as a result turned *pagal* (crazy). That is to say that my mostly male informants expressed a disconcern about her bodily health after she was possessed by a spirit. "Once the spirit possessed her, she would not take care of her appearance anymore. She did not take care of her hair anymore and did not take care of cleaning her cloth anymore" is how one informant recalled the possession of the worker. I learned from visiting the ritual healers who resided in the area that there were several stories of ghost possession in the sand mine but some of them were also related to male workers. For example, I visited a ritual healer living close by—the so-called Kanchan Lama—who was widely respected in the mine as he not only had healed people but also had three students in the mine. When I visited him at his home, he told me a story about a male kaniwalla who had fallen ill four years ago and came to him to be healed. Kanchan Lama diagnosed his malaise as not being able to speak anymore after a malevolent spirit attacked him. To get the evil spirit out of the worker's body, Kanchan Lama had to undergo a spiritual journey and undertake a very complex ritual until the ailing sand miner was healed again.

Given Nepal's more recent political history, it may be little surprising that not all workers shared such beliefs in evil spirits roaming the sand mine at night, and as I learned over time, there was considerable doubt among workers in the mine about the existence of such malevolent spirits and ghosts in the area. In fact, when I talked to the workers, different opinions emerged about the realness of such supernatural beings. For example, Pun Magar did not believe in the existence of ghosts. According to him, such beliefs in ghosts and malevolent spirits were a relic of the past and it was only rural villagers who still believed in supernatural concepts. Other informants encountered in the sand mine expressed that the belief in ghosts and spirits was simply *andhabishwas* (superstition).

How can the practice of visiting ritual healers in order to deal with the insecurities and risks associated with sand mining be understood? Should the story of the possession of the workers by evil spirits be read as a more subtle cultural expression of resistance to workplace-based exploitation, similarly to the ways Aihwa Ong (1987) has suggested in the context of Malaysian factory workers? Or may it be more accurate—following Jean and John Comaroff (2000)—to generally view the practices of shamanism and spirit possession in the wider area as a cultural response from the many who are left out of the benefits of new forms of capitalism? The answer, I believe, is both, but there is also a third reading of such practices. Undoubtedly, the persistence of beliefs in spirit possession and ghosts in the mine carries shades of the conventional exploitation patterns suggested above by Ong (1987) and Comaroff and Comaroff (2000) since workers find themselves working under difficult conditions for a patron who siphons off the profit, and try to use established patterns of ritual healing and fortune-telling in town to their own advantage. But the side-effect of visiting ritual healers to find out auspicious days for migration abroad or to heal oneself from illness due to sand mining was that such practices somewhat legitimized the power of the don in the sand mine. This was because according to the ritual healers in the area, sand miners became sick because of the persistence of masans in the mine, rather than because of the sand-mine work itself. Hence, such ideas, discourses, and practices of shamanic advice to the miners provided legitimacy to the contractor of the mine.

Conclusion: The Dark Side of Urbanization

This chapter has focused on a descriptive analysis of the working lives of sand workers near Pokhara. In doing so, the chapter has described the daily experience of work in a relatively new extractive industry, as well as the encounter of Nepalese workers with emerging mafia-like assemblages. It is difficult to say how widespread such entanglements between local mafia groups and the sand-mining industry really are. But it seems likely that such groups will continue to have a role in the sand-mining sector as it expands along with the current construction boom (Hirslund 2021). The general lack of jobs in many parts of the country, and the fact that many Nepalis have already moved away to find work in other parts of the world, could make these new sand mines a much-needed source of employment for local groups. But, as I have argued in this chapter, it is necessary to understand how workers experience such new work environments and how criminal groups have "conquered" the sand business in Nepal. The fact that many workers do not hold a grudge against their mafia-style employers, and the mixed attitude of workers toward sand mining (i.e., sand mining is used as a means to find better work elsewhere), are likely shared characteristics of sand-mining operations across the country.

In this chapter, I characterized the relationship between the mafia-like employer in the mine and the workforce as a patron-client relationship. While I claim that there was a kind of mafia assemblage governing the mine, for most workers the complex network that existed behind the figure of the don was largely invisible, yet it provided a relatively stable work regime. Two factors helped stabilize this new mafia-like system. First, the emigration of laborers was in the interest of the mafia-like regime as it prevented the emergence of a more serious confrontation with their workers. Second, the fact that some of the miners were under the influence of shamans who defined the "evil" in the mine as originating from supernatural beings, rather than exploitative work regimes, also contributed to the stability of this complex wealth-extraction scheme in the sand mine.

These insights raise the question: what new trends and social forces might undermine and destabilize the formation of such mafia-like assemblages in Nepal? Rather than providing a fully elaborated answer to such a complex question, I would like to conclude by briefly raising two potential scenarios that might help destabilize such mafia-like assemblages. First, given that it seems highly likely that the newly minted Communist Party of Nepal has become involved in such mafia-like formations, an attempt to "follow the money" of sand mines might not only expose but also destabilize such political-economic formations around the country. Second, environmental groups and activists who expose the environmental damage of sand mining might further destabilize such new wealth-extraction schemes. For example, progress might be achieved through an open critique of the Communist Party's very optimistic belief in the power of science over nature—a position that echoes that of many Western governments (see Pearson 2017). Further anthropological research is needed into what could be called the "dark side" of urbanization, and how various forms of critique can be effective in documenting and describing such wealth-extraction schemes as those of the sand mines in Nepal.

Notes

Parts of this chapter have been used in "Digging for Sand after the Revolution: Mafia, Labor, and Shamanism in a Nepali Sand Mine," *Dialectical Anthropology* 45(2): 117–133. I gratefully acknowledge permission to reprint this revised version.

1. The extent to which the mafia-like structure described in this chapter resembles mafias in the Italian context (for example, see Schneider and Schneider 2011 and Pardo 1996) would be interesting to examine but goes beyond the scope of this chapter.
2. Deepak Thapa has argued that the UML, which took over power from the Maoist-led coalition in May 2009, took a hardline approach to control the activities of armed

groups, particularly in eastern Nepal and the Tarai region. Accordingly, by the time of the 2013 Constituent Assembly elections, armed group activity had been largely ceased, "although reports of attempts of extortion have continued" (Thapa 2017:108).

3. The number of workers in the mine varied by the day and remained influenced by the Hindu festival calendar throughout the year. For example, throughout the Tihar festival, there were significantly less people working in the mine.

4. These labor migrants slept in "dormitories" set up next to the mine. The one dormitory I know best was run by a Magar entrepreneur and mostly inhabited by male Magar carriers who came here to carry the sand. The dormitory was a large tent that contained a small kitchen and about twenty-five bunk beds made of wood. Workers who slept here paid 120 NR per day for food and accommodations.

5. Terry Eugene Bollea (aka Hulk Hogan), Mark William Calaway (aka the Undertaker), and John Cena are American professional wrestlers. Tony Ramos is a retired American amateur wrestler.

6. Ina Zharkevich has pointed out that international labor migration from Nepal is a highly gendered phenomenon. Nearly nine out of ten labor migrants from Nepal to other places abroad are men (2019b:682), and on a daily basis an estimated 1,500 Nepali men are leaving the country to find better employment elsewhere (2019b:686).

Conclusion
Glimpses of Hope

Introduction

This book has explored how Nepal's industrial working class has been affected by the country's entangled processes of rapid urbanization, a growing middle class, and the emergence of new forms of industrial production. By following the hidden lives of those working in such environments, we can better understand how workers and managers conceptualize and enact class, and explore the centrality of labor politics in such processes. Throughout, I have described working-class formations in these new settings in terms of their inflection by the broader political context and the recent history of the country. In the process, my ethnography has revealed that many of those working in these new environments see themselves first of all as wage workers, rather than identifying predominantly along the lines of caste, ethnicity, or gender. Operating in a rapidly changing political context, the experiences of the (industrial) urban workers examined here contradict the widely held assumption that there is a global shift from permanent to casual work. Instead, much of the book has shown how Maoism has affected labor relations in these new industrial and urban work environments and in some cases has helped make labor more, instead of less, secure.

In this concluding chapter, I briefly summarize my findings and reiterate the main arguments put forward in this book. I then discuss the notion of the working class with a wider view on Nepal, comparing it with descriptions of the working classes in neighboring India, and in Bolivia and Egypt, which have also experienced revolutionary or quasi-revolutionary political conditions. After establishing this broader discussion of the Nepalese working class, I then comment on more recent developments with regard to broader political-economic forces. One central aim of this concluding chapter is to ask: Is this a story of hope? This is, first of all, a question of interpretation: to call a narrative hopeful implies a deeper understanding of the objects of people's hopes and their attempts to fulfill them (see Jansen 2021). Certainly from an emic perspective, this seems to be the case: permanent contracts are generally regarded among workers in both Nepalgunj and Pokhara as a valuable asset that raises one's own chances to climb the social ladder. Seen from this point of view, there are good reasons to label the story told here as hopeful. From an etic perspective, however, the situation is less clear. This becomes evident when we explore the conditions for the possibility of hoping through a wider examination of the more recent changes in Nepal's political economy, which is the core subject of this concluding chapter.

Class and Labor Politics at Different Workplaces

This book has shown how urban-industrial working classes have emerged in two distinct places in Nepal: Nepalgunj and Pokhara. This analysis was evidenced in two parts of the book. Part I explored the development of industrial working classes by discussing work in food-processing factories in Nepalgunj, a town in the country's periphery close to the Indian border. Part II examined industrial work and the surrounding informal economy in Pokhara, a town in the mid-hills that has been developed as a destination for foreign tourists during the last few decades. Taken together, the analysis shows a striking similarity: in both cases the contrast between isthai and asthai labor was a significant marker of division inside the factories, echoing the emic distinction between *naukri* and *kam* in the Indian context (see Parry 2020). This type of analysis should not be regarded as a "foreign" or "Western" imposition, as informants themselves distinguished between permanent and casual labor, and regarded this division as the dominant marker of the industrial workforces inside the food-processing factories.

Importantly, as I outlined in chapters 1 through 3, the Maoist unions have played a key role in providing more permanent jobs to casual workers over the years, a successful labor action that has been crucial in the "making" of this bifurcated industrial working class. Chapter 1 posed the question of what Nepal's industrial working class looks like from within a modern industrial factory, and how the broader political-economic context has shaped the textures of class. To address this, I focused on a discussion of work in a modern industrial food-processing factory near the urban municipality Nepalgunj in the Banke district. I showed that, over the past few years, labor in the food-processing factory has become more secure for the Madheshi segment of the workforce. For this ethnic group, moreover, a minimum wage had been implemented, and in contrast with the situation common elsewhere in the region, workers were now represented by leaders from their own social stratum. I argued that all these changes were a product of the pressure placed on management by the Maoist union operating in the factory. As a result, the Maoist union also protected labor from the intensification of work that neoliberal conditions have promoted elsewhere.

Chapter 2 looked more closely at the casual labor force of the same company, who largely hailed from the Tharu ethnic community, some of whom had previously worked as bonded laborers in the wider region. The chapter reflected upon their current life as precarious laborers in a modern industrial food-processing factory. It described how former bonded laborers have begun working as contract workers at the factory with the help of contractors related to them by kin. The chapter further showed that one of the defining features of their new lives as casual laborers was chronic precariousness. Undisguised forms of confrontation, such as open disregard for management's instructions, were also part of their new reality in the labor market. Contract laborers were often strongly assertive in the face of managerial authority, and this assertiveness had been shaped largely by either past experiences or memories of bonded labor. The chapter concluded with a reflection on the limitation of Maoism in the modern food-processing factory. Chapter 3 examined the role of ritual offerings made to religious deities within the new work environments, and how such religious practices propped up the social order. By focusing on such marginal movements, the chapter revealed a hierarchy of ritual practices that maps onto a hierarchy of workers. I argued that such rituals show how industrial elites have made use of spiritual practices in their efforts to integrate a new and diverse labor force. Workers also engaged in religious practices to negotiate their industrial environment as well as the financial and physical stress it caused them. Such new forms of spirituality in the industrial context in western Nepal are inextricably related to the recent political history of the country as well as to broader trends in South Asian industrial development.

Part II (chapters 4–7) expanded on the discussion of the divisions among the working class, as well as the broader influence of the wider politics of labor, albeit in a different setting. Chapter 4 zoomed out of Nepalgunj and reentered the ethnographic terrain through what one may call a "grounded snapshot" of class. Similar to the previous chapters on the lowland region, this chapter showed that militant (Maoist) unionism also affected labor relations in industries within an industrial area in Pokhara in the mid-hills of Nepal. This successful challenging of precarious labor conditions by the Maoist unionists may seem surprising given that the city of Pokhara witnessed little violence during the civil war compared to the lowland region. But successful union interventions in the relationship between capital and labor were limited to large factories, and union activism has been in decline in recent years. I provided various reasons for this decline, including the changing political context, the antagonistic relationship between Nepal's two major unions (which was historically rooted in violence), and the shift from radical militant unionism to a more bureaucratic and standardized organization at the central level. Taken together, then, these four chapters describe what class looks like in Pokhara and Nepalgunj in the context of the food-processing industry, and how the Maoist revolution has shaped the formation of class among these factory workers.

Chapter 5 further developed this analysis of the interplay between revolutionary ideology and industrial labor by looking at the case of the water-bottling industry in the mid-hills of Nepal, where Maoism was largely experienced through its absence. Even though the emergence of the water-bottling industry and the popularity of bottled water can be traced back to revolutionary activism in Nepal's rural countryside, I showed how the hierarchy of labor in the industry remains highly gendered, ethnically stratified, and with little activism occurring in the work environment. This view not only brings to the fore perceptions of change and continuity on the workplace or shop floor, but also indicates that the Maoist revolution had an impact in only certain pockets of industrial labor in Nepal.

The last two ethnographic chapters of the book (chapters 6 and 7) discussed class and its labor politics in the informal economy of Pokhara through an ethno-historical and anthropological discussion of labor in the local construction industry, and the related sand-mining industries near the riverbeds of the city. Chapter 6 focused on the life-worlds of builders and their workforces in this town in the mid-hills of Nepal. In the chapter, I examined the character of the construction industry and how the class situation of builders differed from those of their workforces. I argued that builders (who often engage in both manual and managerial work) and manual laborers (e.g., masons, helpers) often live in two different economic worlds and thereby constitute two different class segments. Furthermore, the chapter sheds light on the class differentiation among manual laborers in the construction industry, highlighting how this population remains divided along lines of locality, ethnicity, and gender. I argued that laborers have not been able to unite politically as a working class and challenge their employers because years of post-revolutionary unionization efforts in the construction industry have benefited largely only the builders to the detriment of the manual laborers. The chapter concluded that this process of dual economic stratification mirrors the broader trends in Nepal.

In chapter 7, I offered a descriptive analysis of the working worlds of sand miners along a river near Pokhara. I argued that the sand mines in the region were effectively mafia-run, but those who worked in them did not resent their mafioso employers and instead viewed them as patrons who provide much-needed employment. Focusing on the everyday work practices in a sand mine, the chapter highlighted workers' understanding of sand-mine work, which ranged from viewing sand mines as springboards to better-paid jobs in faraway countries, to more negative renderings of sand mines as dangerous, risky places. It further showed that workers mediate this tension between their attempts to achieve "big dreams" of upward socioeconomic mobility and their fears of workplace accidents by engaging in shamanistic practices.

Taken together, these "grounded snapshots of class" offer an image of the contemporary condition of Nepal's working class. As in neighboring India (Parry 2020; Strümpell 2014b), Nepali workers identify themselves nowadays primarily as wage laborers rather than through the lenses of caste, ethnicity, and gender. They have a clear sense of the importance of the distinction between permanent and casual work, and the relationship between those who have a permanent job and those who have casual work seemed to be an oppositional one—at least within the food-processing factories I examined. The relationship between them may even be one of exploitation. Importantly, at the heart of the different grounded snapshots of class was the interplay between gender, ethnicity, and class at such workplaces. In the case of Nepalgunj, ethnicity mapped neatly onto the hierarchies of labor. Those who had a permanent job were most likely Madheshi locals or were from an Indian background. Those who worked as casual laborers were more likely from the Tharu ethnic group. In Pokhara, the division was less about permanent versus casual and more about larger versus smaller factories. It was in the larger factories that laborers from indigenous backgrounds benefited substantially from Maoist activism. In small factories, there was little Maoist activism and many of the workers still had casual contracts.

Similarly, in the discussions of Pokhara's informal economy, an image of a divided working class emerged. In the construction industry, I encountered workers who had moved up to the position of contractor and were leading what was considered a middle-class lifestyle. In the sand mine, we encountered workers whose forms of upward mobility were achieved either through becoming a contractor or, more frequently, by using the earnings from mine work to move abroad, save money there, and then return to open a small business back in Nepal.

The overall image that this book tries to convey is that there is a division in the informal economy between the labor elites and the common workers, and that ethnic identities map upon this division in important ways. Each chapter demonstrates the increasing importance of class as a marker of identity, while the importance of caste has been in decline. Another significant point is the extent to which classes have been mobilized by the revolutionary Maoists in the immediate aftermath of the conflict. Importantly, as I have shown in chapters 1–4, such activism has been in decline, and there has been a return to more moderate measures.

The Contrast to Other Settings

Self-identification as a wage worker is central to the sense of self among many of the workers in Nepalgunj and Pokhara. How do such findings compare to other ethnographic settings in Nepal and elsewhere? To begin this discussion, it should be noted that Mallika Shakya's (2018) ethnography among garment workers in Kathmandu emphasizes the importance of skill in the way workers identify themselves, rather than the division between isthai and asthai kam. Accordingly, international trade politics mattered much more in the case of the Kathmandu garment workers than in the cases examined in this book. As detailed by Shakya (2018), the garment industry emerged in Kathmandu's streets after Nepal signed the Multi-Fiber Agreement (MFA) with the United States. The latter encouraged countries such as Nepal, Bangladesh, and Sri Lanka to produce a certain quantity of garments per year. After the ratification of the treaty, the Kathmandu-based garment industry evolved quickly, and at its height it employed some ten thousand workers in Kathmandu. But the MFA was canceled in 2004, and with it the industry quickly declined, culminating in the death of an industry. As in the cases described in this book, the Maoist unions were very active toward the end of this decline and began to organize workers who felt betrayed by their traditional union representatives. Their activism, however, only contributed to the decline of the industry, giving it the final push over the cliff. In contrast, the activism of the Maoists in the food and housing industry was less destructive, as food companies operated in a sector that was very profitable, and less impacted by changes at the international trade level.

Beyond Nepal, this book invites a direct comparison with the situation of labor in other revolutionary situations. Thomas Grisaffi's (2019) outstanding ethnographic study of a union of coca growers in Bolivia under the rule of Evo Morales, and Dina Makram-Ebeid's (2012, 2015, 2019) seminal discussions of steel workers in the wake of the Egyptian revolution remain important reference points. While one might argue that both ethnographic accounts are unique since they deal with quite iconic workers—coca growers who saw their leader become president and public-sector steel workers who were once seen as nation-builders—both accounts allow us to gain a better understanding of how labor has experienced periods of rapid political change in different contexts. To begin with, in his vivid ethnography, Grisaffi shows how Bolivian coca growers transformed from a criminalized union into a strong social movement with a vernacular vision of "radical democracy." Focusing his ethnographic account on coca growers in the tropical Chapare region, Grisaffi's account reveals two important insights regarding what happens when a strong labor-based movement comes into power. First, once in power, Evo Morales faced the difficulty of having to appease both his constituency of coca growers and the international community that lobbied for its eradication. By trying to appease both, Morales gradually lost the support of his base. Second, the account shows how, in the process of achieving power, an alternative "direct-action" vision of democracy got lost. The coca growers—with whom Grisaffi spent his time during fieldwork—were demanding that their leadership follow the principle of "leading by obeying" (2019:11). But once in power, Morales had to adopt the liberal vision of democracy. Unsurprisingly, then, the rise of the revolutionary MAS movement led by Morales caused much disillusionment among the coca growers. This scenario is not so far from the situation described in the food industries in

Nepalgunj. Once in power, the Maoists only focused on empowering a certain ethnic segment of the workforce—the Madheshis—thereby alienating other workers from the ethnic Tharu community and leading to an uneven distribution of disappointment with the Maoist movement.

Similarly, Makram-Ebeid's work (2012, 2015, 2019) on the Egyptian Iron and Steel Company (EISCO) located in the company town of Helwan, close to Cairo, explores workers' lives under conditions of revolutionary change. Her account emphasizes that in contemporary Helwan, workers identify themselves through wage work rather than through more traditional identities. As in the food-processing factories considered in this book, the crucial distinction in Helwan was between those who had a permanent job (*muwazzfa*) and those who remained employed on the basis of a casual contract (*urzuquia*). But Makram-Ebeid's writings impressively show how Egypt's "revolution" was in fact a mere political reform that only benefited those who had a permanent contract, while neglecting many casual workers. As in Grisaffi's case, Makram-Ebeid's writings movingly tell the story of how the Egyptian revolution unfolded differently for different types of steel workers and gave way to disappointment and a sense of betrayal among ordinary workers. Similar to her account, this book has described the complicated reasons for the decline of activism in the various workplaces discussed. At the risk of oversimplification, it should be noted, however, that it was a combination of political reform for a tiny working-class elite and the loss of hope in the workers invested in the Maoist cause that precipitated the decline in activism.

Recent Developments and the Room to Maneuver Left

In recent years, several geographers and anthropologists have focused on the role of Chinese aid after the disastrous earthquakes of 2015, and on Nepal's recent inclusion into China's Belt and Road Initiative (BRI) (Campbell 2010, 2013). From this new emerging corpus of work on Nepal-China relations, it appears that in recent years China has begun to expand its political and economic influence in Nepal. This is evidenced by new forms of infrastructure-oriented aid, the cultivation of public-private partnerships involving Chinese firms, as well as the intensification of "trans-Himalayan" trade, the latter being characterized by Galen Murton and colleagues (2016) as a "handshake across the Himalayas" (ibid 2016:403). In fact, in more recent years trans-Himalayan power corridors have appeared in the mountainous areas of the country (Murton and Lord 2020), and it is estimated that around 90 percent of foreign direct assistance to Nepal now comes from China (Paudel 2019).

Of course, Chinese-led investment in infrastructure projects in Nepal is nothing new. It is known that ever since Nepal established formal diplomatic relations with China on 1 August 1955, China has been investing in the building of various infrastructure projects in Nepal, which often leads to diplomatic tensions between Nepal and India. What is new is the scale of Chinese investment in Nepal, and the fact that Nepal's government has recently changed the law to allow foreign companies to own a company in Nepal. For example, Li Hongxuan and Huang Dekai point out that "in terms of economic and trade investment, in 2019, China's project contract value and turnover in Nepal increased by 12.9 percent and 39.6 percent year-on-year, China's non-financial direct investment in Nepal increased by 96.1 percent, and the total bilateral trade between China and Nepal increased by 37.9 percent year-on-year" (2019:1).

Although China's growing influence over the political economy of Nepal is thus undisputed, the question remains: what consequences might this have for industrial and construction labor across the country? The pessimistic view might be that new Chinese-led investments in Nepal and the establishment of Chinese-owned industries across the country might mean bad news for the small industrial workforce of the country, as Chinese-owned companies might bring their own laborers and not create new employment opportunities for Nepalese laborers. At best, such a view might suggest that China will establish new industries but will deprive the workers of their right to organize and collectively bargain for better pay and employment conditions.

Anthropological insights on labor in the context of the Zambian Copperbelt in Africa, however, might be able to fend off such predictable, stereotypical arguments. For example, the anthropologist Ching Kwan Lee writes in her ethnographic work on Zambian copper mines that "despite widespread rumors, scholarly research has not found any empirical evidence to substantiate the claim that Chinese companies bring their own manual workers rather than hiring local Africans" (2018:42). Furthermore, of the three Copperbelt mining companies she studied, the Chinese-owned one has had the most effective labor union, as it hired through a single contractor.

The insights from this book suggest that, at least in some pockets of the economy, Nepal's labor force displayed a strong assertiveness and successfully claimed its labor rights. In this regard, Nepal remains an outlier in the context of the global decline in labor activism and the continuing devaluation of labor by capital around the world. The same insights also make me more optimistic about the most recent Chinese-led investments in Nepal and the possible reconfigurations of Nepal's working classes. It might be—as in the African Copperbelt—that Nepalese labor will successfully adapt to the new proliferation of Chinese investments across the country, and such initiatives might even strengthen Nepal's union activism. But it is also true that historical trajectories are hard to predict and could also develop in the opposite direction. Time will tell, and I leave it to future anthropologists to engage with this wider research agenda. What I hope to have clearly established throughout this book, however, is that there remain glimpses of hope for a better future.

GLOSSARY

aafno manchhe	one's own people
allare	carefree
andhabishwas	superstition
andolan	protest
asthai kam	temporary work
bandh	strike
bhut	ghost
chanda	voluntary donation
chowk	road junction
chuwa-choot	untouchability
dashain	religious festival
daru	alcoholic beverage
dainik jaladari kam	daily wage work
dhalai	the pouring of concrete
dhoka puja	worship of the door
guruwar	shaman
isthai kam	permanent work
ijjat	honor
janajati	indigenous group
jhakri	shaman

Kali	Hindu goddess
kamaiya	debt-bonded laborer
kaniwalla	sand miner
khataranāka	dangerous
Madheshi	lowland dweller
masan	malevolent spirit
mehnat	hardworking
mela	fair
mistriharu	mason workers
namlo	headscarf
paledar	loader
peshgi	advance
phaida	profit
phohari kura	dirty talk
PLA	People's Liberation Army
pujari	priest
rudhiwadi	conservative
sardar	boss
swatantra	freedom
thekedar	contractor
thunse	basket
Vastuu Shastra	Practice of Geomancy
Vishwakarma	Hindu god
Yarsagumbaa	caterpillar fungus
YCL	Young Communist League

REFERENCES

Adhikari, Aditya. 2014. *The Bullet and the Ballot Box: The Story of Nepal's Maoist Revolution*. London: Verso.

Adhikari, Jagannath, and David Seddon. 2002. *Pokhara: Biography of a Town*. Kathmandu: Mandala Book Point.

Adhikari, R. 2013. "Empowered Wives and Frustrated Husbands: Nursing, Gender and Migrant Nepali in the UK." *Int Migr* 51: 168–179.

"Agreement with Maoist Fighters Offers New Hope for Nepali Government." 2011. The National, 3 November. Retrieved 27 September 2017 from https://www.thenational.ae/world/asia/agreement-with-maoist-fighters-offers-new-hope-for-nepali-government-1.452061.

Bampton, James, and Bruno Cammaert. 2007. "How Can Timber Rents Better Contribute to Poverty Reduction through Community Forestry in the Terai Region of Nepal?" *Journal of Forest and Livelihood* 6(1): 28–47.

Baral, Umanath. 2018. "Impact of Trade Union in the Hotel Workers." *Journal of Political Science* 18: 143–166.

Beiser, Vince. 2018. *The World in a Grain*. New York: Riverhead Books.

Bernstein, Henry. 2006. "Is There an Agrarian Question in the 21st Century?" *Canadian Journal of Development Studies* 27(4): 449–460.

Bhatterai, Baburam. 2003. *The Nature of Underdevelopment and Regional Structure in Nepal: A Marxist Analysis*. Delhi, Androit.

——. 2004. "The Question of Building a New Type of State." *The Worker* 9: 1–26.

Blaikie, Piers, John Cameron, and David Seddon. 2002. "Understanding 20 Years of Change in West-Central Nepal: Continuity and Change in Lives and Ideas." *World Development* 30(7): 1255–1270.

Blaikie, Piers M., John Cameron, and John David Seddon. 2005 [1980]. *Nepal in Crisis: Growth and Stagnation at the Periphery*. Revised and Enlarged, Kindle edition. New Delhi: Adroit Publishers.

Blanchette, Alexander. 2018. "Industrial Meat Production." *Annual Review of Anthropology* 47: 185–199.

Blanchette, Alexander. 2020. *Porkopolis: Standardized Life, American Animality, and the "Factory" Farm*. Durham, NC: Duke University Press.

Blom Hansen, Thomas. 1999. *The Saffron Wave: Democracy and Hindu Nationalism in Modern India*. Princeton, NJ: Princeton University Press.

Braverman, Harry. 1974. *Labor and Monopoly Capital: The Degradation of Work in the Twentieth Century*. New York: Monthly Review Press.

Breman, Jan. 1994. *Wage Hunters and Gatherers: Search for Work in the Urban and Rural Economy of South Gujarat*. Delhi: Oxford University Press.

———. 1996. *Footloose Labor: Working in India's Informal Economy*. Cambridge: Cambridge University Press.

———. 2004. *The Making and Unmaking of an Industrial Working Class: Sliding Down the Labor Hierarchy in Ahmedabad*. New York: Oxford University Press.

———. 2013. "A Bogus Concept?" *New Left Review* 84: 130–138.

Bren d'Amour, C., Pandey, M. Reba, S. Ahmad, F. Creutzig, and K. C. Seto. 2020. "Urbanization, Processed Foods, and Eating Out in India." *Global Food Security* 25: 100361.

Bruslé, T. 2010a. "Nepalese Migrations: Introduction." *European Bulletin of Himalayan Research* (35–36): 16–23.

———. 2010b. "Who's in a Labor Camp? A Socio-Economic Analysis of Nepalese Migrants in Qatar." *European Bulletin of Himalayan Research* (35–36): 154–170.

Burawoy, Michael. 1979. *Manufacturing Consent: Changes in the Labor Process under Monopoly Capitalism*. Chicago: University of Chicago Press.

———. 1985. *The Politics of Production: Factory Regimes Under Capitalism and Socialism*. London: Verso.

Campbell, B. 2013. "From Remote Area to Thoroughfare of Globalisation: Shifting Territorialisations of Development and Border Peasantry in Nepal." In *Territorial Changes and Territorial Restructurings in the Himalayas*, ed. J. Smadja, 269–285. New Delhi: Adroit Publishers.

Campbell, Ben. 2010. "Rhetorical Routes for Development: a Road Project in Nepal." *Contemporary South Asia* 18(3): 267–279.

Carrier, James G. 2012. "The Trouble with Class." *European Journal of Sociology* 53(3): 263–284.

Carrier, James. 2015. "The Concept of Class." In *Anthropologies of Class: Power, Practice and Inequality*, ed. James Carrier and Don Kalb, 28–41. Cambridge: Cambridge University Press.

Carrier, James, and Don Kalb. 2015. *Anthropologies of Class: Power, Practice and Inequality*. Cambridge: Cambridge University Press.

Chaudhary, Binod. 2016. *Making It Big: The Inspiring Story of Nepal's First Billionaire in His Own Words*. London: Penguin.

Chhetri, R. B. 2005. "The Plight of the Tharu Kamaiyas in Nepal: A Review of the Social, Economic and Political Facets." *Occasional Papers in Sociology and Anthropology* 9: 22–46.

Comaroff, Jean, and John L. Comaroff. 1999. "Occult Economies and the Violence of Abstraction: Notes from the South African Postcolony." *American Ethnologist* 26(2): 279–303.

Comaroff, Jean, and John Comaroff. 2000. *Millennial Capitalism and the Culture of Neoliberalism*. Durham, NC: Duke University Press.

Crawford, Mary, Gregory Kerwin, Alka Gurung, Deepti Khati, Pinky Jha, and Anjana Chalise Regmi. 2008. "Globalizing Beauty: Attitudes toward Beauty Pageants among Nepali Women." *Feminism & Psychology* 18(1): 61–86.

Cross, Jamie. 2012. "Technological Intimacy: Re-engaging with Gender and Technology in the Global Factory." *Ethnography* 13(2): 119–143.

———. 2014. *Dream Zones: Anticipating Capitalism and Development in India*. London: Pluto Press.

———. 2019. "The Solar Good: Energy Ethics in Poor Markets." *Journal of the Royal Anthropological Institute* 25(S1): 47–66.

Da Col, Giovanni. 2007. "The View from Somewhen: Events, Bodies and the Perspective of Fortune around Khawa Kapro, a Tibetan Sacred Mountain in Yunnan Province." *Inner Asia* 9(2): 215–235.

Davies, James, and Dimitrina Spencer. 2010. *Emotions in the Field: The Psychology and Anthropology of Fieldwork Experience*. Stanford, CA: Stanford University Press.

De Neve, Geert. 1999. "Asking for and Giving Baki: Neo-bondage, or the Interplay of Bondage and Resistance in the Tamil Nadu Power-Loom Industry." *Contributions to Indian Sociology* 33(1–2): 379–406.

———. 2000. "Patronage and 'Community': The Role of a Tamil 'Village' Festival in the Integration of a Town." *Journal of the Royal Anthropological Institute* 6(3): 501–519.

———. 2005. *The Everyday Politics of Labor: Working Lives in India's Informal Economy*. New Delhi: Social Science Press.

De Sales, Anne. 2000. "The Kham-Magar Country, Nepal: Between Ethnic Claims and Maoism." *European Bulletin of Himalayan Research* 19: 41–71.

Dhakal, Gita. 2009. "Women's Experiences of Sexual Harassment in Carpet Factories." *Journal of Nepal Health Research Council* 7(15): 98–102.

Dhruba, Kumar. 2010. *Electoral Violence and Volatility in Nepal*. Kathmandu: Vajra.

Donner, Henrike, ed. 2011. *Being Middle Class in India: A Way of Life*. London: Routledge.

Dunn, Elizabeth. 2004. *Baby Food, Big Business, and the Remaking of Labor*. Ithaca, NY: Cornell University Press.

Eerington, Frederick, Tatsuro Fujikura, Deborah Gewertz. 2013. *The Noodle Narratives: The Global Rise of an Industrial Food into the Twenty-First Century*. Berkeley: University of California Press.

Engelshoven, Miranda. 1999. "Diamond and Patels: A Report on the Diamond Industry in Surat." *Contributions to Indian Sociology* 33(1–2): 353–377.

Ferguson, James. 1999. *Expectations of Modernity: Myths and Meanings of Urban Life on the Zambian Cooperbelt*. Berkeley: University of California Press.

Fernandes, Leela. 1997. *Producing Workers. The Politics of Gender, Class, and Culture in the Calcutta Jute Mills*. Philadelphia: University of Pennsylvania Press.

Forbes. 2020. *Binod Chaudhary*. Retrieved on 20 November 2020 from https://www.forbes.com/profile/binod-chaudhary/

Fujikura, Tatsuro. 2001. "Emancipation of Kamaiyas: Development, Social movement, and Youth Activism in Post-Jana Andolan Nepal." *Himalayan Research Bulletin* XXI: 29–35.

———. 2003. "The Role of Collective Imagination in the Maoist Conflict in Nepal." *Himalaya* XXIII: 21–30.

———. 2007. "The Bonded Agricultural Laborers' Freedom Movement in Western Nepal." In *Political and Social Transformations in North India and Nepal*, vol. 2, ed. Hiroshi Ishii, David N. Gellner, and Katsuo Nawa, 319–359. New Delhi: Manohar Books.

Gardener, Andrew. 2010. *City of Strangers: Gulf Migration and the Indian Community in Bahrain*. Cornell, NY: Cornell University Press.

———. 2012. "Why Do They Keep Coming? Labor Migrants in the Persian Gulf States." In *Migrant Labor in the Persian Gulf*, ed. Mehran Kamrava and Zahra Babar, 41–58. New York: Columbia University Press.

Gautam, Meera. 2018. "Role of Manufacturing Industries in Nepalese Economy." *Management Dynamics* 21(1): 36–45.

Geertz, Clifford. 1973. *Thick Description: Towards an Interpretative Theory of Culture*. New York: Basic Books.

Gellner, David. 1994. "Priests, Healers, Mediums and Witches: The Context of Possession in the Kathmandu Valley, Nepal." *Man* 29(1): 27–48.

Gill, T. 2001. *Men of Uncertainty: The Social Organization of Day Laborers in Contemporary Japan*. Albany: State University of New York Press.

Gleick, Peter. 2010. *Bottled and Sold: The Story Behind Our Obsession with Bottled Water*. Washington: Island Press.

Gosh, Kaushik. 1982. "A Market for Aboriginality: Primitivism and Race Classification in the Indentured Labor Market of Colonial India." *Subaltern Studies* 10: 8–48.

Grisaffi, Thomas. 2019. *Coca Yes, Cocaine No: How Bolivia's Coca Growers Reshaped Democracy*. Durham, NC: Duke University Press.

Guardian. 2018. "French Journalists Labelled Spies over Indian Mining Investigation." Retrieved on 18 May 2019 from https://www.theguardian.com/world/2018/dec/05/french-journalists-labelled-spies-india-sand mining-assignment.

Guneratne, Arun. 2002. *Many Tongues, One People: The Making of Tharu Identity in Nepal.* Ithaca, NY: Cornell University Press.

Hagen, Tony. 1969. *Report on the Geological Survey of Nepal: Preliminary Reconnaissance. Denkschriften der Schweizerischen Naturforschenden Gesellschaft.* 86. Art. Institut Orell Füssli.

Hann, Chris, and Jonathan Parry. 2018. *Industrial Labor on the Margins of Capitalism: Precarity, Class, and the Neoliberal Subject.* New York: Berghahn Books.

Harriss-White, Barbara. 2003. *India Working: Essays on Society and Economy.* Cambridge: Cambridge University Press.

Harriss-White, Barbara, and Lucia Michelutti. 2020. *The Wild East: Criminal Political Economies in South Asia.* Chicago: University of Chicago Press.

Harvey, David. 2003. *The New Imperialism.* Oxford: Oxford University Press.

Hirslund, Dan. 2021. "Brokering Labor: The Politics of Markets in the Kathmandu Construction Industry." *Ethnography* 22(4): 495–514.

Hoffmann, Michael Peter. 2014a. "Red Salute at Work: Brick Factory Work in Postconflict Kailali, Western Nepal." *Focaal* 70: 67–80.

———. 2014b. "A Symbiotic Coexistence: Nepal's Maoist Movement and Labor Unions in an Urban Municipality in Post-Conflict Far-Western Tarai." *Journal of South Asian Development* 9: 213–234.

———. 2015. "In the Shadows of the Maoist Revolution: On the Role of the 'People's War' in Facilitating the Occupation of Symbolic Space in Western Nepal." *Critique of Anthropology* 35(4): 389–406.

———. 2017. "Unfree Labour after the Maoist Revolution in Western Nepal." *Contributions to Indian Sociology* 51(2): 139–162.

———. 2018a. *The Partial Revolution: Labour, Social Movements and the Invisible Hand of Mao in Western Nepal.* New York: Berghahn Books.

———. 2018b. "From Casual to Permanent Work: Maoist Unionists and the Regularization of Contract Labor in the Industries of Western Nepal." In *Industrial Labor on the Margins of Capitalism: Precarity, Class, and the Neoliberal Subject*, ed. Chris Hann and Jonathan Parry, 336–354. New York: Berghahn Books.

———. 2018c. "From Bonded to Industrial Labor: Precarity, Maoism and Ethnicity in a Modern-Industrial Food Processing Factory in Western Nepal." *Modern Asian Studies* 52(6): 1917–1937.

———. 2020. "Work, Precarity and Militant Unionism in an Industrial Area in the Mid-Hills of Nepal." *History and Anthropology* (early online publication): 1–16.

———. 2021. "Digging for Sand after the Revolution: Mafia, Labor, and Shamanism in a Nepali Sand Mine." *Dialectical Anthropology* 45(2): 117–133.

———. 2023. "Uneven and Combined Development in Nepal: Industrial Food Factories, Unions and the Urban Anticipation Economy." In *Industrial Labor in an Unequal World*, ed. Christian Strümpell and Michael Hoffmann. Berlin: De Gruyter.

Holmstroem, Mark. 1976. South Indian Factory Workers: Their Life and Their World. Cambridge: Cambridge University Press.

———. 1984. *Industry and Inequality: The Social Anthropology of Indian Labor.* Cambridge: Cambridge University Press.

Hongxuan, Li, and Huang Dekai. 2021. "Connected by the Highest Peak of the World: A Review of Nepal-China Friendship." Retrieved 11 March 2022 from https://english.onlinekhabar.com/connected-by-the-highest-peak-of-the-world-a-review-of-nepal-china-friendship.html.

Hoque, Ashraf, and Lucia Michelutti. 2018. "Brushing with Organized Crime and Democracy: The Art of Making do in South Asia." *Journal of Asian Studies* 77(4): 991–1011.

ILO. 2005. *Sexual Harassment at the Workplace in Nepal*. International Labor Office, Geneva: ILO Press.

Ingold, Tim. 2001. "Beyond Art and Technology: The Anthropology of Skill." In *Anthropological Perspectives on Technology*, ed. Michael Schiffer, 17–31. Albuquerque: University of New Mexico Press.

Ismail, Feyzi, and Alpa Shah. 2015. "Class Struggle, the Maoists and the Indigenous Question in Nepal." *Economic and Political Weekly* 50(35): 112–123.

Jansen, Stef. 2021. "The Anthropology of Hope." *Oxford Research Encyclopedia of Anthropology.* 22 January 2021. Retrieved 6 March 2022 from https://oxfordre.com/anthropology/view/10.1093/acrefore/9780190854584.001.0001/acrefore-9780190854584-e-182.

Jeffrey, Craig. 2010. *Timepass: Youth, Class, and the Politics of Waiting in India*. Stanford, CA: Stanford University Press.

Jewell, John. 2014. "Bottled Water Is the Marketing Trick of the Century." Retrieved 12 March 2022 from https://theconversation.com/bottled-water-is-the-marketing-trick-of-the-century-25842.

Jha, Manish. 2016. "Waiting for an Industrial Revolution." *Nepali Times* 827: 23–29. Retrieved 12 March 2022 from https://archive.nepalitimes.com/regular-columns/Economic-Class/waiting-for-an-industrial-revolution,784.

Joshi, Chitra. 2003. *Lost Worlds: Indian Labour and Its Forgotten Histories*. New Delhi: Permanent Black.

Kalb, Don. 1997. *Expanding Class: Power and Everyday Politics in Industrial Communities, The Netherlands, 1850–1950*. Durham, NC: Duke University Press.

———. "Class: The Urban Commons and the Empty Sign of 'the Middle Class' in the Twenty-First Century." In *A Companion to Urban Anthropology*, ed. Donald M. Nonini, 155–176. New York: Wiley.

Kantha, Pramoud. 2010. "Maoist-Madheshi Dynamics and Nepal's Peace Process." In *The Maoist Insurgency in Nepal: Revolution in the Twenty-First Century*, ed. Mahendra Lawoti, 156–171. Contemporary South Asia Series 20. New York. Routledge.

Kapadia, Karin. 1995. "The Profitability of Bonded Labor: The Gem-Cutting Industry in Rural South India." *Journal of Peasant Studies* 22(3): 446–483.

Kathmandu Post. 2014. "Pokhara 'at Risk' Due to Rampant Sand Mining." 12 July 2014. Retrieved 7 July 2020 from https://kathmandupost.com/national/2014/07/12/pokhara-at-risk-due-to-rampant-sand mining.

———. 2017. "Illegal Extraction of Sand on the Rise." 30 July 2017. Retrieved 2 July 2017 from https://kathmandupost.com/money/2017/07/30/illegal-extraction-of-sand-on-the-rise.

———. 2018. "Indian Construction Workers Coming to Nepal in Droves." 21 January 2018. Retrieved 30 January 2019 from https://kathmandupost.com/money/2018/01/21/indian-construction-workers-coming-to-nepal-in-droves.

———. 2019. "Everything You Need to Know about the Biggest Gold Smuggling Racket in Nepal." Retrieved 2 July 2020 from https://kathmandupost.com/national/2019/03/13/everything-you-need-to-know-about-the-biggest-gold-smuggling-racket-in-nepal.

———. 2020. "Government Sets Maximum Retail Price of Bottled Water." Retrieved 12 March 2022 from https://kathmandupost.com/money/2020/08/10/government-sets-maximum-retail-price-of-bottled-water-prices-reduced.

Keskülla, Eeva. 2018. "Miners and Their Children: The Re-making of the Soviet Working Class in Kazakhstan." In *Industrial Labor on the Margins of Capitalism: Precarity, Class, and the Neoliberal Subject*, ed. Chris Hann and Jonathan Parry, 61–84. New York: Berghahn Books.

Khadka, Narayan. 2000. "U.S. Aid to Nepal in the Cold War Period: Lessons for the Future." *Pacific Affairs* 73(1): 77–95.

Khilnani, Sunil. 1997. *The Idea of India*. London: Hamish Hamilton Ltd.

Kofti, Dimitra. 2018. "Regular Work in Decline, Precarious Households, and Changing Solidarities in Bulgaria." In *Industrial Labor on the Margins of Capitalism: Precarity, Class, and the Neoliberal Subject*, ed. Chris Hann and Jonathan Parry, 111–133. New York: Berghahn Books.

Koirala, Srijana, and Megh Raj Koirala. 2019. "Nepal Is Going Urban." *MyRepublica*. Retrieved 10 March 2022 from https://myrepublica.nagariknetwork.com/news/nepal-is-going-urban/.

Kondos, Alex. 1991. "A Preliminary Study of the Private Sector of Nepal's Manufacturing Industry." *Contributions to Nepalese Studies* 18(1): 29–39.

Kondos, Alex, Vivienne Kondos, and Indra Ban. 1991. "Some Sociocultural Aspects of Private Industrial Capital in Nepal." *Contributions to Nepalese Studies* 18(2): 175–197.

———. 1992. "Nepal's Industrial Capitalist Class: 'Origin' and 'Behaviour.'" *South Asia: Journal of South Asian Studies* 15(1): 81–103.

Kumar, Nita. 1988. *The Artisans of Banaras: Popular Culture and Identity, 1880–1986*. Princeton, NJ: Princeton University Press.

Kwan Lee, Ching. 2018. "Varieties of Capital, Fracture of Labor: A Comparative Ethnography of Subcontracting and Labor Precarity on the Zambian Copperbelt." In *Industrial Labor on the Margins of Capitalism: Precarity, Class, and the Neoliberal Subject*, ed. Chris Hann and Jonathan Parry, 39–60. New York: Berghahn Books.

Lawoti, Mahendra. 2005. *Towards a Democratic Nepal: Inclusive Political Institutions for a Multicultural Society*. New Delhi: SAGE Publications.

Lawoti, Mahendra, and Anup Pahari. 2010. *Maoist Insurgency in Nepal*. New York: Routledge.

Lazar, Sian. 2012. "Disjunctive Comparison: Citizenship and Trade Unionism in Bolivia and Argentina." *Journal of the Royal Anthropological Institute* 18(2): 349–368.

Lazar, Sian, and Andrew Sanchez. 2019. "Understanding Labor Politics in an Age of Precarity." *Dialectical Anthropology* 43(1): 3–14.

Liechty, Marc. 2003. *Suitably Modern: Making Middle-Class Culture in a New Consumer Society*. Princeton, NJ: Princeton University Press.

———. 2017. *Far Out: Countercultural Seekers and the Tourist Encounter in Nepal*. Chicago: University of Chicago Press.

Lüdtke, Alf. 1993. *Eigen-Sinn. Fabrikalltag, Arbeitserfahrungen und Politik vom Kaiserreich bis in den Faschismus*. Hamburg: Ergebnisse Verlag.

Makram-Ebeid, Dina. 2012. "Manufacturing Stability: Everyday Politics of Work in an Industrial Steel Town in Helwan, Egypt." Retrieved 12 March 2022 from http://etheses.lse.ac.uk/780/.

———. 2015. "Labour Struggles and the Quest for Permanent Employment in Revolutionary Egypt." In *The Political Economy of the New Egyptian Republic*, ed. Nicholas S. Hopkins, 65–84. Cairo: American University in Cairo Press.

———. 2018. "Between God and the State: Class, Precarity, and Cosmology on the Margins of an Egyptian Steel Town." In *Industrial Labor on the Margins of Capitalism: Precarity, Class, and the Neoliberal Subject*, ed. Chris Hann and Jonathan Parry, 180–196. New York: Berghahn Books.

———. 2019. "Precarious Revolution: Labor and Neoliberal Securitization in Egypt." *Dialectical Anthropology* 43(1): 139–154.

Marcus, George. 1995. "Ethnography in/of the World System: The Emergence of Multi-Sited Ethnography." *Annual Review of Anthropology* 24(1): 95–117.

Marschke, Melissa, Jean-Francois Francois, Laura Schönberger, and Michael Hoffmann. 2020. "Roving Bandits and Looted Coastlines: How the Global Appetite for Sand is Fuelling a Crisis." *The Conversation*. 3 May 2020. Retrieved 2 July 2020 from https://theconversation.com/roving-bandits-and-looted-coastlines-how-the-global-appetite-for-sand-is-fuelling-a-crisis-132412.

Martin, Nicolas, and Lucia Michelutti. 2017. "Protection Rackets and Party Machines: Comparative Ethnographies of 'Mafia Raj' in North India." *Asian Journal of Social Science* 45(6): 692–722.

Marx, Karl. 1977 [1848]. "The Communist Manifesto." In *Karl Marx: Selected Writings*, ed. D. McLellan, 221–247. Oxford: Oxford University Press.

Maycock, Matthew. 2015. "Hegemonic at Home and Subaltern Abroad: Kamaiya Masculinities and Changing Mobility in Nepal." *Gender, Place & Culture: A Journal of Feminist Geography* 24(6): 812–822.

———. 2018. *Masculinity and Modern Slavery in Nepal: Transitions into Freedom*. London: Routledge.

Michelutti, Lucia. 2020. "The Inter-State Criminal Life of Sand and Oil in North India, Western Uttar Pradesh." In *The Wild East*, ed. Barbara Harriss-White and Lucia Michelutti, 168–193. London: UCL Press.

Michelutti, Lucia, Ashraf Hoque, Nicolas Martin, David Picherit, Paul Rollier, Arild Ruud, and Clarinda Still. 2018. *Mafia Raj: The Rule of Bosses in South Asia*. Stanford, CA: Stanford University Press.

Miklian, Jason. 2009. "Nepal's Tarai: Constructing an Ethnic Conflict." *South Asia Briefing Paper* No 1., Prio paper. Oslo: PRIO.

Millar, Kathleen. 2015. "The Tempo of Wageless Work: E.P. Thompson's Time-Sense at the Edges of Rio de Janeiro." *Focaal* 73(13): 28–40.

Mohapatra, Prabhu Prasad. 1985. "Coolies and Colliers: A Study of the Agrarian Context of Labor Migration from Chotanagpur,1880–1920." *Studies in History* 1(2): 247–303.

Mollona, Massimiliano. 2009a. *Made in Sheffield: An Ethnography of Industrial Work and Politics*. Oxford: Berghahn Books.

———. 2009b. 'Community Unionism versus Business Unionism: The Return of the Moral Economy in Trade Union Studies', *American Ethnologist* 36(4): 651–666.

———. 2020. *Brazilian Steel Town. Machines, Land, Money and Commoning in the Making of the Working Class*. New York: Berghahn Books.

Mollona, Massimiliano, Geert De Neve, and Jonathan Parry, eds. 2020. *Industrial Work and Life: An Anthropological Reader*. London: Routledge.

Mosse, David. 2005. *Cultivating Development: An Ethnography of Aid Policy and Practice*. London: Pluto Press.

Murton, Galen, and Austin Lord. 2020. "Trans-Himalayan Power Corridors: Infrastructural Politics and China's Belt and Road Initiative in Nepal." *Political Geography* 77: 102100.

Murton, Galen, Austin Lord, and Robert Beazley. 2016. "A Handshake across the Himalayas: Chinese Investment, Hydropower Development, and State Formation in Nepal." *Eurasian Geography and Economics* 57(3): 403–432.

Nash, June. 1979. *We Eat the Mines and the Mines Eat Us: Dependency and Exploitation in Bolivian Tin Mines*. New York: Columbia University Press.

Nelson, Andrew. 2015. "Classquake: What the Global Media Missed in Nepal Earthquake Coverage." *The Conversation*. Retrieved 12 March 2022 from http://theconversation .com/classquake-what-the-global-media-missed-in-nepal-earthquake-coverage-41063.

Nepali Labour Act. 1997. *Government of Nepal: Ministry of Labour and Employment*, 3. Retrieved 27 September 2017 from http://dol.gov.np/.

Ogura, Kiyoko. 2007. "Maoists, People and the State Seen from Rolpa and Rukum." In *Political and Social Transformations in North India and Nepal: Social Dynamics in Northern South Asia*, ed. H. Ishii, D. Gellner, and K. Nawa, 435–475. New Delhi: Manohar.

Ong, Aihwa. 1987. *Spirits of Resistance and Capitalist Discipline: Factory Women in Malaysia*. Albany: State University of New York Press.

Padel, Felix, and Samarendra Das. 2010. *Out of This Earth: East India Adivasis and the Aluminium Cartel*. New Delhi: Orient Blackswan.

Pandey, Shubhanga. 2015. "Binod Chaudhary. 2015. Binod Chaudhary—My Story: From the Streets of Kathmandu to a Billion Dollar Empire." Translated by Sanjeev Ghimire. Kathmandu: nepa~laya. *Studies in Nepali History and Society* 20(2).

Pardo, Italo. 1996. *Managing Existence in Naples: Morality, Action, and Structure*. Cambridge: Cambridge University Press.

Parry, Jonathan. 1994. *Death in Benares*. Cambridge. Cambridge University Press.

———. 1999. "Lords of Labor: Working and Shirking in Bhilai." In *The Worlds of Indian Industrial Labor*, ed. Jonathan Parry, Jan Breman, and Karin Kapadia, 107–140. New Delhi: SAGE Publications.

———. 2007. "The Sacrifices of Modernity in a Soviet-Built Steel Town in Central India." In *On the Margins of Religion*, ed. J. Pina-Cabral and Francis Pine. New York: Berghahn Books.

———. 2009. "Sociological Marxism in Central India: Polanyi, Gramsci, and the Case of the Unions." In *Market and Society: The Great Transformation Today*, ed. Chris Hann and Keith Hart, 175–202. Cambridge: Cambridge University Press.

———. 2013. "Company and Contract Labour in a Central Indian Steel Plant." *Economy and Society* 42(3): 348–374.

———. 2014. "Sex, Brick and Mortar. Constructing Class in a Central Indian Steel Town." *Modern Asian Studies* 48(5): 1242–1275.

———. 2020. *Classes of Labor: Work and Life in a Central Indian Steel Town*. New York. Routledge.

Paudel. 2019. "China's Contribution to Foreign Direct Investment in Nepal—CWG." Retrieved 12 March 2022 from https://www.ibanet.org/Article/NewDetail.aspx?ArticleUid=081e7cfa-bebf-4f75-bd27-933d3ba2beaf.

Pearson, Thomas. 2017. *When the Hills Are Gone: Frac Sand Mining and the Struggle for Community*. Minnesota: Minnesota University Press.

Pettigrew, Judith. 2015. *Maoists at the Hearth: Everyday Life in Nepal's Civil War*. Philadelphia: University of Pennsylvania Press.

Picherit, David. 2012. "Migrant Laborers' Struggles between Village and Urban Migration Sites: Labor Standards, Rural Development and Politics in South India." *Global Labor Journal* 3(1): 143–162.

Pink, Sarah, Dylan Tutt, and Andrew Dainty. 2012. *Ethnographic Research in the Construction Industry*. London: Routledge University Press.

Pradhan, B., R. Gruendlinger, I. Fuerhapper, P. Pradhan, and S. Pradhanang. 2005. "Knowledge of Water Quality and Water Borne Disease in Rural Kathmandu Valley, Nepal." *Aquatic Ecosystem Health & Management* 8(3): 277–284.

Ramaswamy, E. A. 1977. *The Worker and His Union: A Study in South India*. Bombay: Allied Publishers.

———. 1981. *Industry and Labour: An Introduction*. Delhi: Oxford University Press.

Rankin, K. 1999. "The Predicament of Labor: Kamaiya Practices and the Ideology of Freedom." In *Nepal: Tharu and Tarai Neighbors*, ed. H. Skar, 27–45. Kathmandu: BibliotecaHimalayica.

Raj, Jayaseelan, and Richard Axelby. 2019. "From Labor Contractors to Worker-Agents: Transformations in the Recruitment of Migrant Laborers in India." *Contributions to Indian Sociology* 52(3): 272–298.

Rege, Aunshul. 2016. "Not Biting the Dust: Using a Tripartite Model of Organized Crime to Examine India's Sandmafia." *International Journal of Comparative and Applied Criminal Justice* 40(2): 101–121.

Rege, Aunshul, and Anita Lavorgna. 2017. "Organization, Operations, and Success of Environmental Organized Crime in Italy and India: A Comparative Analysis." *European Journal of Criminology* 14(2): 160–182.

Rudnyckyj, Daromir. 2009. "Spiritual Economies: Islam and Neoliberalism in Contemporary Indonesia." *Cultural Anthropology* 24: 104–141

———. 2018. "Regimes of Precarity: Buruh, Karyawan, and the Politics of Labor Identity in Indonesia." In *Industrial Labor on the Margins of Capitalism: Precarity, Class, and the Neoliberal Subject*, ed. Chris Hann and Jonathan Parry, 155–179. New York: Berghahn Books.

Sanchez, Andrew. 2016. *Criminal Capital: Violence, Corruption and Class in Industrial India*. New York: Routledge.

Sanchez, Andrew, and Christian Strümpell. 2014. "Anthropological and Historical Perspectives on India's Working Classes." *Modern Asian Studies* 48(5): 1233–1241.

Sanchez, Andrew, and Eeva Kesküla. 2019. "Everyday Barricades: Bureaucracy and the Affect of Struggle in Trade Unions." *Dialectical Anthropology* 43(1): 109–125.

Sax, William. 2009. *God of Justice: Ritual Healing and Social Justice in the Central Himalayas*. New York: Oxford University Press.

Schneider, Jane, and Peter Schneider. 2011. "The Mafia and Capitalism: An Emerging Paradigm." *Sociologica* 2: 15–22.

Scott, James. 1987. *Weapons of the Weak: Everyday Forms of Peasant Resistance*. New Haven, CT: Yale University Press.

Seddon, David, Pierre Blaikie, and James Cameron. 2002. *Peasants and Workers in Nepal*. Delhi: Adroit Publishers.

Sethi, Aman. 2011. *A Free Man*. Noida: Random House India.

Shah, Alpa. 2006. "The Labor of Love: Seasonal Migration from Jharkhand to the Brickkilns of Other States in India." *Contributions to Indian Sociology* 40(1): 91–118.

———. 2007. "Keeping the State Away: Democracy, Politics and Imaginations of the State in India's Jharkhand." *Journal of the Royal Anthropological Institute* 13(1): 129–145.

———. 2010. *In the Shadows of the State: Indigenous Politics, Environmentalism and Insurgency in Jharkhand, India*. Durham, NC: Duke University Press.

———. 2011. "Alcoholics Anonymous: The Maoist Movement in Jharkhand, India." *Modern Asian Studies* 45(5): 1095–1117.

Shah, Sukhdev. 1981. "Developing an Economy—Nepal's Experience." *Asian Survey* 21(10): 1060–1079.

Shakya, Mallika. 2007. "Our Hymns Are Different but Our Gods Are the Same: Religious Rituals in Modern Garment Factories in Nepal." *European Bulletin of Himalayan Research*, 31, 67–81.

———. 2014. "Nepali Economic History through the Ethnic Lens: Changing State Relationships with Entrepreneurial Elites." In *The Changing Face of Ethnic Movements in Nepal*, ed. M. Lawoti and S. Hangen. London: Routledge.

———. 2015a. "Ethnicity in Nepal's New Constitution." *Focaalblog*, 28 September 2015. Retrieved 16 September 2017 from http://www.focaalblog.com/2015/09/28/mallika-shakya-ethnicity-in-nepals-new-constitution/.

———. 2015b. "Marwari Traders between Hindu Neoliberalism and Democratic Socialism in Nepal." In *People, Money and Power in the Economic Crisis: Perspectives from the Global South*, ed. Keith Hart and John Sharp, 190–206. New York: Berghahn Books.

———. 2018. *Death of an Industry: The Cultural Politics of Garment Manufacturing during the Maoist Revolution in Nepal*. Cambridge: Cambridge University Press.

———. 2020. "The Politics of Border and Nation in Nepal in the Time of Pandemic." *Dialectical Anthropology* 44: 223–231.

Shrivastava, Aseem, and Ashish Kothari. 2012. *Churning the Earth: The Making of Global India*. London: Penguin.

Sinwell, Luke, and Siphiwe Mbatha. 2016. *The Spirit of Marikana: The Rise of Insurgent Trade Unionism in South Africa*. London: Pluto Press.

Snellinger, Amanda. 2018. *Making New Nepal: From Student Activism to Mainstream Politics.* Seattle: University of Washington Press.

Spotlight Nepal. 2017. "Maoism Revisited: A Brief Sketch of the Communist Party of Nepal Led by Netra Bikram Chand." Retrieved 3 May 2019 from https://www.spot lightnepal.com/2019/03/17/maoism-revisited-brief-sketch-communist-party-nepal-led-netra-bikram-chand/.

Standing, Guy. 2011. *The Precariat: The New Dangerous Class.* New York: Bloomsbury.

———. 2014. "Why the Precariat Is Not a 'Bogus Concept.'" Open Democracy. Retrieved 2 May 2019 from https://www.opendemocracy.net/guy-standing/why-precariat-is-not-percentE2 percent80 percent9Cbogus-concept percentE2 percent80 percent9D.

Steinmüller, Hans. 2010. "Communities of Complicity: Notes on State Formation and Local Sociality in Rural China." *American Ethnologist* 37(3): 539–549.

———. 2013. *Communities of Complicity: Everyday Ethics in Rural China.* New York: Berghahn Books.

Stracke, Stefan, and Birte Homann. 2017. *Branchenanalyse Getränkeindustrie. Marktentwicklung und Beschäftigung in der Brauwirtschaft, Erfrischungsgetränke und Mineralbrunnenindustrie.* Hans Böckler Stiftung. Band 368.

Strümpell, Christian. 2014a. "The Politics of Dispossession in an Odishan Steel Town." *Contributions to Indian Sociology* (n.s.) 48(3): 45–72.

———. 2014b. "The Making and Unmaking of an Adivasi Working Class in Western Orissa." In *Savage Attack: Adivasi Insurgency in India,* ed. Alpha Shah and Crispin Bates, 200–227. Delhi: Social Science Press.

———. 2018. "Precarious Labour and Precarious Livelihoods in an Indian Company Town." In *Industrial Labor on the Margins of Capitalism: Precarity, Class, and the Neoliberal Subject,* ed. Chris Hann and Jonathan Parry, 134–154. New York: Berghahn Books.

Subramanian, Dilip. 2009. "Work and Autonomy in the Assembly of Printed Circuit Boards: An Ethnographic Account." *Contributions to Indian Sociology* 43(2): 183–213.

Thapa, Deepak. 2017. "Post-War Armed Groups in Nepal." Accord. Issue 26. Retrieved 9 July 2020 from https://www.c-r.org/accord/nepal/post-war-armed-groups-nepal.

———. 2019. *The Politics of Change: Reflections on Contemporary Nepal.* Kathmandu: Social Science Baha.

Thapa, Hari Bahadur. 2019. "Cold War in Nepal. In The Annapurna Express." Retrieved 10 March 2022 from https://theannapurnaexpress.com/news/cold-war-in-nepal-1950

Thiel, Darren. 2010. "Contacts and Contracts: Economic Embeddedness and Ethnic Stratification in London's Construction Market." *Ethnography* 11(3): 443–471.

———. 2012a. *Builders: Class, Gender and Ethnicity in the Construction Industry.* London: Routledge Press.

———. 2012b. "Builders, Bodies and Bifurcations: How London Construction Workers 'Learn to Labor.'" *Ethnography* 14(4): 412–430.

Thompson, E. P. 1963. *The Making of the English Working Class.* New York: Random House.

Trevisani, Tommaso. 2018. "Work, Precarity and Resistance: Company and Contract Labour in Kazakhstan's Former Soviet Steel Town." In *Industrial Labor on the Margins of Capitalism: Precarity, Class, and the Neoliberal Subject,* ed. Chris Hann and Jonathan Parry, 85–110. New York: Berghahn Books.

———. 2019. "The Veterans' Gala: The Use of Tradition in an Industrial Labor Conflict in Contemporary Kazakhstan." *Central Asian Survey* 38(3): 381–399.

United Nations. 2010. *Nepal: Urban Housing Sector Profile.* Nairobi: UNON, Publishing Services Section.

———. 2014. *World Urbanization Prospects.* Department of Economic and Social Affairs (DESA). New York: United Nations Publications.

Van de Loop, Theo. 1996. *Industrial Dynamics and Fragmented Labor Markets: Construction Firms and Laborers in India.* Thousand Oaks, CA: SAGE Publications.

Van der Geer, Alexandra, Michael Dermitzakis, and John Vos. 2008. "Fossil Folklore from India: The SiwalikHills and the Mahâbhârata." *Folklore* 119: 71–92.

Volkov, Vadim. 2002. *Violent Entrepreneurs: The Use of Force in the Making of Russian Capitalism*. Ithaca, NY: Cornell University Press.

Waldinger, R. 2005. "Networks and Niches: The Continuing Significance of Ethnic Connections." In *Ethnicity, Social Mobility and Public Policy: Comparing the USA and the UK*, ed. Glenn C. Loury, Tariq Modood, and Steven M. Teles, 342–362. Cambridge: Cambridge University Press.

Walters, Damian. 2001. "The Medium of the Message: Shamanism as Localised Practice in the Nepal Himalayas." In *The Archaeology of Shamanism*, ed. Neil Price, 105–122. London: Routledge.

——. 2003. "Among Spirits and Dieties: Diverse Shamanisms in the Nepal Himalayas." *Cultural Survival Quarterly Magazine*. Retrieved 12 March 2022 from https://www .culturalsurvival.org/publications/cultural-survival-quarterly/among-spirits-and-dietiesdiverse-shamanisms-nepal.

Walters, Holly. 2020. *Shaligram Pilgrimage in the Nepal Himalayas*. Amsterdam: Amsterdam University Press.

Weber, Max. 2001 [1930]. *The Protestant Ethic and the Spirit of Capitalism*. New York: Routledge.

Weinstein, Liza. 2008. "Mumbai's Development Mafias: Globalization, Organized Crime and Land Development." *International Journal of Urban and Regional Research* 32(1): 22–39.

Witsoe, Jeffrey. 2012. "Everyday Corruption and the Political Mediation of the Indian State: An Ethnographic Exploration of Brokers in Bihar." *Economic and Political Weekly* xlvii(6): 47–54.

Woodward, Donald. 2002. *Men at Work: Laborers and Building Craftsmen in the Towns of Northern England, 1450–1750*. Cambridge: Cambridge University Press.

Wright, Erik Olin. 2002. "The Shadow of Exploitation in Weber's Class Analysis." *American Sociological Review* 67(6): 832–853.

Yami, Hisila, and Baburam Bhattarai. 1996. "Problems and Prospects of Revolution in Nepal." Retrieved 27 September 2017 from http://www.bannedthought.net/Nepal/ Problems-Prospects/bb_nationalq.html.

Zharkevich, Ina. 2019a. *Maoist People's War and the Revolution of Everyday Life in Nepal*. Cambridge: Cambridge University Press.

——. 2019b. "Gender, Marriage, and the Dynamic of (Im)mobility in the Mid-Western Hills of Nepal." *Mobilities* 14(5): 681–695.

——. 2020. "'We Are in the Process': The Exploitation of Hope and the Political Economy of Waiting among the Aspiring Irregular Migrants in Nepal." *Environment and Planning D: Society & Space* (early online publication): 1–17.

INDEX